Credit & Collection Guidebook

Third Edition

Steven M. Bragg

Published by AccountingTools, Inc., Centennial, Colorado.

For more information about AccountingTools® products, visit our Web site at www.accountingtools.com.

ISBN-13: 978-1-938910-95-1

Table of Contents

Preface

The credit and collection functions have the conflicting roles of assisting in increasing company sales, while at the same time only extending credit in a sufficiently prudent manner that bad debts are not excessive. In the *Credit & Collection Guidebook*, we explore how these dual roles are achieved, as well as the methods by which the functions are managed and risk is reduced.

The *Credit & Collection Guidebook* shows how to most efficiently and effectively run the credit and collection functions, while also addressing the following topics:

- Which job descriptions to use for employees
- How to structure credit and collection procedures and controls
- What to include in a corporate credit policy
- What to include in the credit application form sent to customers
- How to assign credit ratings to customers
- How to interpret the financial statements submitted by customers
- How to mitigate credit risk
- Which methods to use to collect cash from customers
- How to manage payment deductions taken by customers
- How to locate customers who do not want to be found
- When to use collection agencies
- How to employ technology in the credit and collection functions
- Which laws apply to credit and collections

The *Credit & Collection Guidebook* is designed for both professional accountants and students, since both can benefit from its detailed descriptions of credit and collection procedures, controls, information technology, and operational techniques. The book also provides the information you need to support sales while keeping bad debts at a reasonable level. As such, it may earn a place on your book shelf as a reference tool for years to come.

Centennial, Colorado
October, 2017

About the Author

Steven Bragg, CPA, has been the chief financial officer or controller of four companies, as well as a consulting manager at Ernst & Young. He received a master's degree in finance from Bentley College, an MBA from Babson College, and a Bachelor's degree in Economics from the University of Maine. He has been a two-time president of the Colorado Mountain Club, and is an avid alpine skier, mountain biker, and certified master diver. Mr. Bragg resides in Centennial, Colorado. He has written the following books and courses:

7 Habits of Effective CEOs	Cost Accounting (college textbook)
7 Habits of Effective CFOs	Cost Accounting Fundamentals
7 Habits of Effective Controllers	Cost Management Guidebook
Accountant Ethics [for multiple states]	Credit & Collection Guidebook
Accountants' Guidebook	Crowdfunding
Accounting Changes and Error Corrections	Developing and Managing Teams
Accounting Controls Guidebook	Effective Collections
Accounting for Casinos and Gaming	Employee Onboarding
Accounting for Derivatives and Hedges	Enterprise Risk Management
Accounting for Earnings per Share	Fair Value Accounting
Accounting for Inventory	Financial Analysis
Accounting for Investments	Financial Forecasting and Modeling
Accounting for Intangible Assets	Fixed Asset Accounting
Accounting for Leases	Foreign Currency Accounting
Accounting for Managers	Fraud Examination
Accounting for Stock-Based Compensation	Fraud Schemes
Accounting Procedures Guidebook	GAAP Guidebook
Agricultural Accounting	Governmental Accounting
Behavioral Ethics	Health Care Accounting
Bookkeeping Guidebook	Hospitality Accounting
Budgeting	How to Audit Fixed Assets
Business Combinations and Consolidations	How to Audit Inventory
Business Insurance Fundamentals	How to Audit Receivables
Business Ratios	How to Run a Meeting
Business Valuation	Human Resources Guidebook
Capital Budgeting	IFRS Guidebook
CFO Guidebook	Interpretation of Financial Statements
Change Management	Inventory Management
Closing the Books	Investor Relations Guidebook
Coaching and Mentoring	Lean Accounting Guidebook
Conflict Management	Mergers & Acquisitions
Constraint Management	Negotiation
Construction Accounting	New Controller Guidebook
Corporate Cash Management	Nonprofit Accounting
Corporate Finance	Partnership Accounting

(continued)

Payables Management
Payroll Management
Project Accounting
Project Management
Public Company Accounting
Purchasing Guidebook
Real Estate Accounting
Records Management
Recruiting and Hiring

Revenue Recognition
Sales and Use Tax Accounting
The MBA Guidebook
The Soft Close
The Statement of Cash Flows
The Year-End Close
Treasurer's Guidebook
Working Capital Management

On-Line Resources by Steven Bragg

Steven maintains the accountingtools.com web site, which contains continuing professional education courses, the Accounting Best Practices podcast, and thousands of articles on accounting subjects.

The *Credit & Collection Guidebook* is also available as a continuing professional education (CPE) course. You can purchase the course (and many other courses) and take an on-line exam at:

www.accountingtools.com/cpe

Chapter 1
Credit and Collection Operations

Introduction

Credit and collection activities refer to the granting of credit to customers so that they can defer payments to the seller, and then collecting those funds at a later date. Ideally, it is vastly easier to collect payment in advance or on delivery from all customers, but competitive pressures rarely allow this to be the case. Instead, if a business refuses to grant credit, then customers take their business elsewhere. Accordingly, it is necessary for a business to evaluate its customers to determine how much credit it is safe to grant, as well as the methods required to collect funds.

In this chapter, we describe the structure of the credit and collection functions, key job descriptions, goal setting, staff compensation, management reports, and other issues necessary to the daily operation of credit and collections.

Overview of Credit and Collection Management

In this section, we describe the problems faced by the credit and collection functions, as well as how these areas can be organized. Both functions impact the performance of other parts of a company, which can result in some political maneuvering to see who controls them.

The Credit Conundrum

The credit department is arguably the most unpopular department in a company. The reason is that customers want unlimited credit in order to delay cash payments, while the credit manager must exercise some prudence in only granting credit where invoices are likely to be paid. The result is two types of risk:

- The risk of granting too much credit to a customer that cannot pay
- The risk of denying credit to a customer who can pay

It is extremely difficult to maneuver between these two risks and grant just the right amount of credit, so the credit manager is likely to be abused from all directions. The sales department believes that the credit manager is stifling sales, while the chief financial officer believes that the extension of too much credit is resulting in outsized bad debt losses.

Further, because of the confidential nature of some of the information used to reach credit decisions, the credit staff may not be able to fully explain the reasons for its decisions to the sales department. The result is ongoing frustration on all sides, which can result in the credit manager losing all power and eventually just "rubber stamping" all requests for credit. This scenario can only be avoided through the ongoing support of senior management, which must understand the key role that the credit department plays.

The Collections Janitor Role

The collections team can be considered the janitor that sweeps up after the other parts of a business have completed their work. The analogy is an apt one, for any number of problems may have been caused by other parts of the business, such as incorrect billings, flawed product designs, or damaged goods, which the collections team must work around during its efforts to collect cash from customers. This means that the collection effort may seem inefficient, due to problems that are outside of the control of the collections group. Only by giving feedback to the rest of the company can the collections manager achieve reasonable collection results. Thus, collection management requires expertise in dealing with other departments, as well as collection skill.

Organizational Structure

The credit and collection functions may be separately located within different departments. The credit function is essentially issuing short-term loans to customers, which is a financing function, and so it may report to the treasurer or chief financial officer. The collections function is an extension of the billing function, and so is more likely to report to the controller. Since this means the two areas are organized separately, interactions between the two departments can prolong the time required to resolve issues with customers. To keep this from happening, we recommend that the two functions be combined into a single department. In addition, consider folding the order entry function (which normally reports to the sales manager) into this group. By doing so, a large part of customer interactions are combined under common management, which can shorten the time required to resolve customer problems. It is rarely a good idea to have this merged group report to the sales manager, since doing so gives sales too much control over the granting of credit, which will likely be expanded to accommodate all customer orders.

Job Descriptions

Who works in the credit and collection areas? There is a manager of each function, as well as highly specialized clerical staff. In this section, we describe the job descriptions of the credit manager, credit clerk, collections manager, collector, and skip tracer. We also note the importance of using a probationary period when hiring employees into any of these positions, since this type of work does not appeal to everyone.

Credit Manager Job Description

The credit manager position is responsible for the entire credit granting process, including the consistent application of a credit policy, periodic credit reviews of existing customers, and the assessment of the creditworthiness of potential customers, with the goal of optimizing the mix of company sales and bad debt losses. The position generally reports to the treasurer or chief financial officer. The credit manager should not report to any position in the sales department, since the credit function should act as a counterbalance to that department.

The key elements of the credit manager position are as follows, broken down by tasks related to management and to credit operations:

Management Tasks

- Maintain a department organizational structure sufficient to meet all goals and objectives
- Properly motivate the credit staff
- Measure department performance
- Provide for ongoing training of the credit staff
- Manage relations with credit reporting agencies
- Manage relations with credit insurance providers
- Manage relations with the sales department

Credit Operations Tasks

- Maintain the corporate credit policy
- Monitor industry trends
- Recommend changes in the credit policy to senior management
- Create a credit scoring model
- Update customer credit files
- Monitor the credit granting and updating process
- Accept or reject credit recommendations forwarded by the credit staff
- Conduct on-site visits with the largest customers
- Monitor periodic credit reviews
- Monitor deductions taken from payments by customers
- Monitor the application of late fees to customers
- Monitor the corporate leasing program

The credit manager should have considerable experience in the credit granting field, probably having moved up from a credit clerk position. The position can require a college degree, though it is not necessary. Of more importance than a college degree is an excellent knowledge of credit scoring systems, financial analysis, and how credit-related laws may apply to the business. The position may periodically require travel to investigate or build relations with larger customers. Finally, the credit manager needs significant interpersonal skills, to deal with the sales department and customers on a daily basis.

Credit Clerk Job Description

The credit clerk is responsible for not only reviewing credit applications from new customers, but also monitoring current customers to see if their credit levels should be re-examined. The key elements of this position are:

- Process credit applications from new customers
- Conduct trade and bank reference checks
- Establish credit limits based on credit criteria
- Maintain records of credit reviews and document reasons for credit limits granted
- Monitor credit usage by existing customers
- Monitor financial and credit condition of customers
- Review existing credit limits at regular intervals
- Provide credit information to third parties upon request

It is not necessary for a credit clerk to have a college degree, though it is necessary to have a thorough understanding of financial statement analysis and how it relates to the granting of credit.

Collections Manager Job Description

The collections manager position is responsible for all collection activities, including all collection interactions with customers and the management of collection agencies and collection attorneys. This manager is also responsible for accumulating information about the reasons for collection problems and passing the information back to the rest of the company for resolution. The position usually reports to the controller.

The key elements of the collections manager position are as follows, broken down by tasks related to management and departmental interactions:

Management Tasks

- Maintain a department organizational structure that can meet all goals and objectives
- Monitor the use of collection techniques
- Monitor payment deductions taken by customers
- Properly motivate the collections staff
- Measure department performance
- Conduct staff training as needed
- Review and approve negotiated settlements with customers

Third Party Interactions

- Provide feedback to other departments regarding collection issues originating internally
- Manage relations with collection agencies

- Manage relations with collection attorneys
- Manage relations with outside skip tracers

A key aspect of this position is to standardize the process used for contacting customers. This does not necessarily mean a highly regimented process, but rather one in which boundaries for acceptable collection behavior are firmly enforced. Also, the collections manager must ensure that customers are uniformly dealt with in a manner that abides by all applicable laws.

One of the more useful aspects of the collections manager position is monitoring the general trend of collections to see if there is a pattern that may require a change in credit policy. The collections manager is in the unique position of being able to monitor *all* collection activities, which makes it easier to discern subtle increases in days sales outstanding across the entire customer base, or within specific customer concentrations. It can be difficult to allocate time for this analysis in the midst of day-to-day department operations, but it can lead to credit changes that can ultimately save a company from incurring inordinately large bad debts.

Collector Job Description

The collector position is responsible for collecting the maximum amount of overdue funds from customers, which may include a variety of collection techniques, legal claims, and the selective use of outside collection services. The position is not strictly that of a clerk, since the best collector should operate with a more independent orientation than a procedure-bound clerk, taking those steps needed to collect funds. The key elements of the collector position are as follows:

- Stratify collection activities to maximize cash receipts
- Issue dunning letters to overdue accounts
- Use skip tracing techniques to locate customers
- Contact customers regarding overdue accounts and determine reasons for non-payment
- Issue payment commitment letters
- Negotiate the return of unpaid merchandise
- Repossess merchandise when payment is unlikely
- Monitor cash on delivery payments
- Issue credit hold notifications
- Recommend that accounts be shifted to a collection agency
- Process small claims court complaints
- Recommend bad debt write-offs
- Maintain accurate records about interactions with customers

It is not necessary for a collector to have any type of college degree. Instead, it is much more important for a collector to have dogged persistence in contacting customers at regular intervals and the negotiation skills necessary to extract payments from customers. If the company uses computerized collection monitoring software and auto-dialers, a collector should be comfortable with the use of this technology.

A productive collector who enjoys the work is a rare find indeed. These individuals commonly achieve much higher collection rates than normal. The collections manager would be well advised to create a special environment for such employees, including especially quiet work environments, some measure of privacy, bonus pay, and any other inducements necessary to retain their services.

Skip Tracer Job Description

A skip tracer is essentially a private investigator who locates people who do not necessarily want to be found. The orientation of this position is toward research into a variety of databases, so computer skills are paramount. Work hours can be long, and are likely to be self-directed, especially if the skip tracer works from home.

A skip tracer is more likely to be an introvert, given the amount of research involved. However, there is also a need for sufficient social skills to extract location information from the associates of a person who is missing. Obtaining information in this manner requires that a skip tracer be good at posing the correct questions, listening carefully to answers, and interpreting this information "on the fly" to obtain additional information with just the right questions.

In short, a skip tracer is a unique individual, whose personality is inquisitive and research-oriented, and self-directed. It is quite difficult to find a qualified skip tracer, which is why this position is so frequently outsourced.

Probationary Period

When hiring a person into any of the preceding positions, be aware that credit and collections activities are not for everyone, so a certain proportion of new hires will not work out. Accordingly, this is an area in which a mandatory probationary period is useful for deciding whether someone can be an effective part of credit and collections. If not, it is best for the company and for them if they are terminated by the end of the probationary period. Otherwise, the rest of the department will be consumed by the ongoing training requirements, errors, and morale problems of these employees. The result should be a more cohesive group that is entirely comprised of the types of people who thrive in the high-pressure credit and collections environment.

Work Allocations

As is the case in any department, the types of work assigned will vary for new hires and more experienced personnel. This is more of an issue in the collections area, where it takes time to develop collection skills. In this area, a new collector has no knowledge of a company's customers, the company billing processes, which collection techniques have been approved for use, or the types of payment problems that customers usually have. To give a new hire the time to acquire the requisite knowledge, there are several ways to allocate work. Some suggestions are:

- *Courtesy calls.* A new hire can contact the larger accounts in advance of payment due dates to see if there are any issues with the expected payments. This approach keeps a menial task away from more experienced collectors, while giving new hires a chance to interact with customers and learn about their problems. It may also uncover situations that would have resulted in late payments, but which can now be dealt with sooner.
- *Collection call preparation.* Have new hires act as assistants to the more experienced collectors, assembling any information needed for their collection calls, and tracking down information requested by customers. This is useful for learning about company systems and where to locate information.
- *Easy customers.* New hires can be assigned to the smaller accounts that have the fewest problems, after which larger and more difficult accounts are gradually added. The collections manager can also meet with new hires to discuss the characteristics of each of the more difficult accounts.

Tip: If new hires are assigned easier accounts, be aware of the impact on performance measurement systems, which may report high collection performance on these accounts.

The assignment of work for experienced collectors is substantially different. In this case, the collections manager wants to maximize the use of their expertise. This means that the best collectors are assigned to the most intractable customers. The result should increase the overall proportion of cash collected. However, doing so may also mean that the measured performance of experienced collectors appears to decline, since they no longer have any "fluff" accounts for which payments are made in a reliable manner. Despite the measurement problem, this approach is the most effective way to collect cash.

The collections manager should regularly monitor the aged accounts receivable report to determine which customers are the worst, and apportion them to the best collectors. It will be necessary to examine the list of assigned accounts with some care in order to avoid overburdening a few collectors with unusually intractable customers.

Over time, it is possible that a collector may become overly sympathetic to the needs of the accounts assigned to him or her, and so becomes more willing to allow delayed payments. The collections manager should monitor collection rates by account and discuss longer payment intervals with the collectors to see if this is a problem. If so, it may make sense to occasionally shift accounts to different collectors. Though doing so may improve collection rates, it also means that collectors may have to spend time familiarizing themselves with their new accounts and training the recipients of their old accounts.

Tip: Have each outgoing collector enter notes in the files of customers whose accounts are being shifted to a new collector, detailing payment characteristics and tips on ways to obtain payment.

Another variation on work allocations is to adopt staggered working hours that match the time zones to be contacted. For example, one group of collectors can be assigned to those customers located in the Eastern time zone, with other groups assigned to the Central, Mountain, and Pacific time zones. Doing so does not improve collections in these regions, but does afford collectors the opportunity to work in a group that best meets the hours that match their personal activities. Thus, a collector can shift from one group to another to achieve a modified form of flex time.

Staff Training

The credit and collection functions require the use of skilled labor; it is not possible to assign work in either area to a raw recruit and expect reasonable results. A credit department employee must have an understanding of financial analysis and risk mitigation in order to properly evaluate the risk posed by the extension of credit to a customer. Similarly, a collector must have a unique set of organizational and negotiation skills to obtain overdue funds from customers. Thus, a significant amount of training is required in both areas before employees can be considered effective.

If the manager of these areas is dealing with a group of completely untrained employees, it may be possible to impose a standard training regimen on all of them. However, in most cases new hires have a mix of skills, and so must be trained on an individual basis. Accordingly, here are several training steps to consider:

1. Conduct a skills assessment to learn the experience level of new hires.
2. Create a preliminary training plan and review it with each new hire to see if they agree.
3. Itemize the types of training to be conducted for each targeted area, such as off-site seminars, webinars, on-site training, training materials, books, and so forth.
4. Ensure that a budget exists for all of the contemplated training expenditures.
5. Schedule training into the work calendar of each employee.
6. Immediately following training, assess the knowledge level of each employee and decide whether additional training is needed.

In many cases, staff training is conducted internally, since businesses want their employees to learn a specific process flow, or a unique way of examining credit that cannot be learned elsewhere.

> **Tip:** If there is no one available to conduct in-house training, consider hiring a consultant to develop training materials and conduct training as needed.

> **Tip:** If certain errors keep recurring that are leading to customer non-payment, consider recommending additional employee training in those parts of the company where the errors are occurring. For example, billing errors may be rectified with additional training of the billing staff.

The use of case studies is highly recommended in the credit and collection areas. Take specific real-life scenarios from the recent past involving the granting of credit based on a certain set of information, or dealing with a specific nonpayment excuse from a customer, and discuss the various ways in which these situations could have been handled. This type of hands-on approach to training can be more useful than a theoretical analysis of how to generally deal with credit and collection situations.

Goal Setting

Both the credit function and the collections function are essentially engaged in reactive activities. The credit staff analyzes credit applications as submitted, while the collections team only has collection work if receivables have been generated by the rest of the company. This makes it relatively easy to set goals for certain outcomes. The following example illustrates the concept.

EXAMPLE

The collections manager of Luminescence Corporation is setting goals for her collectors for the month of March. She has the following information about receivables:

Month	Receivables Outstanding	Historical Collection %	Collection Goal
January	$2,200,000	50%*	$1,100,000
February	3,500,000	65%**	2,275,000
		Total	$3,375,000

*   For receivables two months old
** For receivables one month old

In addition, she anticipates that total receivables for March will be $3,800,000. Historically, 5% of current-month receivables are collected in the month in which they are billed, so she expects to collect $190,000 of March receivables by the end of the month. If she bases collections on these historical averages, her collection goal for March should be $3,565,000.

This goal can be adjusted for changes in the number of available collectors. For example, a large proportion of collectors taking vacation time could reduce the goal, while adding experienced collectors to the department could increase the collection goal.

The monthly collection goal described in the preceding example can also be broken down into goals for each collection. For example, using the total department collection goal of $3,565,000 in the example, and assuming 10 collectors in the department, each one could be assigned a collection goal of $356,500 for March. This goal assignment only works if there is an approximately equal distribution of invoices across the collector group that are equally likely to be collected.

The goal assignment could be altered to account for the experience level of the collectors. Thus, an experienced collector could be assigned 125% of the baseline goal, while a first-year collector might be assigned 80% and a trainee just 40%. The goal could be more precisely apportioned based on an assessment of the relative difficulty of collecting from each customer, though doing so takes a fair amount of analysis.

The same concept can be used in the credit department, since the credit manager also has a reasonable idea of the amount of work to be expected. The following example illustrates the concept from the perspective of the credit function.

EXAMPLE

The credit manager of Dillinger Designs is setting goals for her credit staff for the month of June. Historically, the department has received between 300 and 350 credit requests from new customers in each month. In addition, there is an ongoing monthly expectation that the credit files of 2% of the company's 5,000 existing customers will be examined. Further, there are usually about 50 emergency credit reviews that are triggered by the receipt of not sufficient funds checks or sudden drops in customer credit ratings. Based on this information, the credit manager expects the following credit review volume in June:

Type of Request	Expected Reviews
300 to 350 new customers	325
2% of 5,000 existing customers	100
50 emergency reviews	50
Total	475

There are 6 employees in the department who are trained in conducting credit reviews. Based on the expected review volume, the credit manager should set an expectation of 80 credit reviews per employee, per month.

Goals can be quite useful when employed on a daily basis, so the department is aware of how far behind or ahead of the target it is as each month progresses. This information can be used to adjust capacity levels with the use of overtime, outsourced work, or changes in staffing levels.

The Watch List

The preceding examples set relatively high-level goals for employees. The department manager might want to be a bit more pointed in directing collectors toward certain customers. This may take the form of a watch list, which includes those customers about which the manager is most concerned. This watch list is regularly updated and distributed to collectors, who can also expect the manager to make regular inquiries about the status of these accounts.

Counterproductive Goals

It is not useful and may be counterproductive to focus attention on certain types of goals. The following items can lead to especially pernicious results if included in department goals:

- *Call time*. A measurement area to be avoided is the monitoring of the amount of time spent on individual collection calls. The collection staff should not feel that it has to rush its customer contacts. In many cases, it makes sense to do the reverse and prolong a call in order to build rapport with a customer or to plumb the other party for additional information regarding the reason for a late payment. An experienced collector may very well have the longest call durations in the department, and yet be the most effective at collecting money.
- *Overtime*. It makes little sense to minimize the percentage of staff overtime, since the additional cost of overtime should be vastly outweighed by the incremental amount of collections resulting from these efforts. Only in cases where there are egregious amounts of overtime being taken with no corresponding collections should overtime reduction be considered a valid goal.

Staff Compensation

The compensation system in the credit and collection functions should not be oriented excessively toward individual performance. If this were the case, and especially in the collections area, the staff would have an incentive to hoard those customers that are the best payers. A better approach is to compensate the entire group for its combined performance. For example, there could be a bonus if both the credit and collection employees were to achieve a full-year target of keeping the bad debt percentage below 1%. With that kind of incentive, everyone would band together to ensure that credit is doled out in a suitably parsimonious manner, while the most difficult accounts would attract the best collectors, who even volunteer to take them on. A group compensation plan also means that employees are more likely to police each other's performance and apply pressure to those who are not performing well.

A potential downside of a performance-based compensation system is an overly aggressive collection attitude toward customers, perhaps to the extent that customers elect not to do business with the company again. This problem can be mitigated with proper training, as well as by monitoring calls made to customers.

> **Tip:** Consider using small bonuses as marks of appreciation to the sales staff on those occasions when they are particularly helpful in collecting an overdue account.

Interdepartmental Relations

The credit function must coordinate its activities with those of the sales department, since credit requests are likely to be referred to the credit staff through the sales department. This calls for astute management of the sales staff, which will continually demand that full credit be granted to all and sundry. There will be cases where credit is *not* granted, so relations between the departments must be cordial enough to prevent warfare over these instances.

The collections function has an even greater need for excellent relations with the sales department, since it may call upon the sales staff to assist it in making collection calls to customers. In addition, if collection problems are being caused by issues occurring within the company (such as damaged or flawed goods), the collections manager must be able to pass along this information in an effective manner to the departments causing the problems. The level of interaction could even lead to the collections manager chairing or participating in various meetings to resolve these underlying problems.

Both the credit and collection managers also need to provide regular feedback to other parts of the company regarding the payment habits of customers. It is entirely possible that senior management is pushing the sales department to sell into market niches that are heavily populated with low-rated customers that cannot pay, or that more sales are being made to customers that do not even deserve the amount of credit they are currently being granted. There should be regularly-scheduled meetings to address the credit and collections view of these issues, so that the entire management team is fully aware of customer payment problems.

> **Tip:** Prepare a profitability report by customer, including the cost of bad debts, and issue it to management at regular intervals. This can provide evidence in favor of any arguments presented to cut back on credit to certain customers.

When a large bad debt is incurred, there should be a meeting with the relevant departments to discuss why the bad debt took place. For example, the sales manager may have placed undue pressure on the credit manager to grant credit for a large sale to a new customer. As another example, a customer refused to pay because the product shipped was of such poor design that it broke down repeatedly. In both examples, internal issues caused the bad debts, which should be rectified to keep them from occurring again. To be most effective, bad debt reviews should require the taking of meeting minutes, the assignment of responsibilities, and reporting to senior management regarding actions taken to mitigate bad debts in the future.

In short, credit and collections are directly impacted by other company functions, so the credit manager and collections manager must have the rare ability to both request their help and occasionally deliver bad news to them.

Reports

There are a variety of reports that can be used to oversee the operation of the credit and collection functions. In most cases, these reports should be designed to highlight problem areas requiring management attention, rather than simply presenting massive amounts of information that a manager must wade through in order to find those few nuggets of actionable information. In this section, we address a number of these reports, and how they can be configured to best present critical information.

Credit Levels Report

The credit manager wants to know which customers are routinely bumping up against the upper end of their allowed credit levels, since this may call for a credit review. To concentrate attention on just this subset of customers, consider a report that only shows this information for those customers who have been within 20% of their credit limits in the past month. A sample report format is:

Sample Credit Levels Report

Customer Name	Customer ID	Credit Limit	Max Credit in Past Month	Percent of Credit Limit
Albertson Clothiers	ALB02	$25,000	$26,000	104%
Bombay Nightgowns	BOM04	40,000	38,000	95%
Charleston Formal	CHA01	15,000	14,500	97%
Denver Nightclub Attire	DEN03	80,000	72,000	90%

Receivables Aging Report

The receivables aging report is the most familiar of all collection reports. It lists all unpaid invoices, usually in 30-day time buckets. This format focuses attention on those invoices that are overdue for payment. The standard format is shown below, with individual invoices aggregated at the account level.

Sample Receivables Aging Report

Customer Name	0 – 30 Days	31 – 60 Days	61 – 90 Days	90+ Days	Totals
Albertson Clothiers	$5,000	$13,000	$6,000	$2,000	$26,000
Bombay Nightgowns		30,000	8,000		38,000
Charleston Formal	14,500				14,500
Denver Nightclub Attire	32,000	39,000		1,000	72,000
Totals	$51,500	$82,000	$14,000	$3,000	$150,500

This format can be altered to yield more targeted information for its various users. For example, it could be printed by salesperson, so that only those customers for which a particular salesperson is responsible are shown. This report can be issued to the sales department on a regular basis. The same approach can be used for collectors.

Another variation is to alter the time buckets in the report to reflect the different stages in the collection process. For example, a 40-50 day time bucket could be used that indicates those accounts to which dunning letters should be sent, while the 51-70 day bucket reveals all accounts for which collection calls are being made, and so forth. The following sample report format illustrates the concept; note that no current accounts are listed at all.

Sample Aging Report for Collection Activities

Customer Name	Dunning Letters 40 – 50 Days	Collection Calls 51 – 80 Days	Attorney Letters 81 – 90 Days	Collection Agency 90+ Days	Totals
Albertson Clothiers	$1,000	$12,000	$6,000	$2,000	$21,000
Bombay Nightgowns	20,000	10,000	8,000		38,000
Denver Nightclub Attire	22,000	1,000		1,000	24,000
Totals	$43,000	$23,000	$14,000	$3,000	$83,000

The preceding report concept only works well in cases where the collection effort is highly regimented, so that certain activities are always used during certain time buckets.

Bad Debt Report

Both the credit manager and collections manager should have access to a report that itemizes bad debts, probably with a lower threshold that drops out the smallest bad debts. This report should not just state the raw numbers written off, but also focus on the reasons for the bad debts. Note in the following example how a reason code is included for each bad debt listed, which is useful for aggregating bad debts by category.

Sample Bad Debt Report

Invoice Number	Customer	Amount	Invoice Date	Reason Code	Notes
3478	Albertson Clothiers	$5,412	5/03/X3	(1)	Filed creditor claim
3502	Nighttime Designs	$4,002	5/11/X3	(3)	Claim disallowed but did not pay
3609	Nighttime Designs	10,499	5/19/X3	(2)	Freight company was Overnight Transport
3651	Albertson Clothiers	6,375	5/29/X3	(1)	Filed creditor claim

(1) Customer bankruptcy
(2) Goods damaged in transit
(3) Marketing allowance

Customer Profitability Report

A business tends to be bogged down in the day-to-day procedures of granting credit and following up with collection activities, without seeing the bigger picture of whether a particular customer is profitable. The amount of profitability can vary dramatically by customer, since some may buy more lower-margin goods than others. The following sample report shows how variable costs can be offset against customer revenues to arrive at an estimate of profitability by customer. In the example, a standard 5% commission applies to all customer sales, but differences in the profitability of the products sold, as well as bad debts, result in significant differences in profits by customer.

Sample Customer Profitability Report

Customer Name	Revenues	Cost of Sales	Commissions	Bad Debts	Profit	Profit %
Albertson Clothiers	$2,500,000	$1,550,000	$125,000	$14,000	$811,000	32%
Bombay Nightgowns	400,000	220,000	20,000	5,000	155,000	39%
Charleston Formal	900,000	720,000	45,000	85,000	50,000	6%
Denver Nightclub Attire	3,200,000	2,590,000	160,000	108,000	342,000	11%

Additional columns can be added to this report, such as the incremental cost of uncompensated rush deliveries to a customer, or the incremental amount of customer service labor required to service a customer. If these columns are added, be sure that the costs stated in the report are truly variable – that is, the cost will disappear if the customer goes away. Otherwise, the costs are really in the general overhead classification, and so should not be assigned to specific customers.

The customer profitability report can be a difficult one to construct, so it may only be cost-effective to prepare it at longer intervals, such as on a quarterly or annual basis.

Employee Experience

The ability of the collections department to collect overdue receivables is based to a considerable extent on the experience of the collections staff. Someone who has dealt with many customers and who knows how to deal with their issues will be much better at collections than a neophyte. However, there is also some amount of natural flair for the position that overrides experience. Also, being fully trained in credit and collection scenarios can be of considerable importance. Given these issues, the following reports could be employed:

- *Employee turnover.* Note the percentage of employee turnover per year. This information should be reported on a trend line, so that it can be compared to prior years. Turnover is a high-level measure, and so provides only a general idea of employee experience.

- *Time in position.* Note the average years in credit and collection roles. This report works best when shown in detail by person, or at least in aggregate by position.
- *Training.* Use a matrix grid to show the training received by each employee. While useful, this report only reveals the adequacy of training, not how it translates into work efficiency or improved judgment.

Summary

A key point in setting up the operations of the credit and collection areas is to ensure that the employees in these areas are as free of bureaucracy as possible. They must have the time to focus on credit analysis and collection tasks, which is how they add value to the business. If there are an unending stream of meetings and reports to fill out, their work will be interrupted to such an extent that efficiency levels will inevitably decline. Thus, the sign of an effective manager in these areas is to minimize or offload these issues, or at least to shift them to less-critical time slots at the end of the day.

This chapter presented the roles of the credit and collection functions and the tasks of the people working in these areas. In the following four chapters, we address the specific procedures and controls required to operate the underlying credit and collection processes.

Chapter 2
Credit Procedures

Introduction

Credit management is an area in which a company attempts to ensure that all customer orders being fulfilled on credit are capable of eventually being paid. This requires an order processing flow that forces sales orders through the credit department, where they can be examined for creditworthiness in accordance with various credit rules.

In this chapter, we begin with a discussion of the key terms used in credit examinations, provide examples of the forms resulting from or used in the credit process, and then move on to the various credit-related procedures. We provide separate procedures for:

- Credit examination (manual system)
- Credit examination (integrated system)

Procedural improvement tips are provided throughout the text, as well as flowcharts showing a streamlined view of each procedure.

Forms: Sales Order Form

The sales order form is used to translate a customer order into a standardized format for internal use by a business. The form should always be assigned a unique identification number, so that it can be tracked. If the company pays commissions, there should also be a space on the form to state the name of the person who is being credited with the sale. A sample format follows.

Sample Sales Order Form

Sales Order Number	Sales Order Date	Sales Order Form

Customer Billing Address Block	Customer Shipping Address Block

Salesperson	Ship by Date	Delivery Via	Payment	Cash	Check	C/C	Invoice

Item Nbr.	Item Description	Quantity	Unit Price	Total Price
	Sales Order Detail Block			
			Subtotal	
			Freight Charge	
			Sales Tax	
			Grand Total	

Credit Card Payment:	Check Payment:	Shipping and Handling:	
Card Type: MC Visa Amex	Check Number:_____	Total up to $50	$4.95
Card #:_____	Check Date:_____	Total $51-$100	$6.95
Expiration: ___/___/___	Check Amount: $_____	Total $101-$200	$9.95
		Total > $200	Free

The sample form includes a large amount of payment information, which is only needed if the order entry staff is also responsible for accepting payments from customers. In situations where customers are always invoiced, there is no need for this information on the sales order form.

If multiple copies of a sales order are to be issued, it may not be wise to include credit card information on the form, since this information will be spread throughout the company. An alternative is to use a stamp on just the order entry department's copy of the sales order, on which are noted the credit card payment details.

Forms: Credit Application

The credit department routinely issues a credit application to those customers wanting to set up credit with the company. The following sample credit application is designed to require a sufficient amount of information for the credit staff to render a well-informed decision regarding the amount of credit (if any) to grant to an applicant.

Sample Credit Application

Credit Application

Customer Address Block	Date Started	For Company Use
	Business Type	Credit Amount
	Incorporation State	Date
	Corporate Parent	Approved By

Customer Financial Information

| Last Year Sales | Current Cash | Current Debt Level |
| Last Year Profits/Losses | Current Working Capital | Current Retained Earnings |

☐ Financial Statements Attached

References

Supplier Reference #1	Contact Information
Supplier Reference #2	Contact Information
Supplier Reference #3	Contact Information
Bank Reference	Checking Account Number
	Savings Account Number

I authorize the above suppliers and bank to release credit information to the Company for its evaluation of this credit application.

| Customer Officer: [signature] | Date |

The credit application form may also include a field in the "For Company Use" section, in which the credit staff can insert the payment terms negotiated with a customer. The form may also include a number of legal clauses, such as an agreement to reimburse the company for collection fees, personal guarantees, and permission for the company to obtain payment by ACH debit. These clauses are typically included on the back of the credit application.

The Credit Examination Procedure (Manual System)

The credit department may receive paper copies of sales orders from the order entry department, documenting each order requested by a customer. In this manual environment, the receipt of a sales order triggers a manual review process where the credit staff can block sales orders from reaching the shipping department unless it forwards an approved copy of the sales order to the shipping manager. The order entry procedure for a manual system is outlined below. A primary assumption of this procedure is that a *new* customer is placing an order; the procedure also shows alternative steps for returning customers (for which a separate flowchart is shown at the end of this procedure).

1. **Receive sales order.** The order entry department sends a copy of each sales order to the credit department. If the customer is a new one, the credit manager assigns it to a credit staff person. A sales order from an existing customer will likely be given to the credit person already assigned to that customer.
   Responsible party: Credit manager

   > **Tip:** It may be possible to grant a small default amount of credit to new customers. By doing so, the credit staff can reserve its analysis time for larger credit requests.

2. **Issue credit application.** If the customer is a new one or has not done business with the company for a long time, send them a credit application and request that it be completed and returned directly to the credit department.
   Responsible party: Credit staff

3. **Collect and review credit application.** Upon receipt of a completed sales order, examine it to ensure that all fields have been completed, and contact the customer for more information if some fields are incomplete. Then collect the following information, if necessary:

   - Credit report
   - Customer financial statements
   - Contacts with customer credit references, including information about average and maximum credit granted, as well as slow payments, discounts taken, and bad debt situations
   - Contacts with bank references concerning the existence of bank accounts, the size range of account balances, and how long the customer has done business with each bank
   - Any previous ordering, payment, bad debt, and dispute history with the company

   Responsible party: Credit staff

   > **Tip:** If a sales order is for a small amount, it may not be necessary to collect some of this information. In particular, it may not be cost-effective to obtain a credit report for a small order, nor may some customers be willing to forward their financial statements.

> **Tip:** It can take some time to assemble the information needed for a credit application, which may drive an impatient customer to a competitor. To keep the credit review process from being prolonged, the credit staff should review the status of all unapproved sales orders every day.

4. **Assign credit level.** Based on the collected information and the company's algorithm for granting credit, determine a credit amount that the company is willing to grant to the customer. The following are all valid approaches to granting credit:

   - Assign a minimum credit amount in all cases; or
   - Assign credit based on the item being ordered (where higher credit levels are allowed for items being cleared from stock); or
   - Assign credit based on estimated annual sales volume with the customer; or
   - Assign credit based the credit score listed in a third party's credit report; or
   - Assign credit based on a decision table developed from the company's overall credit experience; or
   - Assign credit based on an in-house credit granting algorithm

   It may also be possible to adjust the credit level if a customer is willing to sign a personal guarantee.
   Responsible party: Credit staff

5. **Hold order** (optional). If the sales order is from an existing customer and there is an existing unpaid and unresolved invoice from the customer for more than $___, place a hold on the sales order. Contact the customer and inform them that the order will be kept on hold until such time as the outstanding invoice has been paid.
   Responsible party: Credit staff

> **Tip:** Always inform the sales manager before placing a hold on a sales order. The customer will probably contact the sales manager once it learns of the hold, so the sales manager should be prepared in advance for this call.

6. **Obtain credit insurance** (optional). If the company uses credit insurance, forward the relevant customer information to the insurer to see if it will insure the credit risk. The result may alter the amount of credit that the credit staff is willing to grant.
   Responsible party: Credit staff

> **Tip:** It may be possible to bill the customer for the cost of the credit insurance.

7. **Verify remaining credit** (optional). A sales order may have been forwarded from the order entry department for an existing customer who already has been granted credit. In this situation, the credit staff compares the remaining amount of available credit to the amount of the sales order, and approves the order if there is sufficient credit for the order. If not, the credit staff considers a one-time increase in the credit level in order to accept the order, or contacts the customer to arrange for an alternative payment arrangement.
Responsible party: Credit staff
Control issues: The credit manager should review and approve larger one-time credit extensions.

8. **Approve sales order.** If the credit staff approves the credit level needed for a sales order, it stamps the sales order as approved, signs the form, and forwards a copy to the shipping department for fulfillment. It also retains a copy.
Responsible party: Credit staff
Control issues: It may be necessary to maintain control over the credit approval stamp, since someone could use it to fraudulently mark a sales order as having been approved.

> **Tip:** If the customer has agreed to bear the cost of credit insurance, then notify the billing department of the additional amount to be billed to the customer.

9. **File credit documentation.** Create a file for the customer and store all information in it that was collected as part of the credit examination process. This information is useful for future reference, either during periodic reviews or when a customer requests a change in credit level.
Responsible party: Credit staff

> **Tip:** If there are many customers, it may make sense to use a standard methodology to create a unique customer index number for filing purposes. Doing so will reduce the risk that multiple files will be created for the same customer.

The following exhibit shows a streamlined view of the credit procedure for a manual system, excluding most optional steps, and assuming that sales orders are being processed only for new customers.

Credit Process Flow (Manual System for New Customers)

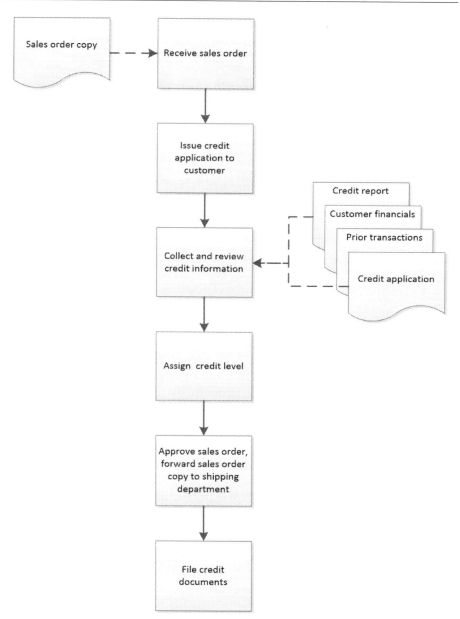

The following exhibit shows a streamlined view of the credit procedure for a manual system, excluding most optional steps, and assuming that sales orders are being processed only for existing customers. In this case, the procedure can be considerably shortened if there is a sufficient amount of unused credit already available to accommodate a sales order.

Credit Process Flow (Manual System for Existing Customers)

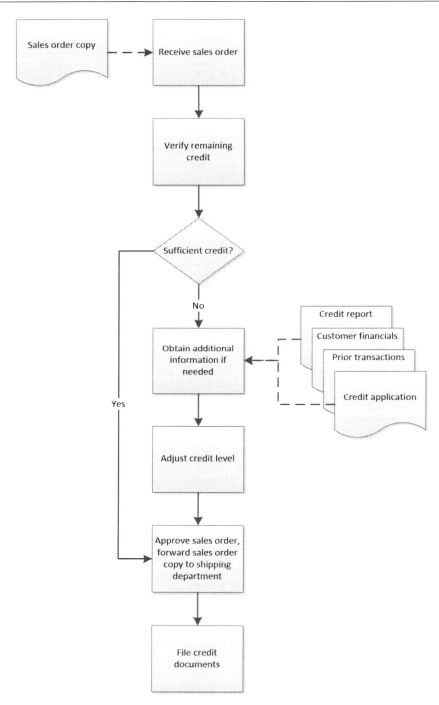

The Credit Examination Procedure (Integrated System)

When the credit department has on-line access to a company-wide integrated computer system, the credit examination process can be streamlined to a considerable extent, particularly in regard to the receipt and forwarding of sales orders. The order entry procedure for an integrated system is outlined below. A primary assumption of this procedure is that a *new* customer is placing an order; the procedure also shows alternative steps for returning customers (which are listed in a separate flowchart at the end of this procedure).

1. **Receive sales order.** The computer system notifies the credit department that a new sales order is now available for viewing. If the customer is a new one, the credit manager assigns it to a credit staff person. A sales order from an existing customer will likely be forwarded automatically to the credit person already assigned to that customer.
    Responsible party: Credit manager

    > **Tip:** Prior to credit analysis, the system should automatically place a hold designation on all sales orders. This keeps sales orders from being accidentally fulfilled.

2. **Issue credit application.** This step is similar to the one shown earlier for the manual system, with two changes. First, the computer system will notify the credit staff that a sales order is ready for its review, rather than the forwarding of a sales order document that is required in a manual system. Second, the company could direct customers to an on-line credit application form that they can complete, and which is routed directly to the credit department for review. This tends to accelerate the credit review process flow.
    Responsible party: None, since these activities are automated

3. **Collect and review credit application.** This is the same step described in the preceding procedure.

4. **Assign credit level.** This is the same step described in the preceding procedure. In addition, it may be possible to automate the process of granting credit for smaller amounts, with the system forwarding its initial credit grants to the staff for approval, or only for larger credit amounts. Also, once a credit level has been determined for a customer, the credit staff enters that amount into the customer master file in the computer system. Once this information has been loaded, the system will automatically approve future sales orders as long as there is sufficient credit available.
    Responsible party: Credit staff
    Control issues: Consider periodically reviewing the credit levels loaded into the customer master file to see how recently they have been updated. This review can spot instances where the credit staff forgot to update the credit limit field.

> **Tip:** The system can automatically monitor the time required to complete the credit review process, and bring excessively delayed sales orders to the attention of the credit manager.

5. **Hold order** (optional). This is the same step described in the preceding procedure. In addition, the system could be designed to automatically place a hold on the indicated types of sales orders and issue related notifications to the credit staff and sales manager.

6. **Obtain credit insurance** (optional). This is the same step described in the preceding procedure.

7. **Verify remaining credit** (optional). This is the same step described in the preceding procedure, except that the system can be set to automatically forward any unusually large credit increases to the credit manager for review.
   Responsible party: Credit manager

8. **Approve sales order.** If the credit staff approves the credit level needed for a sales order, it flags the sales order record as being approved. The system then notifies the shipping department that the sales order is available for fulfillment. There is no need to print a copy of the sales order, since the record is available in the computer system.
   Responsible party: Credit staff

9. **File credit documentation.** This is the same step described in the preceding procedure. In addition, the credit staff may have to create a record for the customer in the customer master file in the computer system.
   Responsible party: Credit staff

> **Tip:** Consider scanning all of the credit-related information described for this step in the preceding procedure and storing the digitized records in the computer system. This makes the credit information more readily available to the credit staff, while also allowing you to eliminate the paper records or at least shift them to off-site storage.

The following exhibit shows a streamlined view of the credit procedure for an integrated system, excluding most optional steps, and assuming that sales orders are being processed for new customers.

Credit Process Flow (Integrated System for New Customers)

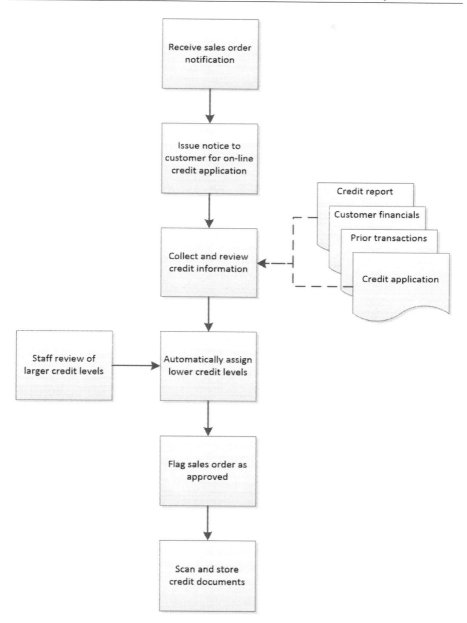

The following exhibit shows a streamlined view of the credit procedure for an integrated system, excluding most optional steps, and assuming that sales orders are being processed for existing customers. In this case, the procedure can be considerably shortened if there is a sufficient amount of unused credit already available to accommodate a sales order.

Credit Process Flow (Integrated System for Existing Customers)

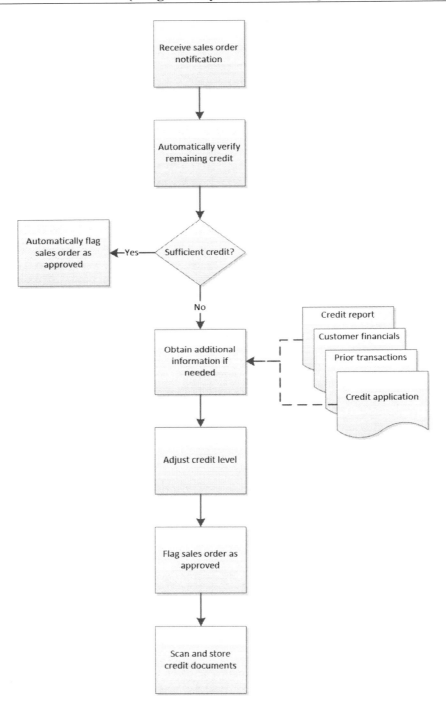

Summary

In many organizations, the credit examination process is considered an annoyance that interferes with the timely shipping of products to customers. Though there is some truth to this perception, the credit department also plays a crucial role – that of reducing the risk of incurring crippling bad debts. Thus, there is certainly a need for the credit function. By paying proper attention to streamlining the credit examination procedure, it is possible to reduce the perceived annoyance level. Possible options are to give the credit department on-line access to sales orders and other credit documents, as well as by automating the credit granting process for the more pedestrian customer orders. These changes will increase the speed of the credit examination process, while focusing the attention of the credit department on the more high-risk customer orders. Controls for the credit process are expanded upon in the next chapter.

Chapter 3
Credit Controls

Introduction

This chapter follows up on the discussion of credit procedures in the preceding chapter by examining how to install control points in a credit process that mitigate the risk of failure. We do so by showing the control systems most likely to be needed for the following situations:

- Credit in a manual order processing system
- Credit in a computerized order processing system

We conclude with a discussion of a number of additional order entry controls and related policies. Please refer back to the Credit Procedures chapter for a discussion of the process flows to which these controls relate.

> **Related Podcast Episode:** Episode 3 of the Accounting Best Practices Podcast discusses credit controls. It is available at: **www.accountingtools.com/podcasts** or **iTunes**

In-Process Credit Controls

In this section, we cover the controls that can be imposed on the core credit activities. In addition, refer to the Additional Credit Controls sections for other controls that are positioned outside of the basic credit process flow.

The main point behind the core group of credit controls is to ensure that a credit review is conducted in those cases where a large amount of credit is involved, and that only approved sales orders are then fulfilled. The following controls address these issues:

- *Require a credit examination for orders from new customers.* When a new customer places an order and requests payment on credit, the order entry staff forwards the resulting sales order to the credit department. The credit department examines the customer's financial information, credit application, and other information, and sets a credit limit for the customer.

> **Associated Policy:** There must be a policy that requires credit approval of orders; this is the reason why the credit department exists. A sample policy is: *The shipping department shall not ship to customers without prior credit approval.*

> **Associated Practice:** It is common for a customer with something to hide to simply not answer a question in a credit application. The credit staff should be particularly cognizant of this missing information, and not be allowed to grant credit without first following up on it.

- *Require a credit examination for orders exceeding credit limits.* When a customer places an order for an amount that exceeds its current unused credit limit, the order entry staff forwards the sales order to the credit department. The credit department should review the customer's payment history and any other information the credit manager believes to be relevant, to see if the order should be accepted.

> **Associated Practice:** From a practical perspective, the credit department does not want to waste time reviewing the credit of existing customers when their orders exceed their credit limits by a small amount. In such cases, the credit manager can grant an automatic one-time credit approval as long as the overage does not exceed a certain percentage of the credit limit.

> **Associated Policy:** A common ploy of the sales staff is to first obtain a large order and then demand that the credit department approve it, since the company will otherwise lose a sale. To mitigate this type of pressure, have a policy that all credit overrides be sent to the credit manager; presumably, the credit manager has sufficient backbone to deal with truculent salespeople. A sample policy is: *All credit overrides shall be approved by the credit manager.*

- *Automatically grant credit for minor orders.* If the credit manager has granted an automatic credit waiver for smaller orders, the order entry staff can stamp a manual sales order as approved, and forward it for immediate fulfillment. In an automated system, the credit waiver level may be built into the software, in which case the sales order is automatically released for immediate fulfillment.
- *Use manual credit granting rules for larger orders.* There is a tendency for the credit staff to be inconsistent in its granting of credit to customers, so they should use a credit decision table to refine who gets credit, and how much those customers are allowed.
- *Use credit rules to grant credit for smaller orders.* Rather than just granting credit automatically for smaller orders, it may be possible to incorporate credit granting rules into the order processing software that do a better job of tailoring credit levels to customers.
- *Stamp sales orders as approved if credit is granted.* A critical control is to stamp sales orders as approved if the credit department finds that a customer has sufficient unused credit for an order. This can take the form of a simple stamp or signature if a company's order processing system is manually op-

erated, or it can be a flag in a sales order record if the process is computerized.

Alternative Credit Control Systems

In this section, we assemble a selection of the controls just described and apply them to the credit management portion of a manual order processing system and a computerized system. The controls for the two systems are largely the same, except for the subsequent handling of sales orders once they are approved.

Control System for Manual Credit Management

In a manual order processing environment, the credit department reviews those sales orders forwarded to it by the order entry staff. This should include the sales orders of new customers, as well as those orders from existing customers that have exceeded their credit limits. The credit staff uses a standard set of credit granting rules to assign credit limits to customers. If the level of credit granted is sufficient for a sales order to be fulfilled by the shipping department, the credit staff stamps its two copies of the sales order, files one copy, and sends the other copy to the shipping department. These controls are noted in the following control chart.

Control System for Manual Credit Management

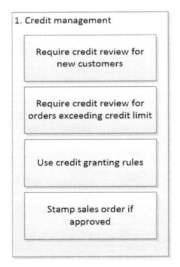

Control System for Computerized Credit Management

The control system for a computerized order processing environment incorporates roughly the same controls as those found in a manual system. The main difference is that the credit staff no longer places an approval stamp on a paper copy of the sales order. Instead, it accesses the sales order record in the computer system and flags it as having been approved. These controls are noted in the following control chart.

Control System for Computerized Credit Management

Additional Credit Controls – Fraud Related

There is a strong incentive for someone to fraudulently move a sales order around the credit department, or to falsify a credit limit, since doing so presents the opportunity to deliver goods to a customer who has no intention of paying. Controls that can prevent or at least detect such activity are:

- *Separation of duties.* Anyone who grants credit to customers should not engage in the issuance of invoices. Otherwise, someone could grant an inordinately large amount of credit to a customer who clearly cannot afford it, and then cover up the sale by issuing a credit memo to cancel the receivable.
- *Password-protect the credit management system.* In a computerized credit management system, always password-protect the system, and require that passwords be changed regularly. By doing so, an unauthorized person cannot access the system and alter customer credit levels or give an unwarranted acceptance to a sales order.
- *Lock up the credit approval stamp.* In a manual credit management system, the credit approval stamp is all that someone needs to fraudulently allow a sales order to be fulfilled. Thus, these stamps should be locked up when not in use.

Additional Credit Controls – Periodic Actions

The following controls are primarily useful for maintaining and updating the level of credit assigned to each customer. They are not part of the basic credit granting process; instead, the credit staff schedules them as separate tasks. These controls are:

- *Review the automatic credit granting level.* The order entry staff may be pre-authorized to grant credit to all new customers whose orders are below a certain dollar value. It is useful to periodically compare bad debts to this credit granting cutoff point to see if bad debt levels are unusually high for receivables arising from these automatic grants. The cutoff point may have to be adjusted over time, depending on the general economic environment and the ability of customers to pay.
- *Periodically review credit levels for all customers.* The credit department approves a certain amount of credit for a new customer based on its financial condition at the time of its initial credit application. However, a customer's financial condition immediately begins to change from that point onward, so it makes sense to periodically review credit levels on a regular basis.

> **Associated Practice:** Given the amount of time involved for an in-depth credit review, it may make more sense to review credit levels most frequently for the largest customers, and at longer intervals for smaller customers.

- *Periodically review credit granting rules.* If there have been changes in the ability of customers to pay their bills in a timely manner, or if management wants to alter sales by loosening or tightening its credit standards, the credit manager will probably need to alter the credit granting rules.

> **Associated Practice:** The review of credit granting rules tends to take place in response to an event, such as an economic downturn, or a corporate strategy planning session, rather than a review that occurs at fixed intervals. Nonetheless, there should be a scheduled review at least once a year, just to ensure that the credit granting rules reasonably reflect the business environment.

- *Match credit terms to database.* When a company has a computerized order management system, the credit department loads customer credit limits into the customer master file. Someone should periodically compare the written credit limit calculations to the amount listed in the customer master file to ensure that they are the same. It is fairly common for employees to update a credit limit calculation, but not to load it into the computer system.
- *Periodically conduct credit training classes.* Whenever the rules used to grant credit are changed, be sure to conduct a training class with the credit staff to ensure that everyone understands how the new rules are to be used.
- *Audit compliance with credit granting rules.* The credit manager or the internal audit staff should periodically review how the credit staff calculates credit levels for customers, based on the company's credit granting rules. Any unexplained results may be cause for follow-up discussions with the credit staff.

- *Subscribe to a credit score notification service.* Though it can be expensive, consider subscribing to a service that sends an e-mail to the credit department whenever a credit rating service alters its credit score for a customer. This can give early warning of a financial collapse, allowing the credit team to cut back on or eliminate the amount of credit granted.

Additional Accounting Policies

There are several supplemental accounting policies that were not mentioned earlier in association with specific credit controls. The following policies are mostly designed to require credit reviews under a variety of circumstances, as well as to keep from issuing too much credit. The policies are:

- *The business status of new customers shall be investigated if the order amount exceeds $___.* This policy is needed to ascertain whether a new customer might be a fraudulent shell company that has no intention of paying for a shipment. The policy usually involves buying a credit report from a third-party credit investigation firm. The cutoff level for this policy needs to be set at a level where the cost of the credit report is substantially lower than the profit to be expected from the proposed sale.
- *Customers shall submit a new credit application if they have not ordered from the company in [time period].* This policy is intended to give the credit department a fresh look at the finances of any company with which it does not have a recent order or accounts receivable payment history.

> **Associated Practice:** This policy can be onerous for customers placing small orders, so only apply it for larger orders. Otherwise, some customers will take their business elsewhere.

- *All customer credit limits shall be placed on hold if there have been no customer orders in [period of time].* This policy is similar to the preceding one – to require a new credit review when the company has had no experience with a customer for a fairly long period of time.
- *The credit of all customers issuing not sufficient funds (NSF) checks shall be suspended.* Whenever a customer issues an NSF check, it is very likely that it has little or no remaining cash, and so is a high credit risk. This policy immediately suspends the credit of such customers, and can be used to also put a credit hold on any customer orders already in process within the company and not yet shipped.
- *Report on customers who stop taking early payment discounts.* Some customers consistently take early payment discounts, if the discount is sufficiently tempting. When they stop doing so, it can be a sign that their cash position is worsening. This behavior can be tracked by creating a custom report that shows discounts taken by customer on a trend line.

> **Associated Practice:** A change in early payment discount terms may also trigger a change in the payment behavior of customers. Thus, a reduced early payment discount will result in fewer customers taking advantage of it; this has nothing to do with their financial condition.

- *The sales staff shall obtain prior credit approval for orders expected to exceed $___.* This policy is designed to avoid the common conflict between a sales department that already has a customer order in hand, and a credit department that refuses to allow credit for the order. By engaging in a credit review in advance, the sales staff can be prevented from wasting time on orders that have no hope of being granted credit.

> **Associated Practice:** In reality, obtaining prior credit approval can be quite difficult. There may not be sufficient information about a customer to generate a credit figure, and the sales staff needs to be on sufficiently good terms with the credit department to want to follow this approach. Also, some orders are quite unexpected, so there is no time in which to gain prior approval. Still, this policy is useful as a general guideline.

- *The credit manager must approve all increases in credit of more than ___% or $___.* This policy is useful for situations where an unusually large credit increase is about to be enacted. Even if the increase is valid, it ensures that an experienced person looks at the transaction.

Summary

The credit department is, in effect, one very large control, since its entire purpose is to mitigate the risk of not being paid by customers. Thus, the department has two key objectives to be concerned with:

- *That sales orders be routed to the credit department.* There should be an iron-clad system to make it as difficult as possible for a sales order to be routed around the credit department.
- *That proper credit granting rules be used.* There should be a reliable methodology for granting credit that will consistently yield the same results, no matter who uses it.

As long as the system of controls of the credit department fulfills these two objectives, a company will have mitigated a significant risk of issuing too much credit to customers.

Chapter 4
Collection Procedures

Introduction

Once customer invoices have been issued, it is entirely possible that customers will not pay some of them by the agreed-upon payment dates. There are a large number of possible reasons for this, including lost invoices, late deliveries, incorrect shipments, and so forth. It is the job of the collections department to uncover and resolve these issues, hopefully resulting in the collection of overdue payments within a reasonable period of time.

In this chapter, we begin with a discussion of the key terms used in collections, provide examples of the forms used in the collection process, and then move on to the various collection procedures. We provide separate procedures for:

- Collections
- Credit memo request
- Allowance for doubtful accounts calculation

Procedural improvement tips are provided throughout the text, as well as flowcharts showing a streamlined view of each procedure.

Forms: The Credit Memo Approval Form

There should be an approval form that explains the need for a credit memo and the amount being requested. The form should also specify whether the credit memo will be a standard one that is issued to the customer, or an internal one that is not issued. If possible, the form should also state the number of the invoice that is to be offset by the credit, which is used to reduce the invoice amount in the aged accounts receivable report. A sample credit memo approval form is shown next.

Sample Credit Memo Approval Form

Credit Memo Approval Form

Customer Name

Credit Memo

Customer Number

Internal Credit Memo

Credit Amount Requested

Reason for Request

Invoice to Offset (if any)

Supervisor Approval Block

The Collection Procedure

The collections staff may deal with an enormous number of overdue invoices. If so, the collection manager needs a procedure for dealing with customers in a standardized manner to resolve payment issues. The detailed collection procedure, including responsibilities and basic controls, is listed below. However, the process flow noted here only generally represents the stages of interaction with a customer. These steps might be shuffled, supplemented, or eliminated, depending on the payment status of each invoice.

> **Tip:** The following procedure assumes the presence of a large number of overdue invoices. In some businesses, there may instead be a small number of large invoices, each of which requires a considerable amount of personalized attention. In this latter case, it may be considerably less necessary to impose a formalized collection procedure on the collections staff.

1. **Assign overdue invoices** (optional). When an invoice becomes overdue for payment, assign it to a collections person for collection activities.
   Responsible party: Collection manager
   Control issues: The collection manager should maintain a list of which collections staff are assigned to each invoice or customer.

> **Tip:** In a well-run collections department, all customers are already assigned to specific collections staff. Doing so allows the collections staff to build familiarity with certain customers. In this situation, assigning specific invoices to collections personnel is not required.

2. **Verify allowed deductions** (optional). A customer may submit a form detailing a deduction claim under the company's marketing plan. If so, verify the claim with the marketing manager and match it against deductions taken by the customer. If a deduction can be traced to the allowed deduction, submit a credit memo approval form to offset the amount of the deduction.
   Responsible party: Collections staff
   Control issues: Have the marketing manager sign the customer's deduction form to authorize it, and attach the form to the credit memo approval form. This provides evidence of the reason for the credit.

> **Tip:** This can be an area of considerable dispute, since customers tend to have a broad interpretation of what can be deducted under a marketing plan. It is best to involve the marketing director in disputes. Also, consider advising the marketing director on definitions of allowable deductions before a marketing plan is released to customers.

3. **Issue dunning letters.** Use the accounting software to print dunning letters at fixed intervals, with each one pointing out overdue invoices to customers. Review the letters and extract any for which other collection activities are already in progress. Mail the other dunning letters to customers.
   Responsible party: Collections staff

> **Tip:** If the accounting system has this feature, e-mail the dunning letters rather than mailing them. Doing so eliminates the delay caused by mail float.

4. **Initiate direct contact.** If there are still overdue invoices outstanding, call customers to discuss the reasons for lack of payment. Following each call, record the details of the call, including the date, person contacted, reasons given for late payment, and promises to pay.
   Responsible party: Collections staff
   Control issues: The collection manager should review the documentation of customer contacts on a regular basis, to see if there are any potentially large collection issues that require accelerated action.

> **Tip:** Where possible, use a collections management system that is integrated into the accounts receivable file. Doing so not only increases the efficiency of the department, but also consolidates all collection notes in one place for review by the collection manager.

5. **Settle payment arrangements** (optional). If it is necessary to accept a longer payment period, document the terms of the payments to be made, as well as any interest to be paid and any personal guarantees of payment.
   Responsible party: Collections staff
   Control issues: The collection manager should approve all special payment arrangements.

6. **Adjust credit limit** (optional). At this point, the collections staff should have sufficient information about the financial condition of a customer to recommend to the credit staff if a reduction or termination of a customer's credit limit is in order. The credit staff is responsible for changing a credit limit – the collections staff only provides information.
   Responsible party: Collections staff and credit staff

7. **Monitor payments under settlement arrangements** (optional). If there are special payment plans, compare scheduled payment dates to the dates on which payments are actually received, and contact customers as soon as it appears that they will miss a scheduled payment date. This level of monitoring is required to keep customers from delaying their payments.
   Responsible party: Collections staff
   Control issues: This monitoring function can be given to a clerk who specializes in monitoring payments. Otherwise, the collections staff may forget to do so, resulting in a greater risk of customer default.

8. **Refer to collection agency.** Once all other in-house collection techniques have been attempted, shift invoices to a collection agency. At this point, the customer should certainly be placed on a credit hold list.
   Responsible party: Collection staff
   Control issues: The collection manager should approve the transfer of all invoices to a collection agency, since doing so will result in the payment of large fees if the invoices are eventually collected.

> **Tip:** Notify the sales manager before sending an invoice to a collection agency, since the vigorous collection methods employed by these agencies will likely have a deleterious effect on relations with the customer.

9. **Sue the customer** (optional). If all other alternatives have failed, meet with the company's legal staff to determine whether the company has a sufficient case against a customer to win a judgment against it in court. Also, the customer should have sufficient assets available to pay any judgment against it. If these issues appear favorable, then authorize the legal staff to proceed with a lawsuit.
   Responsible party: Collection staff, collection manager, legal staff

> **Tip:** From a practical perspective, it rarely makes sense to sue a customer. If they refuse to pay, it is typically because they are in significant financial difficulties, and so would not be able to pay a judgment against them.

10. **Write off remaining balance.** If all collection techniques have failed, complete a credit memo approval form in the amount of the invoice(s) to be written off.
    Responsible party: Collection staff
    Control issues: The collection manager should approve all larger credit memo approval forms. An approval is not necessary for smaller, incidental write-offs.

> **Tip:** When an invoice is written off, this means that the amount of credit granted to the customer in the customer master file will now appear to be available for use again, which could lead to the inadvertent sale of more goods to the customer. To prevent this, set the available credit balance to zero, and also configure the customer's record to require that all future business be conducted on cash-in-advance terms.

11. **Conduct post mortem.** If there was a specific problem with the company's systems that caused a bad debt to occur, call a meeting of those people most closely related to the problem to discuss a solution. Assign responsibility for action items, document the meeting, and schedule follow-up meetings as necessary.
    Responsible party: Collection manager
    Control issues: The controller or collection manager should monitor assigned tasks to ensure that the underlying problem is resolved.

The following exhibit shows a streamlined view of the collection procedure, not including a number of optional steps. The flowchart shows the most likely collection activities that apply to the majority of situations.

Collection Procedures

Collection Process Flow

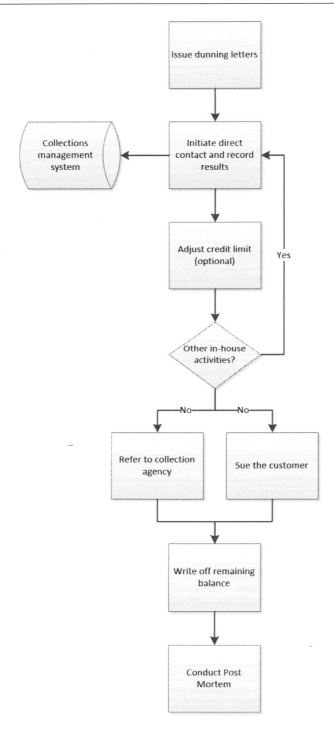

42

The Credit Memo Request Procedure

The collections staff may find it necessary to request that the amount of a customer invoice be reduced or eliminated, usually because it will not be collected. The following procedure shows how a credit memo is requested.

> **Tip:** Schedule a review of the accounts receivable aging report at the end of each month, and issue credit memos for all open accounts receivable that represent small unpaid residual balances. This cleans up the aging report, and usually results in a minimal additional bad debt expense.

1. **Create credit approval form**. On a credit approval form, state the customer name, the invoice for which a credit is requested, the amount of the credit, and the reason for it.
   Responsible party: Collections staff
   Control issues: This step is needed in preparation for obtaining approval for the credit, as noted in the next step. The primary intent of this step is to create documentation for *why* a credit is being issued.

   > **Tip:** The majority of credit memos are issued for very small amounts, such as for eliminating outstanding receivable balances of a few pennies. In these cases, it is not cost-effective to create a credit approval form. Instead, allow the collections staff to process credits for small amounts without any documentation.

2. **Obtain supervisor approval**. Have someone other than the collections clerk who is requesting a credit approve the request. This is usually someone in a supervisory position. The supervisor then forwards the form to the billing clerk.
   Responsible party: Collection manager
   Control issues: This step is needed to prevent the collections clerk from colluding with other accounting staff to fraudulently intercept cash paid to the company by customers, and issue credit memos to hide the missing funds.

   > **Tip:** It may be useful to require the approval of a higher-level person, such as the CFO, for the elimination of really large invoices, if only to bring these invoices to their attention.

Given the brevity of this procedure, no flowchart of the process flow is provided.

The Allowance for Doubtful Accounts Calculation Procedure

The collections staff is responsible for calculating the allowance for doubtful accounts, since it is best able to judge which invoices are at the greatest risk of not being paid. This allowance is a reserve for bad debts that may arise from existing accounts receivable. The procedure for calculating the allowance for doubtful accounts, including responsibilities and basic controls, follows:

1. **Clear out offsetting balances.** Review the accounts receivable aging report for any unapplied credits. Research such credits to see if they can be applied to open accounts receivable. This step is needed to ensure that no reserve is created for older invoices against which credits have already been created.
   Responsible party: Billing clerk

2. **Calculate theoretical reserve.** Print an accounts receivable aging report. Multiply the amount of receivables in each 30 day time bucket on the report by the historical bad debt percentage applicable to that time bucket. Summarize the total amount of theoretical bad debts. In addition, override the percentage calculation and include the full amount of any invoices where:

   - The customer has declared bankruptcy
   - The company is suing the customer for payment
   - The company has sent the invoice to a collection agency
   - Other information exists that indicates a high probability of failure to pay

   Responsible party: Collections staff
   Control issues: The collection manager should verify the amount of this calculation.

   > **Tip:** Verify that the aging report used for this calculation includes *all* invoices. This is not a minor point, since many businesses issue a large number of invoices at the very end of a reporting period, which might be excluded from an aging report that was run too soon.

   > **Tip:** There are multiple methods available for calculating the theoretical amount of the allowance for doubtful accounts. For example, it can be based on the risk level assigned to each customer, or on the risk of nonpayment associated with specific invoices, or an overall historical percentage for the entire amount of accounts receivable.

   > **Tip:** Update the historical bad debt percentage on at least a quarterly basis. Otherwise, using an old percentage when economic conditions are changing rapidly may result in an incorrect theoretical reserve.

3. **Adjust actual reserve.** Forward the approved calculation of the allowance for doubtful accounts to the general ledger accountant. This person adjusts the booked balance of the reserve to match the calculated balance, and includes the calculation in the accompanying journal entry documentation.

Responsible party: General ledger accountant
Control issues: The period-end closing procedure should include a task to update the allowance for doubtful accounts, which makes it more likely that the reserve will be adjusted regularly.

The following exhibit shows a streamlined view of the calculation procedure.

Allowance for Doubtful Accounts Calculation Process Flow

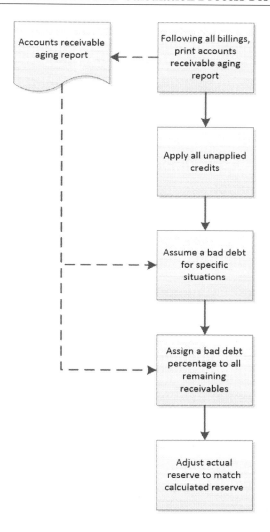

Summary

Collections is an area in which the risk of loss increases rapidly with the passage of time. This means that a strong system of procedures should be in place to ensure that overdue invoices are closely monitored. However, a practiced collections person should be allowed to depart from the standard collections routine if his or her experience indicates that a different approach is warranted. In such cases, the standard collection procedure may be more applicable for trainee collections personnel.

A large number of overdue invoices may not be the fault of the collections staff. The real issue may lie in some other part of the business, such as faulty product designs, late deliveries, or improper packaging that causes damage in transit. Consequently, a key part of the collections procedure may be an analysis of why customers are not paying their invoices on time, rather than timely contact with customers regarding overdue amounts.

Controls for the collection process are expanded upon in the next chapter.

Chapter 5
Collection Controls

Introduction

Collections is an area in which the risk of nonpayment increases rapidly with time, so there needs to be a strong control system in place for monitoring the activities of the collections staff. Additional controls are needed for writing off uncollectible invoices, and estimating the amount that should be recorded in the allowance for doubtful accounts. In this chapter, we describe process-specific controls and then show the baseline system of controls that should be used. We conclude with a discussion of a number of additional collection controls and related policies.

Please refer back to the Collection Procedures chapter for a discussion of the process flows to which these controls relate.

> **Related Podcast Episode:** Episode 171 of the Accounting Best Practices Podcast discusses collection controls. It is available at: **www.accountingtools.com/podcasts** or **iTunes**

In-Process Collection Controls

In this section, we cover the controls that can be imposed on the core collection process. In addition, refer to the Additional Collection Controls section for other controls that are positioned outside of the basic collection activities.

1. Collection Activities

The primary controls over collections are requiring an adequate level of record keeping by the collections staff, and using the resulting information to monitor their activities. The controls are:

- *Use account assignment guidelines*. The collections manager might consider using collection guidelines to decide which collections staff are to be assigned certain accounts. This can have a bearing on situations where certain customers are so difficult to collect from that only the most experienced staff can deal with them.
- *Mandate a collections procedure*. There should be a standard set of activities that the collections staff is required to pursue when contacting customers about collection issues.

> **Associated Practice:** A standard collections procedure may be more applicable for trainee collections personnel, and can be waived to some extent with more experienced employees who know which collection techniques will work with certain customers.

- *Require collections record keeping.* It is impossible to determine the status of an overdue account receivable unless the collections staff maintains adequate records regarding the dates when contacts were made, promises made by customers, and next expected action dates.

> **Associated Practice:** If at all possible, the collections staff should use a collections management system that is integrated into the aged accounts receivable file, which not only increases the efficiency of the department, but also consolidates all collection notes in one place for review by the collections manager.

- *Review collection actions taken.* The collections manager should hold regular meetings with the collections staff to learn about their collection actions taken, as well as expected payments. This is a useful control for ascertaining whether there have been lapses in collection activity.
- *Require supervisory approval of actions taken.* If the collections staff wants to allow delayed or reduced payments, it should first obtain the approval of the collections manager.

> **Associated Practice:** The collections staff should be allowed some leeway in creating payment plans and allowing reduced repayments. Otherwise, the collections manager will be awash in approval forms.

- *Monitor credit levels.* It makes little sense for the collections staff to engage in desperate collection activities against a recalcitrant customer when the company is continuing to sell to the customer. Consequently, a strong control is to give the collections staff input into the termination or reduction of customer credit during (and after) collection activities.

2. Write off Balances

Only one control is needed over writing off invoices, but it is an important one. The control is:

- *Supervisory approval is needed to write off invoices.* The collections manager or controller should approve the write off of invoices requested by the collections staff. This typically involves a review of all collection actions taken thus far, to ensure that all necessary actions have been taken. It is also necessary to prevent collusion by the collections staff with the cash receipts staff, which could abscond with incoming customer cash and then write off the related invoice.

> **Associated Practice:** From a practical perspective, it is a waste of time to review the write off of smaller invoices, so the collections staff should be allowed to write off invoices below a certain dollar level.

Additional Step – Calculate the Allowance for Doubtful Accounts

In addition to the controls over ongoing collection activities that were just noted, there also need to be several controls over the calculation and updating of the allowance for doubtful accounts. The following controls are particularly useful in situations where the amount of bad debt write offs has historically been significant:

- *Verify that the last period-end aging report is the basis for updating the allowance for doubtful accounts.* This control is not a minor one, since a large amount of month-end invoicing is done at many companies, and the calculated allowance will be too low unless all of the invoices are included in the aging report.

> **Associated Practice:** If there is a month-end closing procedure, insert the updating of this allowance into the procedure *after* the completion of all customer billings, so that the receivables aging report will be fully populated.

- *Require controller approval of changes in the formula used to calculate the allowance for doubtful accounts.* The calculation of the allowance could be modified to meet management's wishes to alter the reported level of profitability. To avoid this issue, the calculation method should be locked down from period to period, and only changed with the direct approval of the controller.
- *Any adjustments to the allowance for doubtful accounts are approved by a supervisor.* The collections manager or controller should approve the proposed journal entry in which the allowance for doubtful accounts is updated. The journal entry should have the calculation of the allowance change attached to it.

Alternative Collection Control Systems

In this section, we assemble a selection of the controls just described and apply them to a typical collections system. The key points are to ensure that the collections staff has an adequate record keeping system for their collection activities, and that the collections manager reviews this information on a regular basis to ensure that these activities are being followed on a timely basis. In addition, a supervisor should approve the write off of larger invoices. These controls are noted in the following control chart, where controls are clustered under the basic collection tasks.

Control System for Collections

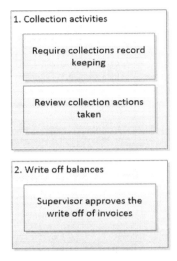

Additional Collection Controls

The following controls are useful for ensuring that the collections staff has the most recent information regarding the status of customer invoices, as well as for tracking collection performance, overseeing the allowance for doubtful accounts, and other matters. They are not necessarily a direct part of the collections process; instead, the collections staff schedules them as separate tasks. These controls are:

- *Use a central collections database.* Install a collections database that is linked to the accounting system, and which the collections staff updates throughout the day. This is perhaps the most effective control that a collections manager can implement, since it gives complete visibility into the workings of the collections staff.
- *Match collection database to aged accounts receivable.* If the collections staff works from a copy of the aged accounts receivable, review the copy to ensure that it matches the most recent information.
- *Require immediate updating of receivable records with cash receipts.* The collections staff may be wasting its time making collection calls on funds that have already been received, so mandate that the cashier apply cash to open accounts receivable at once.
- *Notify the collections staff of changes in credit limits.* The credit manager should notify the collections manager of any prospective or completed changes in customer credit limits.
- *Track collections on a trend line by collections person.* One of the better ways to judge the collections staff is to track their collections percentage over time. This is not a perfect management technique, since some customers are more difficult to collect from than others.

- *Notify the credit manager of collection trends.* The collections manager should inform the credit manager of any clearly worsening trend in collections. This may call for the tightening of the corporate credit policy, so that only the more robust customers are allowed large amounts of credit.
- *Track the allowance for doubtful accounts on a trend line.* It may be useful for the controller to track a comparison of the allowance for doubtful accounts to credit sales or accounts receivable, to see if the proportion is changing. If the proportion is declining, it is likely that the external auditors will question the size of the reserve.
- *Review the formula used for the allowance for doubtful accounts.* The controller and credit manager should occasionally review the formula used to derive the balance in the allowance for doubtful accounts, to see if it arrives at a reasonable reserve. This review may be triggered by an event, such as a downturn in the economy.

Additional Accounting Policies

The following policies relate to accounts receivable collections, and involve the management of the department. The policies are:

- *All collections staff shall be assigned specific customers for collection activities.* It is of some importance to assign collection responsibility to specific collection employees. This allows them to learn about the payment characteristics of specific customers, while also making it clear that they are responsible for overdue payments.

> **Associated Practice:** It may be worthwhile to also assign responsibility for overdue invoices to specific salespeople, and issue aged accounts receivable reports to them that contain only the overdue invoices of the customers for which they are responsible.

- *Account responsibility shall be reassigned at intervals of [time period].* This policy is designed to forcibly shift customers to different collections personnel from time to time. The advantage of doing so is that collectors can begin to identify too closely with customers, and may become more willing to accept excuses for delayed payments.
- *The collections staff can approve account write-offs of up to $__.* It is inefficient for collections personnel to fully document smaller account write-offs and obtain supervisory approval for them. In many cases, these write-offs are for minor payment variances that would be very inefficient to pursue with customers, and which do not present a risk of fraud. Thus, it is reasonable to allow the collections staff to eliminate them as efficiently as possible.
- *The sales manager shall be notified before any accounts are sent to a collection agency or attorney.* Shifting an overdue invoice to a collection

51

agency or an attorney is a serious step, for it implies that the company is willing to terminate its business relationship with the customer. This policy states that the sales manager should be made aware of these actions before they are taken, in case that person wants to make a last attempt at salvaging the relationship.

Summary

The controls used in the collections area differ from those used for other business processes, because there is not really a regimented collections process. There may be general collection guidelines, but the collections staff usually modifies them to meet the circumstances of each individual collection situation. Since there is no iron-clad process, the controls tend to be of a more general nature, with a focus on giving the collections staff the latest receivable information to use, and ensuring that some sort of ongoing collection activities are being engaged in.

Chapter 6
The Credit Policy

Introduction

The credit department is essentially in the business of lending funds to customers – albeit on a very short-term basis and without an interest charge. Like a lender, the credit staff should follow specific guidelines for how this lending function is to be managed. The guidelines are codified in the credit policy, whose contents we discuss in this chapter. We also address how elements of the collections function can be included in the credit policy.

Overview of the Credit Policy

The credit department must deal with a continuing stream of requests from customers for credit terms. Each customer has a different set of characteristics, such as their financial position, years in business, and payment history that must be sorted through and used to make a credit decision. In the absence of any sort of structure to this decision-making process, it is entirely likely that the resulting credit decisions will vary widely, even for customers with relatively similar characteristics.

The credit policy is used to bring a high level of consistency to the credit granting process. To do so, the policy should be constructed with a sufficient level of detail to clarify the following topics:

- The mission of the credit department
- Who is allowed to make credit decisions
- What rules to use for the derivation of credit
- The terms of sale to be used, other than the amount of credit granted

In addition, the credit policy can be designed to encompass collection activities. Doing so means that certain types of collection activities are allowed, others are not allowed, and the approximate timing and duration of various collection steps are laid out. The intention is not to completely regiment the collections process, but rather to set boundaries around how the function shall be managed.

The credit policy should show how to deal with the most common credit and collection decisions that the staff will encounter. Over time, it is likely that additional scenarios will arise that were not covered by the original credit policy, such as unusual types of payment deductions. Accordingly, the policy can be expected to expand to provide coverage of these unusual situations. If a company expands into multiple lines of business, the credit policy will likely have to expand too, to keep pace with the variety of credit and collection scenarios that are likely to arise in this expanded environment.

> **Tip:** The credit policy does not have to cover every scenario, since this would call for an oppressively massive policy. Instead, only create policies for situations that keep occurring with some regularity.

The credit policy is also an excellent training tool for new employees, since it sets guidelines for their activities. Not only does it ensure that they are aware of the policy from their first day on the job, it also sends the message that the company is serious about following the policy.

Credit Policy: Mission

The mission of the credit department sets the tone of the entire credit policy, for it describes the overarching reason why the company grants credit. The mission statement can lie anywhere along a continuum, where one end allows cheap and easy credit (therefore focusing on higher revenues) and the other end dwells on credit risk reduction (therefore focusing on fewer bad debts). Where the company positions itself on this continuum depends on senior management's propensity to expand sales or maintain a prudent financial position. The following factors should be considered when making the decision:

- *Product margins.* If the company sells products that have relatively low margins, then it cannot afford an excess amount of bad debt. Consequently, it has no choice other than to follow a tight credit policy. Conversely, ample profit margins allow management the alternative of granting easier credit in order to expand sales.
- *Economic trends.* The credit policy can fluctuate in accordance with economic trends. If the economy is expanding and customers therefore have more money, it may be acceptable to adopt a looser credit policy, and vice versa. However, adjusting the policy to match the economy also means that the company must follow leading indicators closely to ensure that the policy is modified at regular intervals.
- *Product obsolescence.* If a company has a significant volume of products on the shelf that are approaching obsolescence, it may make sense to grant much looser credit when doing so will sell off these items. Since the company would otherwise take a hefty loss to dispose of these goods, taking a risk granting credit to a lower-quality customer may not really be a risk at all.

Examples of mission statements that encompass the preceding issues are:

[Loose credit version] The credit department exists to facilitate sales. Accordingly, the department shall offer credit to all customers that have been in business for a reasonable period of time, except in those cases where there is a strong indication of probable bad debt losses. Every option will be considered before a customer is denied credit. Consequently, a certain amount of bad debt losses are expected.

[Tight credit version] The credit department exists to maximize company profits. Accordingly, the company shall only offer credit to those customers with verifiable credit histories that indicate on-time payments and no risk of default. All other customers will have mandatory cash on delivery terms until a payment history has been established. Bad debt losses are to be minimized at all times.

[Adjustable credit version] The credit department strikes a balance between the expansion of sales and profits. Accordingly, the department shall regularly examine its margins and liquidity, economic conditions, and other factors in order to set credit levels that yield prudent financial returns.

Credit Policy: Goals

There should be a goals section in the credit policy that states the targets against which the credit department will be judged. Examples of possible goals are:

- *Processing speed.* The department will process 95% of all credit applications within one business day of receipt.
- *Efficiency.* The department will operate with one credit full time equivalent per 500 customers.
- *Results.* The company's average days outstanding (DSO) figure will not exceed 50 days at any time.

Credit Policy: Responsibilities

The ultimate responsibility for making credit decisions should be clearly stated. Otherwise, the credit manager may be involved in ongoing quarrels with the sales manager over the amount of credit that will be granted.

In addition, the policy should clarify who is entitled to place a customer on credit hold status. Once again, the sales manager will want control over this function, even though the responsibility should lie with the credit manager.

> **Tip:** Have a very senior manager sign off on the completed credit policy, which lends force to the stated authorization for who grants credit.

A possible variation on this portion of the credit policy is to include an automatic approval escalation in the policy when the amount of money involved surpasses a predefined threshold level. For example, granting credit above $1,000,000 might call for the approval of the CFO. A variation on this concept is for the sales manager to define a small group of "key customers," who cannot be placed on credit hold status without the prior approval of a senior manager; doing so may be needed if the company has a strategy of pursuing increased market penetration in certain areas.

An example of a credit policy clause concerning responsibilities is:

All credit decisions for the issuance of credit must be approved by the credit manager. When the amount of credit exceeds $50,000, the approval of the president must also be obtained.

Credit hold decisions must be approved by the credit manager. If the credit line to be placed on hold exceeds $50,000, the approval of the president must be obtained.

An additional factor to consider is stating in the credit policy that the credit and collection functions cannot report to anyone within the sales function; or alternatively, to state the position(s) to which these functions report. Doing so keeps the sales manager from gaining direct control over areas that should act as counterbalances to sales. An example of such a credit policy clause is:

The credit manager reports to the chief financial officer. The collections manager may report to either the controller or chief financial officer. Under no circumstances may these positions report to anyone who also supervises the sales function.

Credit Policy: Required Documentation

The credit policy can state the types of information required before a credit judgment can be made about a new customer or a credit revision for an existing customer. For example:

Customer Type	Documentation Required
Individual – new customer	Credit application, credit report, credit references
Individual – existing customer, small increase request	Payment history
Individual – existing customer, large increase request	Credit application, credit report, payment history
Commercial – new customer	Credit application, credit report, financial statements
Commercial – existing customer, small increase request	Payment history
Commercial – existing customer, large increase request	Credit application, credit report, credit references, financial statements, payment history

Particular attention should be paid to the credit application, which is the form upon which the bulk of smaller credit decisions are made. The policy can state the primary responsibility for having applications completed, and note the importance of certain elements of the application. For example:

The salesperson is responsible for delivering credit applications to customers, discussing its contents with them, and ensuring that the forms are completed. No credit application will be accepted for review that has not been signed by the customer. All credit applications will be rejected if the customer has crossed out any portions of the application.

The policy can address the periodic elimination of customer credit records, if the company is no longer doing business with them. For example:

> After the company has not done business with a customer for at least one year, its credit file is to be archived. After an additional period of ___ years, and with the prior approval of the credit manager, the credit files associated with inactive customer accounts are to be shredded.

The policy can also itemize the intervals at which selected information in a customer's credit file should be updated. Rather than being required for every customer at certain intervals, updates could instead be triggered in other ways, such as:

- New credit report when customer renews orders after at least a one-year lapse.
- New credit report whenever a not sufficient funds check is processed.
- Financial statements at annual intervals when the total amount of credit outstanding exceeds $___.
- Financial statements when the credit report indicates a score of less than ___.
- New credit application when there has been a change of control.

Credit Policy: Review Frequency

The policy should note the events that can trigger a review of an account by the credit department, or the intervals at which reviews should take place. Indicators of when these reviews might take place were just noted for the accumulation of required documentation. The following sample policy reveals the level of detail at which the policy can enforce the use of these reviews:

> The credit department shall conduct a review of the credit extended to its customers using the following triggering mechanisms:
>
> - Annually for those customers comprising the top 20% of company sales
> - Annually for those customers whose average days to pay exceeds 20 days past terms
> - Immediately when a not sufficient funds check is processed
> - Immediately when a payment commitment is broken
> - Immediately when there has been a change of control
> - Quarterly for those customers whose average days to pay has increased by 10 or more days in the past year

In addition, when examining the reasons for bad debts, determine whether a change in the credit policy could have prevented a bad debt; this is possible if the company had evidence of a decline in credit quality, but did not act upon the information.

The policy can include mandates to completely cut off all credit in certain situations where there are strong indicators of looming customer failure. For example, a credit score below a predetermined threshold level could trigger a credit stoppage, as could the receipt of two not sufficient funds checks within a one-year period.

Credit Policy: Credit Calculation

The policy can clarify the amount of time that the credit staff is allowed in which to make a credit decision. For example:

> Assuming a normal backlog of credit applications, the credit department is expected to reach a decision on every submitted application within one business day of receipt. If there is not sufficient information available to make a decision, the sales manager shall be notified of the issue within two business days of receipt of a credit application.

The policy can include the detailed methodology for determining the amount of credit to be granted to customers, including the sources of information to be used and how decisions are to be made. The topic is addressed at length in the Customer Credit Ratings chapter.

The credit calculation section should also address a number of common exception conditions that routinely arise in the credit function. For example, what action(s) should be taken if:

- A credit application is not signed by a customer
- A credit decision must be made without certain information
- A trade or bank reference does not respond
- A customer refuses to provide a personal guarantee

The policy can state the forms of payment that a customer is allowed if credit is not granted, or if the amount requested is greater than the credit granted. For example:

> If the amount of credit requested exceeds the amount granted, or if no credit is granted, the customer may still pay using any of the following methods: letter of credit, cash in advance, cash on delivery, or lease financing.

Credit Policy: Terms of Sale

The terms of sale granted to customers are usually kept the same for each business unit, so that each one can provide terms competitive to those found among their competitors. Thus, one business unit may offer net 30 day terms, while another may be compelled to offer 60 day terms.

Within the business unit level, it is best to adopt the same terms of sale for all customers, which makes it easier for the collections department to keep track of when customers are supposed to pay. Otherwise, special dispensations for longer payment terms may mistakenly lead to collection activity before a customer is required to pay. If there is to be an exception to this rule, codify it within the credit policy. An example is:

> Any requests for extended dating beyond normal credit terms must be approved by the credit manager. Extended dating is only granted when doing so is required to meet the terms of a competing sale. Extended dating is not to be granted when it is apparent that the company is simply providing longer-term financing to a customer.

Examples of terms of sale that may be issued by business unit are:

Business Unit	Payment Terms	NSF Fees	Volume Discounts
Book publishing	Net 60 days	None	20% over 100 units
Magazine publishing	20% on order placement, 80% in 30 days	$25	15% over $10,000
Website construction	50% in advance, 50% when complete	$25	None
App store	In advance by credit card	N/A	None

Credit Policy: Collection Methodology

An effective collector knows that a number of collection tools may be required to obtain funds from a recalcitrant customer, and that the use and timing of those tools should be based on the judgment of the individual collector. Nonetheless, the policy should at least contain a listing of those collection techniques that are specifically authorized for use, as well as any techniques *not* authorized, or at least not to be used without the authorization of the collections manager. A sample listing might be:

Collection Techniques Permission List

Authorized for Use	Prior Approval Required	Not Authorized for Use
Courtesy calls	Credit hold	Calls to personal phone of customer
Dunning letters	Order hold	Calls to spouse of customer
Check payment by e-mail	Promissory note	Calls to associates of customer
Take back merchandise	Barter	Personal visits to customer
Split payments	Arbitration	
Postdated checks	Attorney letters	
Salesperson assistance	Final demand letter	
	Referral to collection agency	
	Referral for legal action	

In addition, the policy could state a recommended collection procedure, where certain collection steps are used for a certain period of time, after which other methods are used. This approach is more useful for training new collectors, or when there is a large amount of turnover in the collections department. A sample procedure is:

Collection Procedure

Step	Action	Duration
1	Call in advance of due date if invoice > $10,000	1 week prior to due date
2	First dunning letter	4 days after due date
3	Second dunning letter	8 days after due date
4	Call customer	10 days after due date
5	Follow-up call to customer	Daily until responded to
6	Attorney letter	30 days after due date
7	Credit hold	45 days after due date
8	Forward to collection agency	60 days after due date

The collection procedure may vary by customer type, especially when there are significant differences in the payment histories of these customers. For example, a credit policy may have initially been designed around a business strategy of only dealing with large sales to a small number of high net-worth customers who all know each other, while a new company business unit only sells in small quantities to low net-worth customers who are not closely affiliated. In this case, the collection strategy for the first group may be completely different from the methods used for the latter group. The collections staff knows that news of any aggressive action taken against someone in the first group will quickly spread to the entire customer base, who may then retaliate against the company. The latter group is much larger and not well affiliated, so the collections staff can afford to be more aggressive in its collection activities.

Miscellaneous Provisions

The following additional topics may sometimes be covered in a credit policy. Their inclusion depends upon the level of detail that the credit manager wants the policy to cover and how the business operates its selling, credit, and collection functions. The miscellaneous provisions are:

- *Collection agencies.* The credit policy could include a discussion of collection agencies. For example, it could state the maximum percentage fee that will be paid, the criteria used for selecting and terminating collection agencies, when to refer invoices to them, and who is authorized to make decisions regarding these entities. A sample policy is:

The collections manager is responsible for hiring and terminating collection agencies. These decisions shall be based primarily on the collection efficiency of the agencies, though under no circumstances shall fees exceeding 30% of collected funds be allowed. The basis of compensation paid shall be the successful receipt of funds from customers; under no circumstances are retainers or periodic fees to be paid. All collection agencies must be bonded. Accounts shall be referred to collection agencies as promptly as possible, once all internal collection efforts have clearly failed.

- *Collection attorneys*. The credit policy could include a decision matrix for when accounts are to be shifted to collection attorneys for legal action. The decisions covered would be similar to those used for collection agencies.
- *Confidentiality*. The credit policy can state the degree to which the company reveals the information in a customer's credit file. In short, this information should be treated with a high degree of confidentiality. For example:

    Members of the credit department shall not discuss the contents of customer credit files with anyone outside of the department. If a credit request is rejected, the customer is not to be told which trade references were contacted or the outcome of those discussions. Credit files are to be stored in a locked facility after working hours.

- *Credit balances*. There may be situations where a customer has a credit balance with the company, perhaps because a credit memo was issued and the customer never made use of it. More commonly, a flaw in a customer's billing system may have led to the double payment of an invoice, resulting in a credit balance. Eventually, the company may have to remit these funds to the applicable state government under escheatment laws. To avoid this loss of funds, the credit policy could state that credit balances are subject to an inactivity fee. By doing so, the company gradually reduces the applicable credit balance, and so can retain the related amount of funds. This policy may be subject to applicable state laws. A sample policy is:

    Customers shall be contacted regarding outstanding credit balances when the balances exceed $___. These contacts shall continue on a quarterly basis, and shall note that an inactivity fee is being applied. The fee is $___ per month, beginning six months after the credit balance first appears.

- *Credit holds*. If there has been a history of sparking customer ill will by an excessive use of credit holds, specify in the policy the circumstances under which credit holds can be used, and (more importantly) when they *cannot* be used. The policy can also state that the customer and assigned salesperson must be notified at once of a credit hold, and when a credit hold is removed. A sample policy is:

    The use of credit holds is considered an extreme measure that will not be used unless all other reasonable measures have first been attempted. The credit manager must approve all credit holds. The sales manager must be notified in advance of all credit holds and when credit holds are terminated. Customers must be notified at once of all credit holds and when credit holds are terminated.

- *Customer bankruptcy*. The policy could state the process that the company should follow if a customer were to declare bankruptcy, such as arranging for the return of any goods in transit to the customer, advising the sales staff of the situation, holding all orders in process, and the preparation of a creditor claim.
- *Early payment discounts*. The policy could address how to deal with customers who take early payment discounts, but not within the stated number of days allowed for such a discount. For example, it could address how many days late are allowed before a discount is charged back to the customer. A sample policy is:

  > Early payment discounts are accepted if they are paid within five business days of the final date for which a discount was offered, which is intended to compensate for mail float. All other discounts taken shall be rejected, and the discount amounts separately rebilled to the customers, with "due on receipt" payment terms.

- *Final demand letter*. The policy can state that final demand letters be copied to a specific senior management position at the customer, as well as the company's sales manager. The policy could also specify that this letter be sent by certified mail or overnight delivery, so that there is evidence of receipt.
- *NSF checks*. The policy could mandate the exact forms of payment that the company will accept, following the receipt of a not sufficient funds check. Examples are cash, a wire transfer, or a cashier's check.
- *Payment disputes*. If the company deals with a large number of payment disputes, consider writing a set of policies that describe how to deal with these situations. Such policies can describe the resolutions to be offered and the escalation actions to be taken. If these disputes relate to certain types of problems, such as product failures or marketing discounts, consider creating a separate policy that is tailored to the requirements of each specific situation. Also, if there are very large payment disputes, this may call for a separate policy that accelerates the handling of the process.
- *Resale certificates*. In those cases where a customer would normally be charged a sales tax but claims a sales tax exemption because it intends to resell the goods, the policy should state that a sales tax exemption is only to be granted when a current resale certificate is on file. Otherwise, the seller could be liable for the sales tax that was not collected. A sample policy is:

  > When a customer requests a sales tax exemption, it is only to be granted if a current resale certificate is submitted or already on file. At the option of

the customer, an order will be held until such a document is received. Otherwise, all sales are to be classified as taxable for shipments to those regions in which the company has sales tax nexus.

- *Sales commissions.* A variation on the granting of credit is to institute a policy offering the sales staff a higher commission percentage if they can obtain cash-in-advance payments from customers. Doing so eliminates all credit risk, especially if the payments are non-refundable. Use this approach with caution, since customers with enough cash to pay in advance are unlikely to be inordinate credit risks.

Expanded Use of the Credit Policy

Thus far, we have implied that the credit policy is primarily for the use of the credit department. The document can also be distributed to the sales department, which can use it as background information for how it can expect the credit department to deal with customers. With this information, salespeople are more inclined to work within the credit department's systems to obtain credit for customers. They may also be less inclined to spend time working on sales to potential customers that clearly do not have the financial wherewithal to qualify for credit with the company.

To assist with the sales department's understanding of company credit practices, the policy manual can include examples of typical credit scenarios that customers may present to salespeople, and how they would be handled by the credit department. For example, the manual could note how an increase in credit would be calculated for an existing customer with a long history of timely payments, versus a demand for credit by a new customer that wants to place a large order.

Revision Frequency

It is a rare industry that is staid enough to have little customer turnover and minimal fluctuation in the ability of customers to pay. More commonly, there are ongoing cyclical changes in the economy that may trigger significant changes in how quickly customers are able to pay (if at all). The credit policy should reflect these changes, which means that it should be reviewed and revised at regular intervals. This could mean a mandatory review on set dates, or allowing the credit manager to conduct a review when necessary.

The most common update to the credit policy is a decision to either loosen or tighten the amount of credit issued by the company. It is also possible that changes in the competitive environment may allow (or require) the business to alter its terms of sale, such as lengthening the days over which customers are allowed to pay. However, such changes arise at much longer intervals, since they are triggered by industry trends that tend to become apparent only over long periods of time.

When altering the amount of credit issued, consider the impact of the following issues on the decision:

Has a seasonal pattern emerged?	It is possible that customers, in aggregate, are taking longer to pay at certain times of the year, which may call for credit restrictions to match the seasonal pattern.
What is the competition offering?	If the larger players in the industry are altering their credit terms, this may impact the company's ability to compete, and so may require a reactive change in the credit policy.
How is the economy impacting customers?	It is not sufficient to automatically alter the credit policy if there is a change in economic conditions. Customers may be insulated from these changes or more exposed to them, so the response may vary. For example, a company that caters to high net-worth individuals may not worry much about changes in the economy.
Is the customer profile changing?	The company may have created its credit policy based on a certain customer profile, which may no longer match the types of customers doing business with the company. A review of credit scores and historical profiles may reveal that credit is under- or over-extended in comparison to the actual customer base.
Have company gross margins changed?	The company may be allowing a certain amount of credit on the assumption that its gross margins are sufficiently high to offset projected bad debt losses. If gross margins have changed, the amount of credit granted may also need to change.

The need for a credit policy revision may be indicated when a series of related credit problems arise, such as a sudden spike in a certain class of customer. If so, it may make sense to create a reporting mechanism that tracks a variety of credit and collection measurements on a trend line, and which can be used to trigger a credit policy review if there is a jump in one of these measurements.

Tip: If the credit environment can change quickly, consider running the trend line report as frequently as once a week, to gain early warning of conditions that may require a change in the credit policy.

Distribution of Credit Policy Revisions

When a change is made to the credit policy, be sure to distribute it to everyone who uses the policy. The process for doing so should ensure that all old versions are removed from circulation, so that the wrong policy is not inadvertently followed. Also, everyone must be fully aware of the changes. To ensure that these issues are dealt with, consider the following steps:

1. Create the credit policy in a three-hole punch format, so that each element of the policy can be separately removed from a three-ring binder and replaced.
2. Assign a distribution date and/or version number to each page of the policy.
3. Issue updates to the policy with a cover memo, noting which pages to replace. Require each recipient to sign for the updates received.

> **Tip:** If the credit policy is a small one, consider posting it on the company intranet site, and issuing e-mail notices to users whenever the posted policy is altered.

Though these steps will ensure that the policy will be regularly updated, it does not mean that anyone will follow the policy. Ensuring a reasonable degree of compliance may call for periodic in-person training regarding policy changes, and perhaps even an audit of credit actions taken. Audits will likely spot credit compliance failures, so that the credit manager can follow up with policy violators.

Summary

When the management team discusses the credit policy, it may also want to consider the fact that some customers will inevitably be dropped or take their business elsewhere as a result of the terms of the policy. The amount of sales that will be lost to these customer departures can probably be quantified, based on historical information. If so, managers could consider allocating resources to the ongoing replacement of these customers with new ones, so that revenue levels will not decline over time.

Do not treat the credit policy as a stale document that is created to satisfy a management requirement and is then locked away in a drawer. While it may not be used on a daily basis, the credit policy is intended to set guidelines for how the credit function is managed, and so should be consulted regularly. In addition, be sure to review the policy when conditions change, so that the policy supports the current credit environment in which a business operates. If the credit and collection functions are spread through several locations, it is of particular importance to propagate changes in the policy to these locations, so that credit and collection issues are handled on a consistent basis throughout the organization.

Chapter 7
The Credit Application

Introduction

The credit application is a key source of information that is used by the credit department to make a determination of whether it will grant credit to an applicant. The credit application can also be used as a contract, to impose certain payment, guarantee, and other conditions on the applicant. We address both of these uses in the following section, where we cover the content and format of the credit application, dealing with trade references and incomplete applications, and the frequency with which applications should be re-submitted.

The Credit Application

The credit application is intended to accumulate as much information about a prospective customer as possible, not only to serve as the basis for granting credit, but also to provide information for possible collection efforts in the future. A simplified credit application can be purchased from an office supply store, or can be constructed for the specific needs of a business. A sample credit application appears next.

Sample Credit Application

Credit Application

Customer Address Block	Date Started	For Company Use
	Business Type	Credit Amount
	Incorporation State	Date
	Corporate Parent	Approved By

Customer Financial Information

Last Year Sales	Current Cash	Current Debt Level
Last Year Profits/Losses	Current Working Capital	Current Retained Earnings

☐ Financial Statements Attached

References

Supplier Reference #1	Contact Information
Supplier Reference #2	Contact Information
Supplier Reference #3	Contact Information
Bank Reference	Checking Account Number
	Savings Account Number

I authorize the above suppliers and bank to release credit information to the Company for its evaluation of this credit application.

Customer Officer: [signature]	Date

The preceding sample only contains a basic set of information. In addition, consider including some or all of the following additional items in a more customized application form:

- *Authorized purchasers*. To avoid later problems with a customer claiming that the person placing an order was not authorized to do so, have them list on the application the names of those people who are authorized to place orders. However, this list will require regular updating to stay current with changes at the customer.
- *Contacts*. It is useful to obtain a list of the contact information for all of the people working for the applicant who may be able to assist with payment issues at a later date, such as the accounts payable clerk, accounts payable supervisor, and controller.

- *Credit request*. Allow the applicant to request a certain amount of credit. The credit staff is certainly entitled to ignore the amount requested, but at least should be aware of the expectations of the applicant.
- *DUNS number*. The DUNS number makes it easier for the credit staff to access the correct credit report for the applicant.
- *Officers*. This is not just the names of the company officers, but also their complete contact information, which can be useful for following up regarding unpaid debts or personal guarantees.
- *Principals*. This is somewhat different from corporate officers; it refers to the owners of the business, and should include their home addresses and phone numbers. This information may be better than the contact information for officers, since it may allow a collector to pursue the owners personally for payment.
- *Trade names*. Have the applicant list all trade names under which it does business, which is useful for researching the entity.
- *Type of entity*. The application (if a business) can state the type of business entity. The company will have access to more assets in the event of an account delinquency if the business entity is a sole proprietorship and less if the entity is a corporation. Consequently, knowing that the entity is a corporation could trigger a request for a guarantee of funds owed, since the payment claims of the seller will otherwise be limited to the assets of the corporation.
- *Years in business*. Year in existence is considered a key determinant of the ability to pay by many credit managers.

Adjustments to the Credit Application

The credit application can be considered a legal document, since it may be signed by the applicant. If customers can be persuaded to sign the application, then consider adding a number of clauses to the document to give the company a variety of legal rights. For example:

- *Arbitration*. Both parties agree to arbitration of any payment disputes. By doing so, more expensive litigation is avoided. Include in the clause the exact arbitration steps to be followed, so there are no delays associated with later negotiation of these steps.
- *Binding signature*. The applicant could claim that the person signing the application does not have the authority to do so. A clause could state that the person signing the application *does* have the authority to agree to the terms and conditions stated in the application.
- *Disclaimer*. The applicant acknowledges that the company's liability is limited to replacement or credit following the return of an authorized, unused, and unadulterated product. Doing so mitigates the risk of additional losses from customer lawsuits.

- *Early payment terms affirmation.* The applicant acknowledges that the company will charge back any early payment discounts that are taken too late, possibly including an additional processing fee.
- *Electronic payment.* The customer will pay the company by having the company automatically debit its bank account with an ACH debit transaction for invoiced sales, as of a certain number of days after the invoice date, or as of a certain date in each month.
- *Fee reimbursement.* If the company needs to pay a third party, such as a collection agency or attorney, to collect from the applicant, the applicant agrees to pay these fees. It is not likely that the fees will actually be collected, but it may be worthwhile to insert the clause just to provide the company with extra collection leverage.
- *Inspection.* The customer agrees to inspect goods from the company upon their arrival and issue a complaint about any problems found within a specific period of time. After that time period has expired, the customer revokes the right to continue to claim product damage. This clause reduces the number of options that a customer has for delaying payment.
- *Interest payments.* The applicant agrees to pay a stated rate of interest on any past due balances. The company then has the choice of activating this clause or ignoring it, depending on the circumstances.
- *Legal venue.* The parties agree that, if a legal outcome is necessary, the litigation will be addressed in the state of residence of the company, not the applicant. This reduces the cost of travel for the company.
- *Ownership change notice.* If there is a change in control of the applicant on a future date, it must provide written notice of the change in ownership to the company.
- *Personal guarantee.* The person signing the application agrees to personally guarantee the debts owed by the applicant. This clause is the most frequently objected to by applicants, but is worth attempting in order to establish a legal claim.
- *Returned check fees.* If the applicant pays the company with a check for which there are not sufficient funds, the company is entitled to charge the applicant the amount of the associated bank fees. This results in a minor expense reduction for the company, but can be useful for convincing customers to pay attention to the amount of available cash in their checking accounts.
- *Security interest.* The applicant grants the customer a security interest in any goods sold to the customer. Assuming the company follows up on this right by filing the appropriate paperwork, it will then have a right to those goods that has priority over the claims of unsecured creditors.
- *Tax exemption certificate.* If the applicant has a tax exemption certificate, it should be attached to the completed credit application. Doing so saves time later, when preparing invoices to the applicant for tax-exempt sales.

It is likely that a large number of additional clauses will spill over to the back side of the credit application. If so, include extra lines on the back for signatures or initials. Having these lines filled out provides legal evidence that the applicant has read and agreed to the additional provisions.

> **Tip:** If the signer of the application agrees to a personal guarantee, have a procedure in place for storing the original of the credit application in a secure location, since this is a potentially valuable document.

Some of these clauses will not be applicable, depending on the circumstances. For example, the security interest clause is of no use when the company sells services, rather than goods. Similarly, no one in a publicly-held company is likely to agree to a personal guarantee. In these cases, it is acceptable to either tailor the application to the circumstances, or accept the fact that certain clauses have been crossed out by the applicant.

The On-Line Credit Application

A number of days can pass while the credit department issues a credit application, an applicant fills out the form, and sends it back for review by an analyst. The time delays built into this process can be significantly reduced by installing an on-line credit application that is accessible through the company's website. Customers can fill out the form on-line, after which it is automatically routed by workflow management software to the queue of a credit analyst. The system can even access and attach a third-party credit report that will then be immediately accessible to the analyst.

The on-line credit application can be interactive, so that the information required varies with the information provided. For example, the information requirements for a corporation may vary from the requirements for a sole proprietorship, while more information can be required of an applicant that does not choose to provide financial statements.

An on-line form may not be fully integrated into a company's internal credit review processes. Instead, it may be simpler to design an application form that is sent to a designated person as a text e-mail, with each response listed on a different line. The recipient may use this information to immediately conduct a credit review, or re-enter it into the company database for further analysis or routing. This is a sufficient level of automation if there is only one credit analyst. However, if there are many analysts to whom the form might be routed, then a more complete (and expensive) integration with the in-house credit review process will be necessary.

A lesser alternative is to simply post a credit application in PDF format on the company website. Though this approach puts the credit application into the hands of customers quickly, it does nothing to insert the customer's information into the credit department's database. Thus, the PDF approach does little to reduce the total time required to complete and review a credit application.

Trade References

The trade references that a credit applicant submits on a credit application will have been carefully cultivated by the applicant. This may include paying the trade references well before any of its other suppliers. A particularly weak reference is a landlord or utility, since these entities must be paid on time by the applicant to avoid negative consequences. One way to sidestep this issue is to refuse to accept landlords, utilities, or similar entities as trade references, which forces the applicant to come up with more realistic references. Also, reject all trade references that have been doing business with the applicant for less than one year, on the grounds that it is preferable to obtain references that have an extensive record of payments from the applicant.

> **Tip:** When searching for additional trade references for an applicant, ask the salesperson who deals with the applicant. The salesperson may know which competitors have been selling to it. A trade reference from a competitor is especially valuable, since the applicant may have already been turned away by the competitor because of late payments.

If the supplied list of trade references indicates that they are all being paid on time, purchase a credit report for the applicant and compare their reported experiences with the range of pay dates listed on the report. It may be possible to discern a pattern among the various reported pay dates, where the applicant is paying its most critical customers on time, and delaying payments to its more peripheral suppliers.

The person making inquiries with trade references should ask the same questions of every reference, using a standard checklist. By doing so, the same information is consistently collected every time, and no information is missed. The following is a sample list of inquiries:

- How long the applicant has had an account with the trade reference
- The account balance with the applicant at the current date
- The amount of any past due balance at the current date
- The average number of days that the applicant normally takes to pay
- The highest account balance with the applicant in the past 12 months
- The last date on which the trade reference sold to the applicant
- The terms of sale with the applicant, as well as any guarantees

It is useful to ask for a new set of trade references whenever a customer is asked to supply the company with a new credit application (see the Updating the Credit Application section). Specifically, ask for a different set of trade references with each update, rather than the same set of references. Over time, this means that the credit staff will gain access to a larger pool of references.

> **Tip:** There is a certain amount of skill associated with making inquiries with trade references. If certain credit staffers are exceptionally good at this task, route all trade reference checks to them.

If it proves difficult to contact trade references, it is possible to simply rely upon the payment information contained within a third party credit report. However, the identities of the reporting organizations on these reports are masked, so it is not possible to tell who has submitted payment experience information.

The Incomplete Application

A credit applicant may choose not to complete certain fields on a credit application, or to not sign the application. If so, this is a major warning flag that the applicant is attempting to hide information from the company. For instance, missing financial statements might have revealed that the business is failing, or there are no trade references willing to talk to the credit staff. Whenever there is missing information or an unsigned application, a good rule is to immediately refuse to extend any credit, on the grounds that the other party is already not being honest with the company. Further, make note of the issue in the company's credit database, so the problem will be flagged if the applicant ever submits another credit application in the future.

Updating the Credit Application

When a customer completes a credit application, the information provided is only accurate as of the date on which the form was completed. Thereafter, the actual circumstances of the customer will diverge from what it originally reported to the company. Over time, the credit department will be making credit decisions concerning that customer based primarily on the company's own payment history with it, supplemented by occasional credit reports purchased from a reporting agency. To improve the information available, consider requiring a replacement application from time to time. Here are several possible scenarios for requiring a new application:

- *Bounced check.* When a customer's check payment is returned, due to not sufficient funds.
- *Larger customers.* An annual requirement for a new application if the annual order volume exceeds $___.
- *Near threshold.* When a customer's order volume is consistently near the top end of the allowed credit limit.
- *No recent history.* When a customer has not placed any orders recently and then places a large order.
- *Predetermined time period.* When the customer's last credit application is at least ___ years old.

While it is useful to obtain new credit information, it is also annoying for customers to fill out the form again. To keep from annoying customers, do not require a replacement application if the amount of credit that the customer needs is quite low.

Summary

The credit application is the core document upon which the granting of credit is based. For this reason, the basic rule should be that no credit amount above a minimum threshold level should be granted without a completed and signed credit application. Otherwise, the credit staff is making credit decisions based on incomplete information. Also, if the company grants large amounts of credit, treat the credit application as an important legal document that should adequately protect the rights of the company, and which can be tailored to meet the needs of the company as it relates to each individual applicant.

Chapter 8
Customer Credit Ratings

Introduction

Credit ratings are used to standardize the measurement of a customer's ability to pay. In this chapter, we describe the nature of credit ratings, how to create an internal rating system, the availability of third party systems, and how to evaluate the results of a credit rating system.

The Credit Rating

It is possible to individually judge the merits of each customer's ability to pay for a sale made on credit, based on such information as credit applications, financial statements, and payment history. However, doing so on an individual basis introduces inconsistency into the granting of credit to all customers. It is entirely likely that a credit manager will grant more credit to a customer because he or she likes the customer, or less credit because their accounts payable person is annoying – hardly quantitative reasons, but all too common.

A better approach is to develop a standardized method for granting credit that is based on hard facts, such as customer payment history and liquidity. Doing so results in considerable consistency in how much credit is granted across the entire spectrum of customers, and should also reduce the incidence of bad debt losses. Such a system should ideally reject a request for credit when a customer is likely to default, as well as extend credit when a customer is not likely to default. Though the concept seems obvious, it can be quite difficult for a standardized system to differentiate between acceptable and unacceptable customers. A high-quality credit rating system does the best job of sorting through the credit applications of *marginal* customers; the applications of substantially better and worse customers can be more easily sorted through by even the more pedestrian credit rating systems.

Internal Credit Rating Systems

It is possible to develop an internal credit rating system, since the credit department has access to a large pool of information about customers, especially those that have been doing business with the company for a long time. However, a credit rating system will only be useful if a company has well over a thousand customers, since statistical analysis yields better results across large populations. Trying to develop a credit rating system based on the information from a smaller pool of customers will not yield an accurate credit scoring system.

An internal credit rating system should be based on any factors that a company finds to be important in determining the credit quality of customers in its specific industry. It is entirely possible that a credit determinant of ability to pay in one industry is a relatively minor one in another industry. Thus, the mix and weightings given to factors in the home improvement industry for contractor customers may differ wildly from those used by a sporting goods manufacturer for its retailer customers. Despite the broad potential range of variability in factors, the following are considered to be among the more reliable indicators of creditworthiness:

- *Bankruptcy.* There should not have been a recent bankruptcy filing, or the prospect of one.
- *Legal proceedings.* There should be no tax liens or other judgments against the customer.
- *Liquidity.* The customer's current assets greatly exceed its current liabilities, as measured by the current ratio or quick ratio.
- *Payment history.* The customer should have a track record of reliably paying on time.
- *Profitability.* The customer has a recent history of achieving a profit over the past few years, preferably close to the median profit level for the industry.
- *Stability.* The longer the customer has been in business, the better.
- *Third party credit score.* The credit score assigned to the customer by a credit scoring business should indicate that it is a reliable payer to *all* of its suppliers.

To construct an internal credit rating system, itemize the factors to be used in the system, and assign a range of scores to each of the factors that are either added to or subtracted from a customer's score. The following table illustrates the concept.

Point Assignment for Credit Scoring

Credit Scoring Factor	Excellent	Average	Neutral	Poor
Liquidity	+10	+5	-5	-10
Profitability	+15	+5	-5	-15
Payment history	+20	+5	0	-10
Stability	+5	0	-10	-20
Adverse judgments	0	0	0	-20
Third party credit score	+10	0	-5	-10
Bankruptcy	0	0	0	-100

The scores assigned in the preceding table can vary substantially, depending on the company's experience with how a particular factor appears to impact the ability of a customer to pay in a timely manner. For example, the credit manager may decide that payment history is the most important factor, and so assigns a large number of points to an excellent rating for that factor.

Also, note how some scores in the point assignment table are only activated if there is a negative result. Thus, there are only large negative scores related to bankruptcy or adverse judgments; a customer is not awarded points for the absence of these factors.

The point scoring system should be designed to keep a large cluster of customers from inhabiting the high and low ends of the scoring range. It is not useful when the assigned scores indicate that all customers should be granted maximum credit, or that none of them deserve credit, since this does not provide useful information.

The points assigned under a credit scoring system can be used as thresholds for a variety of actions by the credit department. For example, a score of 60 or more may allow for the automatic granting of credit, while a score between 40 and 50 calls for an escalated review, and scores between 30 and 40 indicate the need for a personal guarantee.

EXAMPLE

The credit manager of Kelvin Corporation is evaluating the credit application of a prospective new customer, which has submitted a complete set of audited financial statements. Further investigation reveals that the applicant has a 3:1 quick ratio, has been solidly profitable for the past five years, and has no adverse judgments against it. The business has been assigned an average credit score by a third party scoring firm. Based on this information, the credit manager assigns the following score to the applicant:

Factor	Issues	Score
Liquidity	High liquidity level	+10
Profitability	High historical profitability	+15
Stability	Five year history	+5
Adverse judgments	None detected	0
Third party credit score	Average ranking	0
	Score	+30

In essence, the ranking indicates that the applicant is an ideal prospective customer. According to Kelvin's credit policy, the applicant should be offered a $10,000 initial maximum credit, with re-evaluation to occur once a payment history has been compiled over the next six months. If the payment history is acceptable, the applicant can then be assigned an additional ten points, which will give it a total credit score of 40 and allow the credit manager to increase its maximum credit to $25,000.

A number of additional features can be applied to an internal credit scoring system that may enhance its usefulness. Consider the following features:

- Adjust credit scores based on the economic environment, where (for example) a contracting economy results in an automatic 5% reduction in all credit scores, thereby contracting the total amount of credit offered.

- Adjust the credit score based on the average or trending number of days past terms that a customer pays, either with the company or according to a third party credit report.
- Cap the amount of credit granted at a certain percentage of the reported net worth of the applicant.
- Cap the amount of credit granted at the amount of credit granted by anyone else to that customer, as stated on the third party credit report.
- Reduce the credit score of a customer located in a country that is perceived to have a high level of political risk.
- Reduce a credit score an increasing amount based on how long the applicant has been unable to report a profit.
- Reduce the number of points assigned to an applicant if its financial statements have not been audited, thereby reflecting the increased unreliability of the underlying information.

A company may conclude that having an internal credit rating system is a competitive advantage, since the in-house system may give a superior ability to grant credit to those customers whose credit fundamentals might lead competitors to reject their requests for credit. The result may be increased sales and profits, but only if the internal system continues to generate high-quality information. It is quite possible that the accuracy of the system will decline over time unless the company continues to compare actual results to what was indicated by the scoring system, and adjusts the system accordingly. If it appears too difficult to maintain an in-house scoring system, then an alternative is to use a third party credit rating system, as described in the following section.

Third Party Credit Ratings

A business may find that it has too few customers to develop a sufficient pool of information for its own in-house credit rating system. Also, it may not compile enough information about its customers to develop a rating system. If so, a common option is to subscribe to a third party credit rating service. Even a business that has an internal credit rating system may buy such a subscription in order to supplement its own system.

A credit rating organization, such as Experian or Dun & Bradstreet, collects information from many customers about their credit experiences with other entities, and also collects public information about liens, bankruptcies, and so forth, and aggregates this information into a credit report. These credit reports can be purchased with varying amounts of information, such as a credit rating, payment performance trend, legal filings, corporate officers, and much more.

The credit rating assigned to a business is based on the credit scoring methodology developed by the credit rating organization, which uses certain types of information and applies weightings that may differ from what a company would use if it were to develop its own credit scores. Nonetheless, these third party credit scores can provide a valuable view of how outside scoring analysts calculate credit scores.

> **Tip:** If a credit reporting subscription is purchased, be sure to include automatic updates of major changes in customer status, so that notifications of large credit downgrades or bankruptcies are received by e-mail as soon as possible.

The range of inputs that a credit rating agency may employ for the scoring of individuals is well beyond what a company could compile on its own. For example, here is a sample of some of the inputs that are reportedly used to derive the FICO score that comprises a large part of the credit rating for an individual:

Age of non-mortgage balance information	Number of accounts with delinquency
Amount of recent installment loan information	Number of bank revolving accounts
Amount owed on accounts	Number of other revolving accounts
Amount owed on revolving accounts	Number of consumer finance accounts
Amount past due on accounts	Number of established accounts
Delinquency on accounts	Number of inquiries in last 12 months
Length of credit history	Number of revolving accounts
Length of revolving credit history	Proportion of balances to credit limits
Number of accounts currently paid	Serious delinquencies
Number of accounts opened in last 12 months	Time since delinquencies recorded
Number of accounts with balances	

In short, a credit rating organization has access to much more information than a business could possibly access on its own, and uses this information to construct comprehensive credit reports about most larger businesses currently in existence, as well as for individuals.

Evaluating Credit Scores

Is it possible to tell which credit scoring methodology issues the highest-quality credit scores? Most companies avoid the issue and subscribe to the most reputable service (a subjective approach at best), or the one with the lowest prices, but either approach may not yield the best results – and results can vary substantially, since the scoring companies input different types of data into their models, as well as assign different weights to the data.

A good way to quantitatively evaluate scoring systems is to conduct a credit score comparison test, with the objective of identifying the scoring model that most clearly polarizes good and bad credit risks. This level of polarization can be measured with the Kolmogorov-Smirnov test, which evaluates the ability of a model to separate data. More information about this test can be found on Wikipedia under the "Kolmogorov-Smirnov Test" topic.

To conduct the comparison test, extract a statistically significant proportion of the account file for the past twelve months and compare its results to the credit scores issued by each credit scoring company. Look in particular for situations where the credit scores differ substantially, and where those differences would have resulted in a credit request being rejected that has subsequently resulted in a bad debt write-off. In addition, look for consistent results by a scoring model over a multi-month period.

If this test results in the decision to change to a new credit scoring methodology, also be sure to conduct a retrospective validation of the results, using both credit scores again, just to ensure that the original analysis held up over time. In addition, this subsequent analysis will allow the company to test which customers have been accepted under the new credit model that would have been rejected under the old model, and whether those additional credit acceptances turned out to be good credit risks. By weighing the benefits of reduced bad debt write-offs against any potential change in the cost of the credit scoring service, you can now arrive at a rational evaluation of which credit scoring methodology works best for your company.

Use of Credit Ratings

Credit ratings are valuable tools, and should be a mandated part of the credit management function. The corporate credit policy should require that a credit rating be developed or purchased for every credit application where doing so is cost-effective. Nonetheless, management may sometimes override the use of credit ratings when it wants to make a sale or increase profits. For example, if the intent is to gain market share, one approach is to acquire higher-risk customers by granting credit that competitors are not willing to issue. Conversely, management can increase the profit percentage (not necessarily total profits) by contracting the use of credit and thereby avoiding bad debt losses.

When management intends to increase or decrease the use of credit, credit ratings should still be used. If credit is to be increased, then the credit manager simply authorizes the extension of credit to customers whose credit scores are further down the continuum of credit ratings, rather than granting extra credit on a spot basis. Conversely, if credit is to be contracted, the reduction occurs at the low end of the current range of approved credit ratings, leaving the credit to higher-scoring customers relatively untouched.

Tip: If management intends to override the use of credit ratings, the amount of bad debt incurred will likely increase. Consequently, document the management override, since responsibility for the override tends to be forgotten when bad debts occur.

Credit Rating Errors

Credit ratings are developed from historical information, and so cannot be expected to perfectly predict the future. For example, a corporate customer with a sterling payment history may suddenly lose its warehouse due to flooding or an earthquake, and no longer be able to pay its bills. Or, an individual with a high credit rating may lose his job, and immediately begin delaying payments. And in general, an escalation or decline in general economic conditions will create a corresponding change in the proportion of bad debts experienced.

Another issue with credit ratings is the information upon which they are based. The information collected about a customer may not be perfect. It could be outdated or incorrect, or may contain fraudulent information (such as false financial statements). Also, key information may be missing, such as the existence of a loan. Consequently, credit ratings are only as accurate as the information upon which they are based.

For both of the preceding reasons, credit ratings will generate misleading results from time to time, which means that bad debts will be incurred. The built-in errors associated with credit rating systems will likely result in an average rate of bad debt losses that is relatively consistent over time, barring the effects of such major systemic changes as a recession.

The Five Cs of Credit

So far in this chapter, we have advocated a quantitative approach to assigning credit ratings to customers. Doing so is the most rational way to assign credit, and is less likely to result in excessively high or low credit level assignments. That being said, many organizations prefer to use a more qualitative approach, known as the Five Cs of Credit. These five items are as follows:

- *Character*. The character of a customer refers to its willingness to pay in a timely manner, usually as evidenced by its payment history. This information is available in a credit report, which is available from one of the credit bureaus. At a deeper level, understanding the character of a customer requires one to delve into the backgrounds of the people who own or manage the business. A good example of character is a business that has paid its bills when due for many years, without having had any litigation with its suppliers. Conversely, a history of late payments and litigation is a clear sign of lack of character.
- *Capacity*. The capacity of a customer refers to its ability to pay back a loan or credit advance. A high level of capacity is evidenced by a history of strong positive cash flow and a reasonable ratio of liabilities to cash flow. An additional issue is whether the customer's projected circumstances will change enough to alter its current cash flow or liquidity position.
- *Capital*. The capital of a customer is its net worth, which is the residual amount of assets left after all liabilities have been subtracted. An examination of capital is intended to give an idea of the asset reserves that a custom-

er has available to pay down its liabilities. A concern when examining this issue is that a customer could have a massive net worth, but it is entirely tied up in fixed assets (such as a factory) that are impossible to liquidate in order to settle outstanding liabilities.

- *Conditions*. The conditions associated with a customer refer to the environment within which it operates. One must investigate the customer's economic environment (such as highly seasonal sales), regulations impacting it, and the possibility of catastrophic events. If a customer's sales are sensitive to any of these issues, it may be difficult to grant a significant amount of credit.

- *Collateral*. Collateral refers to the ability of the customer to make a secondary source of repayment available to the company. This is especially important when the cash flows of the customer are weak or variable. For example, a customer could pledge its receivables, investment securities, or a building as collateral. The company can then seize these assets and sell them off to gain payment of the underlying debt. The investigation of collateral includes an examination of whether a customer's assets have already been pledged to other creditors.

An examination of these five items will give a credit analyst a broad-based view of the ability of a customer to pay in a timely manner. However, we suggest that it be combined with the credit rating concepts noted earlier in this chapter, in order to reduce the level of subjectivity involved in determining the amount of credit to be granted. The Five Cs are especially useful when deciding upon large credit amounts; in these cases, the company is placing itself at risk of default on a significant amount of money, and so needs to employ every possible credit tool to minimize its risk.

Summary

When a credit department first decides to use credit ratings, it is easiest to purchase a subscription from a third party credit rating agency. Once the company has built up its own database of information about customers, which may take several years, it can then consider the option of developing its own credit scoring system, which can supplement or completely replace the information being provided by the credit rating agency. The decision to use an in-house system may be driven by the need to develop a competitive advantage in ascertaining which riskier customers should be granted or denied credit.

The use of credit scoring does not completely mechanize the credit granting function, but it does introduce a high level of consistency in the credit granting process that is probably sufficient for 80% of all customers. The unique circumstances of the remaining customers will likely require more hands-on analysis that may result in adjustments to the baseline credit scores, and therefore to the credit terms offered.

Chapter 9
Ongoing Credit Monitoring

Introduction

Once an initial set of credit terms have been decided upon for a customer, the credit department must initiate an ongoing process of monitoring to ensure that the correct terms and limits continue to be applied to that customer. Monitoring involves the compilation of a baseline set of credit documentation, from which credit analysis and decisions can be made. In this chapter, we address the types of credit documentation to collect, payment delinquency indicators, credit monitoring activities, and related topics.

Credit Documentation

In order to engage in the monitoring of customer credit on an ongoing basis, the credit department should collect the following information, which it uses to reach decisions regarding changes in the credit terms it offers to customers:

- *Credit application.* Every customer asking for more than a minimal amount of credit should be required to complete a credit application. This document details the legal form of the customer, its ownership, financial condition, trade references, and other information.
- *Trade references.* Most credit applications require that an applicant for credit supply the names of at least three trade references. The results of any conversations with these trade references should be included in the credit file.
- *Personal guarantees.* If a party has provided a personal guarantee to pay for the debts of a customer, store the signed copy of this document in the company safe, and a photocopy of it in the credit documentation.
- *Notes payable.* If a customer has agreed to a longer-term payment plan to pay off its debts to the company, store this document in the credit documentation.
- *Credit reports.* If the company purchases credit reports on its customers, keep all of them on file; doing so is useful for developing trend line information for each customer.
- *Balance sheet.* The balance sheet describes the financial condition of a business as of a specific date (which should be listed in the header of this document). The line items in a balance sheet may be excessively aggregated by the issuing customer, so insist on line items describing cash, accounts receivable, inventory, fixed assets, accounts payable, and debt.

- *Income statement.* The income statement describes the financial performance of a business over a specific time period (which should be listed in the header of this document).
- *Statement of cash flows.* The statement of cash flows describes the general types of cash inflows and outflows experienced during a reporting period (which should be listed in the header of this document).
- *Debtor admissions.* Whenever there are communications with a debtor, it is important to document any admission by the debtor that they owe the company money. If this admission is verbal, then document what was said and the date of the admission. This admission is best when issued by the debtor in writing. No matter what form this communication may take, store it alongside the credit documentation, since it can be a valuable tool if a collection issue goes to court.

The preceding credit documentation items should be accumulated into a formal credit file for each customer.

> **Tip:** Enact a procedure for reviewing and purging the documents in the credit files, to keep them from becoming too bulky to be manageable. For example, some types of information can probably be safely eliminated once they are more than a certain number of years old.

The preferred financial statements are ones that have been audited, since this means a certified public accountant (CPA) has examined the underlying financial information and found that the statements fairly represent the results of operations, financial position, and cash flows of a business. However, few businesses have their financial statements audited more than once a year, so if there is a need to collect financial statements more frequently, expect that no outside party will have examined them. Also, it is possible that a company's financial statements will have been reviewed or compiled, rather than being audited. Reviews and compilations involve much less investigatory work by a certified public accountant, and so the quality of these financial statements should not be considered anywhere near as reliable as audited statements.

> **Tip:** When a customer submits financial statements that have not been examined by a CPA in any way, there is an enhanced probability that the statements will contain material errors or exclusions. For example, some smaller businesses only record depreciation expense at the end of each year, which results in the reporting of excessively profitable interim results. These issues can sometimes be spotted by closely examining the line items in the financial statements on a trend line, and looking for anomalies.

When it is time to obtain updated credit documentation for customers, one of the easier ways to obtain it may be through the company's sales department. These people usually have the best relations with customers, and can more easily obtain the necessary information. Alternatively, if the credit staff has built up relations with their contacts at customers via site visits, they may be able to more readily obtain this information themselves.

Indicators of Future Payment Delinquency

When conducting ongoing credit monitoring activities, look for several flags that can indicate future payment difficulties with a debtor. These flags include the following:

- *Bankruptcy*. Once a customer declares bankruptcy, the odds of the seller being paid decline rapidly. Consequently, subscribe to a bankruptcy notification service, under which a credit reporting agency provides immediate notice of bankruptcy filings.
- *Change from proprietorship*. A customer may have originally been granted credit in part because the business was a sole proprietorship, which means that the owner is personally responsible for the debts of the business. If the customer later converts the structure of the business into some form of corporation, this means that the owner is no longer liable for the debts of the business. When this change happens, it may be necessary to reduce the amount of credit to reflect the reduced amount of assets that are now available to the company for collection purposes. A change in the form of legal organization can be detected on a credit report.
- *Credit report results*. It may be that a customer is paying within terms, but is paying everyone else late, perhaps because your business is more important to the customer. If so, a declining payment history on a credit report will reveal this issue, as reported by the other suppliers of the customer.
- *Days to pay*. The main indicator of future delinquency is simply a lengthening of the number of days that a customer takes to pay an invoice. The number of days to pay is most easily monitored with a report that states the trend line of days to pay for each customer. However, since this report may be generated only once a month, there are other more immediate indicators. For example, a check payment may be rejected by the bank on the grounds that there are not sufficient funds in the bank account of the customer. Or, a customer may avoid paying the largest outstanding invoice while still paying a number of smaller invoices on time. Another possibility is that the number of deductions taken will suddenly rise.
- *Decline in financial indicators*. If there is a noticeable decline in the financial condition or results of a customer, the decline will eventually be felt in their accounts payable area, which will not have sufficient cash with which to make timely payments. Of course, it is only possible to notice such issues if the credit staff has arranged for the ongoing receipt of financial statements from its customers.

- *Failed payment promises.* Whenever a debtor states that a payment will be made as of a certain date and in a certain amount, and that payment fails to appear, this represents a significant indicator of severe cash flow difficulties by the debtor. Such an event should be a clear trigger to shut down all credit to a customer.

- *Missing credit application information.* When a customer fills out a credit application, every field on the form should be completed. When this is not the case, it is entirely possible that the customer is attempting to hide information from the credit staff. It is particularly important to delve into this missing information to identify why no information was provided.

- *Order decline.* If a customer is facing financial hardship or a decline in its core business, it should cut back on the volume of its orders to the company. If the credit staff is monitoring the trend of these orders, it should cut back on the amount of credit granted to be more in line with actual order volume. This is not necessarily a case where entirely cutting off credit is warranted – instead, the amount of credit granted should merely be scaled back to meet the needs of the customer.

- *Ownership changes.* Whenever the ownership of a business changes hands, this indicates that the payment history associated with that account becomes much less reliable, since it is now based on the payment habits of the new owner. In essence, a change in ownership could trigger a resetting of credit to that of a new business. This issue is particularly important for a smaller business, where a new owner is more likely to directly impose his or her payment practices on the accounts payable department. It can be difficult to spot a change in ownership. It may be noted on a credit report, or indicated when a collection person's call is routed to a new person at a debtor.

- *Triggering events.* An event may occur that is considered critical to the operations of a customer, such as an armed insurrection in a country where it generates most of its sales, or an earthquake that destroys its facilities. The credit staff needs to monitor news reports to be aware of these events. While rare, they can have a major impact on the credit terms extended to a customer.

The occurrence of any one of these items should certainly trigger a more detailed review by the credit staff, while a cluster of them should be considered a major warning sign that the amount of credit granted should be reduced forthwith.

The real issue with delinquency indicators is formulating a system for bringing them to the attention of the credit staff and ensuring that some action is taken, as described in the next section.

Ongoing Credit Monitoring Actions

The credit staff should decide upon the frequency and type of monitoring that it wants to impose upon its customers, which will be driven by many of the factors described in the preceding section. The *frequency* and *type* of monitoring are two different issues, and can be modified at the individual customer level, based on the circumstances. For example, a new customer that has reported shaky financial results could warrant a full quarterly review, as well as a requirement to issue its financial statements to the company as part of these quarterly reviews, on the grounds that the seller is at substantial risk of loss. Conversely, a cursory annual review may be sufficient for a small but well-established customer with a long history of on-time payments, since the track record is excellent and the amount of receivables at risk is small. In addition, it may be necessary to conduct a review whenever new customer orders result in a customer exceeding its allowed credit limit. This issue is dealt with in more detail in the next section, Requests for Credit Increases.

In addition to formal credit reviews, the credit staff's other main form of credit monitoring activity is centered on the accounts receivable aging report. This is a standard report generated by any accounting system, which classifies the age of unpaid accounts receivable by time bucket (such as for invoices that are 0-30 days old, 31-60 days old, and so forth). The credit staff can skim through this report each day to determine which customer receivables are trending longer than usual before being paid, which can trigger a more active and thorough credit investigation.

An alternative to the accounts receivable aging report is to review the days sales outstanding (DSO) for each customer, tracked on a trend line. If the DSO suddenly trends or spikes upward, this is a strong indicator of customer payment problems that should trigger a credit review. The calculation of DSO is:

$$\frac{\text{Accounts receivable}}{\text{Total credit sales}} \quad \times \quad \text{Number of days}$$

For example, if the credit sales to a customer for the past quarter were $100,000 and the accounts receivable due from that customer were $40,000 at the end of the period, then its DSO would be:

$$\frac{\$40,000 \text{ Accounts receivable}}{\$100,000 \text{ Total credit sales}} \quad \times \quad 90 \text{ Days} \quad = \quad 36 \text{ Days sales outstanding}$$

There is an issue with calculating DSO information over too short a period, such as the last 30 days, since the measurement will likely contain receivables from a prior period that should not be compared to the total credit sales shown in the denominator of the equation. To avoid this comparability problem, consider using a DSO calculation period of no less than 90 days, calculated on a rolling basis for the past 90 days. Thus, DSO could be calculated on a weekly basis for each customer, for the 90 days immediately preceding each calculation date.

The main forms of credit monitoring for many credit departments stop at the use of scheduled credit reviews and DSO analysis. However, there are other types of monitoring available that come from a variety of sources within and outside of the company, all of which provide useful clues regarding the financial condition of customers. Consider using the following additional types and sources of information:

- *Credit report updates.* Subscribe to the credit report updating service of a credit reporting agency. The agency will issue updates whenever there is a significant change in the status of a customer, including a bankruptcy filing.

- *Credit uptake.* A customer typically operates at a level where it does not use all of the credit allowed to it by the credit department. The difference between the amount of credit used and available tends to be fairly steady, except for seasonal industries. When there is a sudden surge from the normal amount of credit taken to a level close to the maximum allowed, this is known as *credit uptake*. A company's computer system can spot these sudden increases and bring them to the attention of the credit department, which can contact the indicated customers to learn more about the reason for the ordering change.

- *Customer service conversations.* Customers may contact the company for a variety of reasons, some of which may provide clues to their financial condition or willingness to pay for a specific invoice. For example, a call about an improper installation of equipment could result in a delayed payment by a customer. The customer service staff should record a summary of all such calls in a database, which the credit staff can peruse for clues regarding credit issues.

- *Data mining.* In some industries, analysis firms can be hired to sift through all available information about an individual or corporate customer, resulting in improved estimates about which customers are more likely to be delinquent in their payments, as well as the appropriate level of credit to extend. This service is most prevalent when customers are individuals.

- *Discounts not taken.* A customer may have been in the habit of taking all early payment discounts offered by the company, and suddenly stops doing so, which can indicate cash flow problems. This is an extremely difficult item to detect, since accounting systems do not monitor it. A possible option is to develop a list of customers that have historically taken early payment discounts, and periodically compare that list to the most recent payments made by customers.

- *Exception payments.* A notable sign of impending cash flow trouble is when a customer pays smaller invoice amounts on time, but not the larger invoices. This issue is most easily discernible by the cash application staff, which can readily see that invoices are not being paid at the point of cash application. They should note these situations in an e-mail to the credit department. This approach gives the credit staff faster notification of a problem than if they simply reviewed the accounts receivable aging report on a periodic basis and gradually became aware that certain invoices were not being paid.

- *Industry rumors.* The sales department is the best-networked group in the company, and so has the best information about any rumors in the industry concerning specific customers. When these rumors could impact customer credit, the information should be forwarded to the credit department. This type of information can be extremely difficult to extract from the sales staff, so consider having the credit manager and sales manager meet on a scheduled basis to discuss and interpret this information.

- *Inquiry rate*. When someone wants to engage in fraud, one of the more clever ways is to establish a shell company that is then kept inactive for a number of years, thereby establishing a historical basis upon which credit requests can be made. It is possible to spot this type of fraud by looking for a sudden spike in the inquiry rate for credit reports on that company, since the operators of the shell will likely begin requesting credit from several companies at once.

- *Not sufficient funds checks*. Someone within the accounting department is responsible for reviewing all notifications from the bank at which the company deposits its checks. These notifications can include a notice that a customer check was rejected, due to insufficient funds in the customer's bank account. Whenever such a notice is received, the credit department should be notified at once, preferably with complete information about the specific check that was rejected.

- *Public filings*. If a customer is publicly-held, it must submit regular filings to the Securities and Exchange Commission (SEC). These filings contain the complete financial statements of the business on the Forms 10-K and 10-Q. In addition, Form 8-K filings contain descriptions of significant events impacting the filing company. The Form 8-K disclosures can be particularly relevant to the credit department, since they reflect the current circumstances of the filing entity. SEC filings are available for public viewing at the www.sec.gov website.

- *Site visits*. The credit department should schedule an ongoing series of site visits with those customers having the most credit with the company, or for those situations where other information indicates that there may be a problem. The credit staff can look for a number of physical indicators of financial difficulty, discuss any issues with the customer's account balance, and establish relations with their counterparts that may create better access to credit information.

Note: A site visit by a credit department representative is one of the few interactions that a customer has with a supplier – the other interactions are with a salesperson and an order entry person. This means that the credit department also has a responsibility to enhance the customer relationship and give feedback to the sales department if the customer mentions any possible sales opportunities.

If the company has installed a comprehensive enterprise resources planning system, it may be possible to collect some of the preceding information from the system, since an ERP system collects every possible scrap of information. If such a system is not available, a separate arrangement will have to be made with each person providing information to send it to the credit department by whatever means is most efficient and foolproof.

Requests for Credit Increases

Customers continually ask for increases in the amount of credit granted to them. There are several ways to deal with these requests, depending upon the perceived duration of the need for credit, and the amount of additional credit requested. Several possible credit-granting scenarios are:

- *One-time small order increase.* A customer may request a small credit increase, perhaps to allow for the acceptance of one incremental order. If so, an option is to grant additional credit just for that order, and then drop the credit level back to its pre-existing level once the order has been paid for by the customer. This approach calls for a small amount of additional monitoring by the credit staff, to reduce the credit level at a later date.
- *Permanent small order increase.* A customer may request a relatively small and permanent increase in its level of credit. If so, this likely results from a gradual, trending increase in the order volume from that customer. This common occurrence calls for a modest review by a credit staff person with a minimal request for additional information by the customer, and probably does not call for an excessive amount of approval escalation within the department.
- *Large increase by old customer.* An existing customer with a lengthy payment history may ask for a large increase in credit. In this case, the credit staff should move the customer to a higher reporting level, such as quarterly financial statements, quarterly credit reports, and oversight by a senior credit employee. Also, the additional amount approved should be escalated to a high level within the organization.
- *Large request by new customer.* The riskiest credit request is a large one from a new customer with which the company has no experience. In this case, the level of investigation is similar to what a lender would impose on a prospective borrower, including financial statements for the past few years, a credit report, an on-site meeting, and approval by the credit manager. Every possible risk mitigation strategy should be considered in this situation (see the Credit Risk Reduction chapter).

Thus, the information requested and the amount of additional analysis and management oversight required will increase in stages, based on the type of credit request. For the largest credit requests from the newest customers, the sheer volume of information needed and analysis to be conducted will require a fair amount of time; this may present a problem when a customer wants a quick decision on a credit increase.

The Riskiest Customers

A prior section described a number of indicators of payment delinquency, which can be used for ongoing credit monitoring purposes. In addition, there are several types of businesses that are worthy of particularly detailed examination on an ongoing basis. These are:

- *New businesses.* Most new businesses fail within a few years. This is an established fact, so be aware that any new business requesting credit is several times more likely to default on its trade receivables than a more established business.
- *Distributors and retailers with newly-granted credit increases.* Whenever a large increase in credit is granted to a customer, the customer is presumably banking on a ramp-up in its own business in order to sell the goods that you have sold to the customer. However, an increase in business by the distributor or retailer may call for a presumed increase in market share, or extra distribution or marketing efforts that will not be realized. If so, the customer will not sell the goods, and so cannot pay the company.
- *Transitional businesses.* Whenever a customer is transitioning out of one line of business and into another, it is essentially encountering the same conditions that an entirely new business must deal with. In these cases, the risk of default is high. Unfortunately, it can be quite difficult to ascertain when such a change is occurring, since a business may give the appearance of having been in operation for years, and give no indication that it is abandoning one line of business and shifting to another.

Whenever a customer falls into this "riskiest" category, the credit staff must monitor every possible indicator of their condition and performance on a very frequent basis. This high level of hands-on monitoring requires a great deal of credit staff time, which brings up the issue of whether it is cost-effective to have such customers. In those cases where the company is not doing much business with a "riskiest" customer and there are few prospects for more revenue, it makes sense to shut down the relationship entirely. Only in cases where sales to such a customer are expected to increase, and the customer will eventually progress beyond the "riskiest" classification does it make sense to extend credit to this class of customer.

The Demanding Customer

There are usually a few customers who are constantly demanding attention in many areas, such as customized products, overnight delivery, and – yes, additional credit on short notice. In these cases, it is useful to examine the situation from a high level to understand the complete picture. In essence, the customer is treating your business as an extension of its own business, in order to obtain a sale that benefits the customer. In addition, your business is funding the customer's operations through the extension of credit to it. Thus, you are relying upon the business sense of the customer's management to continually conclude business deals with *its* customers that allow your customer to pay in a timely manner.

This scenario is a bad one from several perspectives, and can result in both increased costs and the prospect of substantial losses. Here are several examples:

- A distributor is about to close a deal with a large retail chain, and asks Seller Company for $5,000,000 of additional credit on 30-day terms in order to have sufficient goods on hand to sell to the retail chain. At the last minute, the retailer's purchasing manager negotiates 60-day payment terms from the retail chain to the distributor. The distributor does not have the resources to still pay Seller Company within terms, and so asks for 60-day terms. In essence, Seller is financing the distributor's sale to the retailer. If the retailer fails to pay the distributor, Seller will sustain a large loss.

- A retailer wants Seller Company to repackage one of its mainstream products in time for the Christmas selling season. In order to do so, Seller must pay its employees overtime to design the revised packaging and repackage the product, as well as ship the products by overnight delivery service to the retailer's many locations. In this case, if the products do not sell, Seller can take back the goods and repackage them for shipment elsewhere. However, it has incurred the costs of employee overtime, packaging, and shipping for this special deal, and will not be compensated for these expenses. In this case, the retailer benefits from any sales, while the seller incurs greater losses than usual if the promotion fails.

These scenarios might tempt the credit manager to always avoid deals with demanding customers. How to handle these customers depends upon the circumstances, since it is also possible to earn a large profit by doing business with them. The following two factors are paramount in making a decision to extend credit:

- *Track record.* If a customer is very demanding but always pays on time, this is a strong indicator that the customer may be an acceptable risk for the ongoing extension of credit. It is entirely possible that the customer's management team simply treats all of its suppliers in a demanding manner, but is also quite successful in its own business dealings, and so is capable of earning sufficient profits to pay its suppliers in a timely manner.

- *Product margins.* If the products being sold have razor-thin margins, the seller stands to lose more than when its products carry substantial margins. In the first case, the credit manager is much less inclined to take a chance on a demanding customer, since the business is built around the standardized sale of goods in the most cost-efficient manner; there is no margin for error if a customer proves to be *too* demanding. In the latter case, margins are so comfortable for the seller that it can afford to take on a number of demanding customers, meet their special needs, and still earn a respectable profit.

In short, the decision to deal with a demanding customer is driven by both an analysis of the capabilities of the customer's management team and the profitability of a company's own products. The first factor is knowledge that can only be gained over time, which calls for the gradual extension of credit. The second factor is based on a simple profit calculation, of which the credit manager should be well aware at all times.

Effects of Industry Credit Practices

A certain set of credit terms will likely have become widespread within an industry over time. For example, payment terms may be extremely short in one industry (such as overnight delivery services) or quite long in others (such as durable goods). It is very difficult to improve upon these terms (from the perspective of the seller) if the goods and services being offered cannot be easily differentiated from those of competitors.

The dominance of standard industry terms is a particular concern in an industry being severely impacted by a downturn, since industry practice may continue to require relatively generous credit terms. The credit manager may want to tighten credit terms in a variety of ways, but cannot do so, since the seller's offerings are so undifferentiated that customers simply shift their business to competitors.

The best way to deal with rigid industry credit practices is to reformulate the company's offerings to make them more unique. By doing so, customers are more willing to accept more conservative credit terms than would normally be the case, and will continue to do business with the company. Having unique products can have a particularly favorable impact during an industry downturn, since the credit manager can more readily retract credit and still expect customers to do business with the company.

Effects of General Economic Conditions

The state of the world economy is in a constant state of flux, depending on the latest currency crisis, supply constriction, local conflicts, and so forth. These general economic conditions can translate into varying degrees of trouble within local markets. For example, a war anywhere near an oil pipeline can increase the price of fuel, which in turn increases the operating costs of numerous industries. Consequently, there will be times when a company will find that its customer base is either enjoying a state of growth, or suffering through a period of decline. Either condition may call for changes in the amount of credit granted to customers.

When an industry is experiencing boom times, management may be quite justified in expanding the amount of credit offered to nearly all customers, on the grounds that the entire group is more flush with cash than normal. Conversely, if all customers are having financial difficulty, this may call for a retrenchment of the credit policy. The latter case is a particular concern for management. If the company routinely cuts back on credit during industry slowdowns, customers may be turned away by this practice. If so, management might consider selectively maintaining higher credit levels with longer-term customers. Doing so may engender more customer loyalty, perhaps increasing the chance that these customers will remain with the company once economic conditions return to normal.

Summary

This chapter has described the approach that a credit department should take to the ongoing monitoring of customers, as well as a number of conceptual issues related to credit problems with certain classes of customers. The key concept in this chapter is that the credit manager cannot possibly conduct detailed credit reviews of all customers on a continuous basis, and so must use the tools and concepts presented here to focus the attention of the department on those customers most likely to have payment problems; all other customers can be subjected to considerably less credit oversight.

This discussion has not included a major issue that impacts not only the initial credit decision, but also the ongoing extension of credit, which is the interpretation of financial statements. That topic is covered in the next chapter.

Chapter 10
Interpretation of Financial Statements

Introduction

When a customer sends its financial statements to the credit department for review, what information can be extracted from these statements? In this chapter, we cover many types of analyses, mostly related to ratios, that can be used to develop an interpretation of the financial condition of a customer.

Interpretation of Financial Statements

There are two key techniques for analyzing financial statements. The first is the use of horizontal and vertical analysis. Horizontal analysis is the comparison of financial information over a series of reporting periods, while vertical analysis is the proportional analysis of a financial statement, where each line item on a statement is listed as a percentage of another item. Typically, this means that every line item on an income statement is stated as a percentage of gross sales, while every line item on a balance sheet is stated as a percentage of total assets. Thus, horizontal analysis is the review of the results of multiple time periods, while vertical analysis is the review of the proportion of accounts to each other within a single period. Later sections describe horizontal and vertical analysis more fully.

Another heavily-used technique is ratio analysis. Ratios are used to calculate the relative size of one number in relation to another. After a ratio is calculated, compare it to the same ratio calculated for a prior period, or that is based on an industry average, to see if the target company is performing in accordance with expectations. In a typical financial statement analysis, most ratios will be within expectations, leaving a small number of outlier ratios that require additional detailed analysis.

There are several general categories of ratios, each designed to examine a different aspect of a company's performance. These categories are:

- *Liquidity ratios.* This is the most fundamentally important set of ratios, because they measure the ability of a company to remain in business. Samples of ratios in this category are:
  - *Cash coverage ratio.* Shows the amount of cash available to pay interest.
  - *Current ratio.* Measures the amount of liquidity available to pay for current liabilities.
  - *Quick ratio.* The same as the current ratio, but does not include inventory.

- ○ *Liquidity index.* Measures the amount of time required to convert assets into cash.

- *Activity ratios.* These ratios are a strong indicator of the quality of management, since they reveal how well management is utilizing company resources. Samples of ratios in this category are:

  - ○ *Accounts payable turnover ratio.* Measures the speed with which a company pays its suppliers.
  - ○ *Accounts receivable turnover ratio.* Measures a company's ability to collect accounts receivable.
  - ○ *Inventory turnover ratio.* Measures the amount of inventory needed to support a given level of sales.
  - ○ *Fixed asset turnover ratio.* Measures a company's ability to generate sales from a certain base of fixed assets.
  - ○ *Sales to working capital ratio.* Shows the amount of working capital required to support a given amount of sales.

- *Leverage ratios.* These ratios reveal the extent to which a company is relying upon debt to fund its operations, and its ability to pay back the debt. Samples of ratios in the category are:

  - ○ *Debt to equity ratio.* Shows the extent to which management is willing to fund operations with debt, rather than equity.
  - ○ *Fixed charge coverage.* Shows the ability of a company to pay for its fixed costs.

- *Profitability ratios.* These ratios measure how well a company performs in generating a profit. Samples of ratios in this category are:

  - ○ *Breakeven point.* Reveals the sales level at which a company breaks even.
  - ○ *Gross profit ratio.* Shows revenues minus the cost of goods sold, as a proportion of sales.
  - ○ *Net profit ratio.* Calculates the amount of profit after taxes and all expenses have been deducted from net sales.
  - ○ *Return on net assets.* Shows company profits as a percentage of fixed assets and working capital.

An additional measurement that combines elements of several of these categories is the Altman Z score formula, which we include at the end of the chapter.

Each of these ratios is described in more detail in the following sections.

Problems with Financial Statement Analysis

While financial statement analysis is an excellent tool, there are several issues to be aware of that can interfere with the interpretation of results. These issues are:

- *Comparability between periods.* The company preparing the financial statements may have changed the accounts in which it stores financial information, so that results may differ from period to period. For example, an expense may appear in the cost of goods sold in one period, and in administrative expenses in another period.
- *Comparability between companies.* A credit analyst may compare the financial ratios of different companies to see how they match up against each other. However, each company may aggregate financial information differently, so the results of their ratios are not really comparable. This can lead an analyst to draw incorrect conclusions about the results of a company in comparison to its competitors.
- *Operational information.* Financial analysis only reviews a company's financial information, not its operational information, so you cannot see a variety of key indicators of future performance, such as the size of the order backlog, or changes in warranty claims. Thus, financial analysis only presents part of the total picture.

Horizontal Analysis

Horizontal analysis is the comparison of historical financial information over a series of reporting periods, or of the ratios derived from this information. The analysis is most commonly a simple grouping of information that is sorted by period, but the numbers in each succeeding period can also be expressed as a percentage of the amount in the baseline year, with the baseline amount being listed as 100%.

When conducting a horizontal analysis, it is useful to conduct the analysis for all of the financial statements at the same time, so that the complete impact of operational results on the company's financial condition can be seen over the review period. For example, as noted in the next two examples, the income statement analysis shows a company having an excellent second year, but the related balance sheet analysis shows that it is having trouble funding growth, given the decline in cash, increase in accounts payable, and increase in debt.

Horizontal analysis of the income statement is usually in a two-year format such as the one shown next, with a variance also reported that states the difference between the two years for each line item. An alternative format is to simply add as many years as will fit on the page, without showing a variance, in order to see general changes by account over multiple years.

Sample Income Statement Horizontal Analysis

	20X1	20X2	Variance
Sales	$1,000,000	$1,500,000	$500,000
Cost of goods sold	400,000	600,000	-200,000
Gross margin	600,000	900,000	300,000
Salaries and wages	250,000	375,000	-125,000
Office rent	50,000	80,000	-30,000
Supplies	10,000	20,000	-10,000
Utilities	20,000	30,000	-10,000
Other expenses	90,000	110,000	-20,000
Total expenses	420,000	615,000	-195,000
Net profit	$180,000	$285,000	$105,000

Horizontal analysis of the balance sheet is also usually in a two-year format, such as the one shown below, with a variance stating the difference between the two years for each line item. An alternative format is to add as many years as will fit on the page, without showing a variance, in order to see general changes by account over multiple years.

Sample Balance Sheet Horizontal Analysis

	20X1	20X2	Variance
Cash	$100,000	$80,000	-$20,000
Accounts receivable	350,000	525,000	175,000
Inventory	150,000	275,000	125,000
Total current assets	600,000	880,000	280,000
Fixed assets	400,000	800,000	400,000
Total assets	$1,000,000	$1,680,000	$680,000
Accounts payable	$180,000	$300,000	$120,000
Accrued liabilities	70,000	120,000	50,000
Total current liabilities	250,000	420,000	170,000
Notes payable	300,000	525,000	225,000
Total liabilities	550,000	945,000	395,000
Capital stock	200,000	200,000	0
Retained earnings	250,000	535,000	285,000
Total equity	450,000	735,000	285,000
Total liabilities and equity	$1,000,000	$1,680,000	$680,000

Vertical Analysis

Vertical analysis is the proportional analysis of a financial statement, where each line item on a financial statement is listed as a percentage of another item. Typically, this means that every line item on an income statement is stated as a percentage of gross sales, while every line item on a balance sheet is stated as a percentage of total assets.

The most common use of vertical analysis is within a financial statement for a single time period, to see the relative proportions of account balances. Vertical analysis is also useful for timeline analysis, to see relative changes in accounts over time, such as on a comparative basis over a five-year period. For example, if the cost of goods sold has a history of being 40% of sales in each of the past four years, then a new percentage of 48% would be a cause for alarm. An example of vertical analysis for an income statement is shown in the far right column of the following condensed income statement.

Sample Income Statement Vertical Analysis

	$ Totals	Percent
Sales	$1,000,000	100%
Cost of goods sold	400,000	40%
Gross margin	600,000	60%
Salaries and wages	250,000	25%
Office rent	50,000	5%
Supplies	10,000	1%
Utilities	20,000	2%
Other expenses	90,000	9%
Total expenses	420,000	42%
Net profit	$180,000	18%

The information provided by this income statement format is primarily useful for spotting spikes in expenses.

The central issue when creating a vertical analysis of a balance sheet is what to use as the denominator in the percentage calculation. The usual denominator is the asset total, but you can also use the total of all liabilities when calculating all liability line item percentages, and the total of all equity accounts when calculating all equity line item percentages. An example of vertical analysis for a balance sheet is shown in the far right column of the following condensed balance sheet.

Sample Balance Sheet Vertical Analysis

	20X1	Percent
Cash	$100,000	10%
Accounts receivable	350,000	35%
Inventory	150,000	15%
Total current assets	600,000	60%
Fixed assets	400,000	40%
Total assets	$1,000,000	100%
Accounts payable	$180,000	18%
Accrued liabilities	70,000	7%
Total current liabilities	250,000	25%
Notes payable	300,000	30%
Total liabilities	550,000	55%
Capital stock	200,000	20%
Retained earnings	250,000	25%
Total equity	450,000	45%
Total liabilities and equity	$1,000,000	100%

The information provided by this balance sheet format is useful for noting changes in a company's investment in working capital and fixed assets over time, which may indicate an altered business model that requires a different amount of ongoing funding.

We now turn to an explanation of the ratios that may be of use to a credit analyst. Each explanation is accompanied by an example to illustrate how the ratio can be employed.

Cash Coverage Ratio

The cash coverage ratio is useful for determining the amount of cash available to pay for interest, and is expressed as a ratio of the cash available to the amount of interest to be paid. This is a useful ratio when the entity evaluating a company is a prospective lender. The ratio should be substantially greater than 1:1. To calculate this ratio, take the earnings before interest and taxes (EBIT) from the income statement, add back to it all non-cash expenses included in EBIT (such as depreciation and amortization), and divide by the interest expense. The formula is:

$$\frac{\text{Earnings before interest and taxes} + \text{Non-cash expenses}}{\text{Interest expense}}$$

There may be a number of additional non-cash items to subtract in the numerator of the formula. For example, there may have been substantial charges in a period to increase reserves for sales allowances, product returns, bad debts, or inventory obsolescence. If these non-cash items are substantial, be sure to include them in the calculation. Also, the interest expense in the denominator should only include the actual interest expense to be paid – if there is a premium or discount to the amount being paid, it is not a cash payment, and so should not be included in the denominator.

EXAMPLE

The controller of Currency Bank is concerned that a borrower has recently taken on a great deal of debt to pay for a leveraged buyout, and wants to ensure that there is sufficient cash to pay for its new interest burden. The borrower is generating earnings before interest and taxes of $1,200,000 and it records annual depreciation of $800,000. The borrower is scheduled to pay $1,500,000 in interest expenses in the coming year. Based on this information, the borrower has the following cash coverage ratio:

$$\frac{\$1,200,000 \text{ EBIT} + \$800,000 \text{ Depreciation}}{\$1,500,000 \text{ Interest expense}}$$

$$= 1.33 \text{ Cash coverage ratio}$$

The calculation reveals that the borrower can pay for its interest expense, but has very little cash left for any other payments.

Current Ratio

One of the first ratios that a lender or supplier reviews when examining a company is its current ratio. The current ratio measures the short-term liquidity of a business; that is, it gives an indication of the ability of a business to pay its bills. A ratio of 2:1 is preferred, with a lower proportion indicating a reduced ability to pay in a timely manner. Since the ratio is current assets divided by current liabilities, the ratio essentially implies that current assets can be liquidated to pay for current liabilities.

To calculate the current ratio, divide the total of all current assets by the total of all current liabilities. The formula is:

$$\frac{\text{Current assets}}{\text{Current liabilities}}$$

The current ratio can yield misleading results under the following circumstances:

- *Inventory component.* When the current assets figure includes a large proportion of inventory assets, since these assets can be difficult to liquidate. This can be a particular problem if management is using aggressive accounting techniques to apply an unusually large amount of overhead costs to inventory, which further inflates the recorded amount of inventory.
- *Paying from debt.* When a company is drawing upon its line of credit to pay bills as they come due, which means that the cash balance is near zero. In this case, the current ratio could be fairly low, and yet the presence of a line of credit still allows the business to pay in a timely manner.

EXAMPLE

A supplier wants to learn about the financial condition of Lowry Locomotion. The supplier calculates the current ratio of Lowry for the past three years:

	Year 1	Year 2	Year 3
Current assets	$8,000,000	$16,400,000	$23,400,000
Current liabilities	$4,000,000	$9,650,000	$18,000,000
Current ratio	2:1	1.7:1	1.3:1

The sudden rise in current assets over the past two years indicates that Lowry has undergone a rapid expansion of its operations. Of particular concern is the increase in accounts payable in Year 3, which indicates a rapidly deteriorating ability to pay suppliers. Based on this information, the supplier elects to restrict the extension of credit to Lowry.

Quick Ratio

The quick ratio formula matches the most easily liquidated portions of current assets with current liabilities. The intent of this ratio is to see if a business has sufficient assets that are immediately convertible to cash to pay its bills. The key elements of current assets that are included in the quick ratio are cash, marketable securities, and accounts receivable. Inventory is not included in the quick ratio, since it can be quite difficult to sell off in the short term. Because of the exclusion of inventory from the formula, the quick ratio is a better indicator than the current ratio of the ability of a company to pay its obligations.

To calculate the quick ratio, summarize cash, marketable securities and trade receivables, and divide by current liabilities. Do not include in the numerator any excessively old receivables that are unlikely to be paid. The formula is:

$$\frac{\text{Cash + Marketable securities + Accounts receivable}}{\text{Current liabilities}}$$

Despite the absence of inventory from the calculation, the quick ratio may still not yield a good view of immediate liquidity, if current liabilities are payable right now, while receipts from receivables are not expected for several more weeks.

EXAMPLE

Rapunzel Hair Products appears to have a respectable current ratio of 4:1. The breakdown of the ratio components is:

Item	Amount
Cash	$100,000
Marketable securities	50,000
Accounts receivable	420,000
Inventory	3,430,000
Current liabilities	1,000,000
Current ratio	4:1
Quick ratio	0.57:1

The component breakdown reveals that nearly all of Rapunzel's current assets are in the inventory area, where short-term liquidity is questionable. This issue is only visible when the quick ratio is substituted for the current ratio.

Liquidity Index

The liquidity index calculates the days required to convert a company's trade receivables and inventory into cash. The index is used to estimate the ability of a business to generate the cash needed to meet current liabilities. Use the following steps to calculate the liquidity index:

1. Multiply the ending trade receivables balance by the average collection period.
2. Multiply the ending inventory balance by the average inventory liquidation period. This includes the average days to sell inventory and to collect the resulting receivables.
3. Summarize the first two items and divide by the total of all trade receivables and inventory.

The liquidity index formula is:

$$\frac{(\text{Trade receivables} \times \text{Days to liquidate}) + (\text{Inventory} \times \text{Days to liquidate})}{\text{Trade receivables} + \text{inventory}}$$

The liquidation days information in the formula is based on historical averages, which may not translate well to the receivables and inventory currently on hand. Actual cash flows may vary substantially around the averages indicated by the formula.

EXAMPLE

A credit analyst wants to understand the ability of a customer, Hassle Corporation, to convert its receivables and inventory into cash. Hassle has $400,000 of trade receivables on hand, which can normally be converted to cash within 50 days. Hassle also has $650,000 of inventory, which can be liquidated in an average of 90 days. When combined with the receivable collection period, this means it takes 140 days to fully liquidate inventory *and* collect the proceeds. Based on this information, the liquidity index is:

$$\frac{(\$400{,}000 \text{ Receivables} \times 50 \text{ Days to liquidate}) + (\$650{,}000 \text{ Inventory} \times \text{Days to liquidate})}{\$400{,}000 \text{ Receivables} + \$650{,}000 \text{ Inventory}}$$

$$= 106 \text{ Days to convert assets to cash}$$

The larger proportion of inventory in this calculation tends to skew the number of days well past the liquidation days for trade receivables. In short, Hassle will require a lengthy period to convert several current assets to cash, which may impact its ability to pay bills in the short term.

It may appear difficult for a credit analyst to obtain the liquidation days information required for this formula. However, using industry averages can yield a reasonable estimate of the liquidity index for a business.

Accounts Payable Turnover Ratio

Accounts payable turnover measures the speed with which a company pays its suppliers. If the turnover ratio declines from one period to the next, this indicates that the business is paying its suppliers more slowly, and may be an indicator of worsening financial condition. A change in the turnover ratio can also indicate altered payment terms with suppliers, though this rarely has more than a slight impact on the overall outcome of the ratio. If a company is paying its suppliers very quickly, it may mean that the suppliers are demanding fast payment terms.

To calculate the ratio, summarize all purchases from suppliers during the measurement period, and divide by the average amount of accounts payable during that period. The formula is:

$$\frac{\text{Total supplier purchases}}{(\text{Beginning accounts payable} + \text{Ending accounts payable}) \div 2}$$

The formula can be modified to exclude cash payments to suppliers, since the numerator should include only purchases on credit from suppliers. However, the amount of up-front cash payments to suppliers is normally so small that this modification is not necessary.

EXAMPLE

A credit analyst is reviewing Mulligan Imports, and wants to determine the company's accounts payable turnover for the past year. In the beginning of this period, the accounts payable balance was $800,000, and the ending balance was $884,000. Purchases for the last 12 months were $7,500,000. Based on this information, the analyst calculates the accounts payable turnover as:

$$\frac{\$7,500,000 \text{ Purchases}}{(\$800,000 \text{ Beginning payables} + \$884,000 \text{ Ending payables}) \div 2}$$

$$= 8.9 \text{ Accounts payable turns per year}$$

To calculate the accounts payable turnover in days, the analyst divides the 8.9 turns into 365 days, which yields:

$$365 \text{ Days} \div 8.9 \text{ Turns} = 41 \text{ Days}$$

Accounts Receivable Turnover Ratio

Accounts receivable turnover measures the ability of a company to efficiently issue credit to its customers and collect it back in a timely manner. A high turnover ratio indicates a combination of a conservative credit policy and an aggressive collections department, while a low turnover ratio represents an opportunity to collect excessively old receivables that are tying up working capital. This is useful information for a credit analyst, since a customer with its own collection problems is less likely to pay its suppliers on time.

To calculate accounts receivable turnover, add together the beginning and ending accounts receivable to arrive at the average accounts receivable for the measurement period, and divide this amount into the net credit sales for the year. The formula is:

$$\frac{\text{Net annual credit sales}}{(\text{Beginning accounts receivable} + \text{Ending accounts receivable}) \div 2}$$

If the receivables balance is quite variable over the measurement period, the use of just the beginning and ending receivable balances in the denominator may skew the measurement. In this case, consider using a larger number of data points to derive the average.

EXAMPLE

A credit analyst is investigating the credit application of Norrona Software, and wants to see if it is experiencing any of its own collection problems. In the beginning of the measurement period, the beginning receivable balance was $316,000, and the ending balance was $384,000. Net credit sales for the last 12 months were $3,500,000. Based on this information, the analyst calculates the accounts receivable turnover as:

$$\frac{\$3,500,000 \text{ Net credit sales}}{(\$316,000 \text{ Beginning receivables} + \$384,000 \text{ Ending receivables}) \div 2}$$

$$= 10 \text{ Accounts receivable turnover}$$

To calculate the accounts receivable turnover in days, the analyst divides the 10 turns into 365 days, which yields:

$$365 \text{ Days} \div 10 \text{ Turns} = 36.5 \text{ Days}$$

Inventory Turnover Ratio

The inventory turnover ratio is the rate at which inventory is used over a measurement period. This is an important measurement from the credit analysis perspective, for many businesses are burdened by an excessively large investment in inventory, which can consume available cash.

When there is a low rate of inventory turnover, this implies that a business may have a flawed purchasing system that bought too many goods, or that stocks were increased in anticipation of sales that did not occur. In both cases, there is a high risk of inventory aging, in which case it becomes obsolete and has little residual value.

When there is a high rate of inventory turnover, this implies that the purchasing function is tightly managed. However, it may also mean that a business does not have the cash reserves to maintain normal inventory levels, and so is turning away prospective sales. The latter scenario is most likely when the amount of debt is unusually high and there are minimal cash reserves.

To calculate inventory turnover, divide the ending inventory figure into the annualized cost of sales. If the ending inventory figure is not a representative number, then use an average figure instead. The formula is:

$$\frac{\text{Annual cost of goods sold}}{\text{Inventory}}$$

The result of this calculation can be divided into 365 days to arrive at days of inventory on hand. Thus, a turnover rate of 4.0 becomes 91 days of inventory.

EXAMPLE

An analyst is reviewing the inventory situation of the Hegemony Toy Company. The business incurred $8,150,000 of cost of goods sold in the past year, and has ending inventory of $1,630,000. Total inventory turnover is calculated as:

$$\frac{\$8,150,000 \text{ Cost of goods sold}}{\$1,630,000 \text{ Inventory}}$$

$$= 5 \text{ Turns per year}$$

The five turns figure is then divided into 365 days to arrive at 73 days of inventory on hand.

Fixed Asset Turnover Ratio

The fixed asset turnover ratio is the ratio of net sales to net fixed assets. A high ratio indicates that a company is doing an effective job of generating sales with a relatively small amount of fixed assets. Conversely, if the ratio is declining over time, the company has either overinvested in fixed assets or it needs to issue new products to revive its sales. Another possible effect is for a company to make a large investment in fixed assets, with a time delay of several months to a year before the new assets start generating revenues. Finally, a lack of ongoing investment in fixed assets will yield an apparently high turnover ratio over time, as depreciation reduces the reported amount of net fixed assets; this issue can be spotted by reviewing the cash expenditures for fixed assets that are reported in the statement of cash flows.

To derive fixed asset turnover, subtract accumulated depreciation from gross fixed assets, and divide into net annual sales. It may be necessary to obtain an average fixed asset figure, if the amount varies significantly over time. Do not include intangible assets in the denominator, since it can skew the results. The formula is:

$$\frac{\text{Net annual sales}}{\text{Gross fixed assets} - \text{Accumulated depreciation}}$$

This ratio is of most use in a "heavy industry," such as manufacturing, where a large capital investment is required. It is less useful in a services or knowledge-intensive industry, where the amount of fixed assets may be quite small.

If accelerated depreciation is used, it can rapidly reduce the amount of net fixed assets in the denominator, which makes the turnover figure look higher than is really the case.

EXAMPLE

Latham Lumber has gross fixed assets of $5,000,000 and accumulated depreciation of $2,000,000. Sales over the last 12 months totaled $9,000,000. The calculation of Latham's fixed asset turnover ratio is:

$$\frac{\$9{,}000{,}000 \text{ Net sales}}{\$5{,}000{,}000 \text{ Gross fixed assets} - \$2{,}000{,}000 \text{ Accumulated depreciation}}$$

$$= 3.0 \text{ Fixed asset turnover per year}$$

Sales to Working Capital Ratio

It usually takes a certain amount of invested cash to maintain sales. There must be an investment in accounts receivable and inventory, against which accounts payable are offset. Thus, there is typically a ratio of working capital to sales that remains fairly constant in a business, even as sales levels change. This relationship can be measured with the sales to working capital ratio, which should be reported on a trend line to more easily spot spikes or dips. A spike in the ratio could be caused by a decision to grant more credit to customers in order to encourage more sales, while a dip could signal the reverse. A spike might also be triggered by a decision to keep more inventory on hand in order to more easily fulfill customer orders.

The ratio is calculated by dividing annualized net sales by average working capital. The formula is:

$$\frac{\text{Annualized net sales}}{\text{Accounts receivable} + \text{Inventory} - \text{Accounts payable}}$$

EXAMPLE

A credit analyst is reviewing the sales to working capital ratio of Milford Sound, which has applied for credit. Milford has been adjusting its inventory levels over the past few quarters, with the intent of doubling inventory turnover from its current level. The result is shown in the following table:

	Quarter 1	Quarter 2	Quarter 3	Quarter 4
Revenue	$640,000	$620,000	$580,000	$460,000
Accounts receivable	214,000	206,000	194,000	186,000
Inventory	1,280,000	640,000	640,000	640,000
Accounts payable	106,000	104,000	96,000	94,000
Total working capital	1,388,000	742,000	738,000	732,000
Sales to working capital ratio	1.8:1	3.3:1	3.1:1	3.1:1

The table includes a quarterly ratio calculation that is based on annualized sales. The table reveals that Milford achieved its goal of reducing inventory, but at the cost of a significant sales reduction, probably caused by customers turning to competitors that offered a larger selection of inventory.

Debt to Equity Ratio

The debt to equity ratio of a business is closely monitored by the lenders and creditors of the company, since it can provide early warning that an organization is so overwhelmed by debt that it is unable to meet its payment obligations. This may also be triggered by a funding issue. For example, the owners of a business may not want to contribute any more cash to the company, so they acquire more debt to address the cash shortfall. Or, a company may use debt to buy back shares, thereby increasing the return on investment to the remaining shareholders.

Whatever the reason for debt usage, the outcome can be catastrophic, if corporate cash flows are not sufficient to make ongoing debt payments. This is a concern to lenders, whose loans may not be paid back. Suppliers are also concerned about the ratio for the same reason. A lender can protect its interests by imposing collateral requirements or restrictive covenants; suppliers usually offer credit with less restrictive terms, and so can suffer more if a company is unable to meet its payment obligations to them.

To calculate the debt to equity ratio, simply divide total debt by total equity. In this calculation, the debt figure should also include all lease obligations. The formula is:

$$\frac{\text{Long-term debt} + \text{Short-term debt} + \text{Leases}}{\text{Equity}}$$

EXAMPLE

A credit analyst is reviewing the application of New Centurion Corporation for credit. The company reports a $500,000 line of credit, $1,700,000 in long-term debt, and a $200,000 operating lease. The company has $800,000 of equity. Based on this information, New Centurion's debt to equity ratio is:

$$\frac{\$500,000 \text{ Line of credit} + \$1,700,000 \text{ Debt} + \$200,000 \text{ Lease}}{\$800,000 \text{ Equity}}$$

$$= 3{:}1 \text{ debt to equity ratio}$$

The debt to equity ratio exceeds the 2:1 ratio threshold above which the credit analyst is not allowed to grant credit. Consequently, New Centurion is kept on cash in advance payment terms.

Fixed Charge Coverage

A business may incur so many fixed costs that its cash flow is mostly consumed by payments for these costs. The problem is particularly common when a company has incurred a large amount of debt, and must make ongoing interest payments. In this situation, use the fixed charge coverage ratio to determine the extent of the problem.

If the resulting ratio is low, it is a strong indicator that any subsequent drop in the profits of a business may bring about its failure.

To calculate the fixed charge coverage ratio, combine earnings before interest and taxes (EBIT) with any lease expense, and then divide by the combined total of interest expense and lease expense. The formula is:

$$\frac{\text{Earnings before interest and taxes} + \text{Lease expense}}{\text{Interest expense} + \text{Lease expense}}$$

EXAMPLE

Luminescence Corporation recorded earnings before interest and taxes of $800,000 in the preceding year. The company also recorded $200,000 of lease expense and $50,000 of interest expense. Based on this information, its fixed charge coverage is:

$$\frac{\$800,000 \text{ EBIT} + \$200,000 \text{ Lease expense}}{\$50,000 \text{ Interest expense} + \$200,000 \text{ Lease expense}}$$

$$= 4:1 \text{ Fixed charge coverage ratio}$$

Breakeven Point

The breakeven point is the sales volume at which a business earns exactly no money. It is mostly used for internal analysis purposes, but it is also useful for a credit analyst, who can use it to determine the amount of losses that could be sustained if a credit applicant were to suffer a sales downturn.

To calculate the breakeven point, divide total fixed expenses by the contribution margin. Contribution margin is sales minus all variable expenses, divided by sales. The formula is:

$$\frac{\text{Total fixed expenses}}{\text{Contribution margin percentage}}$$

A more refined approach is to eliminate all non-cash expenses (such as depreciation) from the numerator, so that the calculation focuses on the breakeven cash flow level.

EXAMPLE

A credit analyst is reviewing the financial statements of a customer that has a large amount of fixed costs. The industry is highly cyclical, so the analyst wants to know what a large downturn in sales will do to the customer. The customer has total fixed expenses of $3,000,000, sales of $8,000,000, and variable expenses of $4,000,000. Based on this information, the customer's contribution margin is 50%. The breakeven calculation is:

$$\frac{\$3,000,000 \text{ Total fixed costs}}{50\% \text{ Contribution margin}}$$

$$= \$6{,}000{,}000 \text{ Breakeven sales level}$$

Thus, the customer's sales can decline by $2,000,000 from their current level before the customer will begin to lose money.

Gross Profit Ratio

The gross profit ratio shows the proportion of profits generated by the sale of goods or services, before selling and administrative expenses. In essence, it reveals the ability of a business to create sellable products in a cost-effective manner. The ratio is of some importance from a credit analysis perspective, especially when tracked on a trend line, to see if a business is continuing to provide products to the marketplace for which customers are willing to pay.

The gross margin ratio is calculated as sales minus the cost of goods sold, divided by sales. The formula is:

$$\frac{\text{Sales} - \text{Cost of goods sold}}{\text{Sales}}$$

The ratio can vary over time as sales volumes change, since the cost of goods sold contains some fixed cost elements that will not vary with sales volume.

EXAMPLE

A credit analyst is reviewing a credit application from Quest Adventure Gear, which includes financial statements for the past three years. The analyst extracts the following information from the financial statements of Quest:

	20X1	20X2	20X3
Sales	$12,000,000	$13,500,000	$14,800,000
Cost of goods sold	$5,000,000	$5,100,000	$4,700,000
Gross profit ratio	42%	38%	32%

The analysis reveals that Quest is suffering from an ongoing decline in its gross profits, which should certainly be a concern from the perspective of allowing credit.

Net Profit Ratio

The net profit ratio is a comparison of after-tax profits to net sales. It reveals the remaining profit after all costs of production and administration have been deducted from sales, and income taxes recognized. As such, it is one of the best measures of the overall results of a firm, especially when combined with an evaluation of how well it is using its working capital. The measure is commonly reported on a trend line, to judge performance over time. It is also used to compare the results of a business with its competitors.

The net profit ratio is really a short-term measurement, because it does not reveal a company's actions to maintain profitability over the long term, as may be indicated by the level of capital investment or research and development expenditures. Also, a company may delay a variety of discretionary expenses, such as maintenance or training, to make its net profit ratio look better than it normally is. Consequently, evaluate this ratio alongside an array of other metrics to gain a full picture of a company's ability to continue as a going concern.

Another issue with the net profit ratio is that a company may intentionally keep it low through a variety of expense recognition strategies in order to avoid paying taxes. If so, review the statement of cash flows to determine the real cash-generating ability of the business.

To calculate the net profit ratio, divide net profits by net sales and then multiply by 100. The formula is:

$$(\text{Net profit} \div \text{Net sales}) \times 100$$

EXAMPLE

Kelvin Corporation has $1,000,000 of sales in its most recent month, as well as sales returns of $40,000, a cost of goods sold of $550,000, and administrative expenses of $360,000. The income tax rate is 35%. The calculation of its net profit percentage is:

$1,000,000 Sales - $40,000 Sales returns = $960,000 Net sales

$960,000 Net sales - $550,000 Cost of goods - $360,000 Administrative expenses = $50,000 Income before tax

$50,000 Income before tax × (1 − 0.35) = $32,500 Profit after tax

($32,500 Profit after tax ÷ $960,000 Net Sales) × 100 = 3.4% Net profit ratio

Return on Net Assets

The return on net assets measurement compares net profits to net assets to see how well a company is able to utilize its asset base to create profits. A high ratio is an indicator of excellent management performance.

To calculate the return on net assets, add together fixed assets and net working capital, and divide the result into net after-tax profits. Net working capital is defined as current assets minus current liabilities. It is best to eliminate unusual, one-time items from the calculation, since they can skew the results. The calculation is:

$$\frac{\text{Net profit}}{\text{Fixed assets + Net working capital}}$$

The fixed asset figure in the calculation can be net of depreciation, but the type of depreciation calculation used can skew the net amount significantly, since some accelerated depreciation methods can eliminate as much as 40% of an asset's value in its first full year of usage.

EXAMPLE

Quality Cabinets, an old maker of fine mahogany cabinets, has net income of $2,000,000, which includes an unusual, one-time expense of $500,000. It also has fixed assets of $4,000,000 and net working capital of $1,000,000. For the purposes of the return on net assets calculation, the unusual expense item is eliminated, which increases the net income figure to $2,500,000. The calculation of return on net assets is:

$$\frac{\$2,500,000 \text{ Net income}}{\$4,000,000 \text{ Fixed assets} + \$1,000,000 \text{ Net working capital}}$$

$$= 50\% \text{ Return on net assets}$$

Altman Z Score

The Altman Z Score was developed by Edward Altman, and is used to predict the likelihood that a business will go bankrupt within the next two years. The formula is based on information found in the income statement and balance sheet of an organization; as such, it can be readily derived from commonly-available information. In its original form, the Z score formula is as follows:

$$Z = 1.2A \times 1.4B \times 3.3C \times 0.6D \times 0.99E$$

The letters in the formula designate the following measures:

A = Working capital ÷ Total assets [measures the relative amount of liquid assets]
B = Retained earnings ÷ Total assets [determines cumulative profitability]
C = Earnings before interest and taxes ÷ Total assets [measures earnings away from the effects of taxes and leverage]
D = Market value of equity ÷ Book value of total liabilities [incorporates the effects of a decline in market value of a company's shares]
E = Sales ÷ Total assets [measures asset turnover]

A Z score of greater than 2.99 means that the entity being measured is safe from bankruptcy. A score of less than 1.81 means that a business is at considerable risk of going into bankruptcy, while scores in between should be considered a red flag for possible problems. The model has proven to be reasonably accurate in predicting the future bankruptcy of entities under analysis.

This scoring system was originally designed for manufacturing firms having assets of $1 million or more. Given the targeted nature of the model, it has since been modified to be applicable to other types of organizations.

This approach to evaluating organizations is better than using just a single ratio, since it brings together the effects of multiple items - assets, profits, and market value. As such, it is most commonly used by creditors and lenders to determine the risk associated with extending funds to customers and borrowers.

Essential Analysis Tools

Which of the preceding analyses are most critical from the perspective of a credit analyst, and which merely provide useful additional information? Consider using the following tranches of analysis activities to obtain layers of information about customers:

- *Essential information*. The core requirement is to understand whether a customer can pay its bills in the short term. To find this information, use a combination of the quick ratio, accounts payable turnover ratio, and the net profit ratio.
- *Expanded information*. If there is additional time available or the credit request is a large one, supplement the first layer of analysis with the liquidity index, sales to working capital ratio, and fixed charge coverage analysis.
- *Long-term viability*. To understand the long-term ability of a customer to pay its bills, add to the preceding analyses all asset turnover ratios, the debt to equity ratio, and the breakeven point.

When using all three layers of analysis just described, always do so using trend line (horizontal) analysis. By doing so, any declines in profitability or financial position are much more apparent.

Limitations of Ratio Analysis

Ratio analysis is a useful tool for a credit analyst, who needs to create a picture of the financial results and position of a business just from its financial statements. However, there are a number of limitations of ratio analysis to be aware of. They are:

- *Historical*. All of the information used in ratio analysis is derived from actual historical results. This does not mean that the same results will carry forward into the future. However, you can use ratio analysis on pro forma information and compare it to historical results for consistency.
- *Historical versus current cost*. The information on the income statement is stated in current costs (or close to it), whereas some elements of the balance sheet may be stated at historical cost (which could vary substantially from current costs). This disparity can result in unusual ratio results.

- *Aggregation.* The information in a financial statement line item that is being used for a ratio analysis may have been aggregated differently in the past, so that running the ratio analysis on a trend line does not compare the same information through the entire trend period.
- *Accounting policies.* Different companies may have different policies for recording the same accounting transaction. This means that comparing the ratio results of different companies may be like comparing apples and oranges. For example, one company might use accelerated depreciation while another company uses straight-line depreciation, or one company records a sale at gross while the other company does so at net.
- *Business conditions.* Ratio analysis should be placed in the context of the general business environment. For example, 60 days of sales outstanding might be considered poor in a period of rapidly growing sales, but might be excellent during an economic contraction when customers are in severe financial condition and unable to pay their bills.
- *Interpretation.* It can be quite difficult to ascertain the reason for the results of a ratio. For example, a current ratio of 2:1 might appear to be excellent, until you realize that the company just sold a large amount of its stock to bolster its cash position. A more detailed analysis might reveal that the current ratio will only temporarily be at that level, and will probably decline in the near future.
- *Point in time.* Some ratios extract information from the balance sheet. Be aware that the information on the balance sheet is only as of the last day of the reporting period. If there was an unusual spike or decline in the account balance on the last day of the reporting period, this can impact the outcome of the ratio analysis.

In short, ratio analysis has a variety of limitations. However, as long as you are aware of these problems and use alternative and supplemental methods to collect and interpret information, ratio analysis is still useful.

The Going Concern Qualification

Thus far, we have assumed that the credit analyst merely receives financial statements from a customer, without regard to any additional information that might normally accompany the statements. A great deal more information may be available if the financial statements have been audited. In particular, ask for the auditor's opinion letter and read it thoroughly. There may be language in this letter that states the auditor's doubt that the business will continue as a going concern. This statement is not given lightly, and is probably backed by a large amount of auditor analysis. Consequently, if the letter *does* have a going concern qualification, consider it likely that the customer will not be in business by the end of the next 12 months.

Summary

A busy credit analyst is hardly likely to use all of the types of analysis outlined in this chapter. It is more likely that a typical customer asking for a modest amount of credit will be subjected to a few of the basic ratio analyses, if only to reduce the time required of the analyst. However, when a significant amount of credit is being discussed, it makes more sense to use a number of different analyses to arrive at a more complete picture of a company's financial condition. Spending just an extra hour on analysis may uncover a nugget of information that results in a significant adjustment to the amount of credit that would otherwise have been issued to an applicant.

Chapter 11
Credit Risk Reduction

Introduction

The prudent use of a variety of risk reduction techniques can be used to greatly reduce the amount of bad debt that a company must recognize. The risk reduction alternatives noted in this chapter can allow a business to issue a relatively large amount of credit to its customers, while actually being at risk for a significantly smaller amount of receivables.

The Risk Reduction Concept

Every time a company grants credit to a customer, it is at full risk of not collecting the entire billed amount from the customer. In some industries, a remarkably high percentage of these receivables are at considerable risk of default, so there is a potentially massive amount of bad debt associated with credit sales that could bankrupt a company.

There are a variety of ways to deal with the prospect of bad debts. Some businesses grant credit only to the most financially stable customers. Other businesses use credit risk as a competitive weapon, scooping up those customers that no one else wants in exchange for bearing a higher risk of default. Both of these strategies can be improved upon through the judicious use of credit risk reduction. By using the tools described in this chapter, an excessively conservative business can grant credit to more customers, while an aggressive company can reduce its bad debts on credit sales to higher-risk customers.

The suggestions in this chapter can generally be aggregated into the following classifications of risk reduction:

- *Find alternate payer*. Someone besides the customer agrees to also be liable for payments, or to pay insurance claims for bad debts.
- *Retain ownership*. There are a variety of ways to retain a legal interest in goods sold, so that the goods can be recovered.
- *Offload ownership*. Once an invoice is issued, transfer ownership of the invoice to a third party in exchange for cash, so that the new owner bears the risk of default.
- *Pay early*. Require the acceleration of payment by customers, so that only smaller payments are at risk of default, and for shorter periods.

By using a mix of these tools, a credit manager can achieve a significant reduction in the amount of bad debt risk that may be incurred, even while extending credit to customers that are not entirely financially sound.

Payment Guarantees

There are several alternative kinds of guarantee that the seller can request from a customer in order to reduce the risk of non-payment. All of the approaches involve an agreement that gives the seller access to assets located outside of the assets owned by the buying entity. The main sources of these guarantees are the owner of a business, a corporate parent or fellow subsidiary, or a third party. There are two types of guarantee, the guarantee of payment and the guarantee of collection or performance. The *guarantee of payment*, which is the preferred type from the seller's viewpoint, states that the seller can collect payment from the guarantor without first attempting to collect from the buyer. The *guarantee of collection or performance* requires the seller to first attempt to collect from the buyer, and then pursue collection from the guarantor.

The owner of a small business may be willing to personally guarantee that a payment owed by his or her company will be paid, if necessary out of personal assets. While this approach may initially appear satisfactory to the seller, there are actually several problems with it. First, the owner's net worth may be closely tied to the fortunes of the business, so there will be no personal assets left if the business fails. Also, the owner may have issued personal guarantees to many suppliers, so a failure of the business will lead to a scramble by this group to attach the owner's personal assets. And finally, demanding a personal guarantee is hardly a way to obtain the long-term loyalty of a customer. Given these issues, a common path to follow is a personal guarantee requirement when a customer is a new business, followed by its revocation after several years of reliable payment history have been achieved.

If a business is a subsidiary, it can be useful to obtain a payment guarantee from the parent company. Depending on the structure of the organization, the parent entity may have more assets than the subsidiary, and so may be an excellent backup payer. However, some parent companies are essentially shell organizations that contain minimal assets. Accordingly, request the financial statements of the parent company to determine the amount of available assets. If the parent does not appear to be an adequate guarantor, consider demanding a guarantee from another subsidiary that owns more assets.

It is sometimes possible to obtain a guarantee from a third party. This may be a related party that has an interest in the operations of the buyer, such as a member of its board of directors, a key supplier, a manager, or a family member. This type of guarantee can be quite valuable, since the assets of the third party may not be so closely tied to the fortunes of the buyer, and can survive the demise of the business. When researching the possibility of a third party guarantee, be sure to request documentation of the net assets of the third party, as well as any guarantees that may take precedence over the guarantee being negotiated.

A guarantee can be of particular use when the buyer may be on the verge of bankruptcy. If bankruptcy does occur, the third-party guarantee is usually still valid and enforceable, since the guarantor is not being granted relief from creditors – only the entity that actually filed for bankruptcy.

While all of these forms of guarantee can eventually result in payment of an overdue invoice, they tend to require a noticeable amount of staff time and legal fees, while there is also a significant risk that the extra effort and funds expended will not yield any additional cash. Consequently, the use of guarantees may not result in the most cost-effective risk reduction. Instead, it may be considered a backup method for obtaining payment, with some other risk reduction method also being used to collect funds.

> **Tip:** When contemplating the extension of credit based on a third-party guarantee, obtain a credit report for the third party, rather than relying upon the general reputation of the third party. The report may reveal that the third party has a lower net worth than expected, or is already guaranteeing more debt than its asset base.

> **Tip:** If a guarantee is being issued by an individual, have the guarantor's spouse sign onto the guarantee, so that you can pursue the collection of their jointly-held assets. Also have all signatures witnessed.

If it is possible to obtain a guarantee, have the seller's attorney write the language for the guarantee, so that the wording favors the seller. The agreement should contain the following minimum elements:

- *Amounts paid.* The guarantee should cover not only the full amount owed by the buyer, but also any related interest, penalties, and attorney's fees.
- *Immediate liability.* Once the amounts are due for payment, the seller can immediately pursue the guarantor for payment, rather than first having to attempt collection from the buyer.
- *Termination.* There is no termination date to the agreement, after which the guarantee is invalid. Instead, the guarantee continues until the underlying amount is paid.
- *Responsibility.* The guarantor signs the agreement as an individual who is personally responsible for payment, not in his or her capacity as an officer of a business.

Title Retention

It is possible to retain title to goods that are shipped to customers, and only transfer the title to buyers once payment has been made. This can be an effective risk reduction tool, but only if capital goods are being sold – the option is not practical for small-value items, with the exception of a consignment arrangement, as noted below. There are three alternatives for title retention described in this section, which are the UCC-1 financing statement, the purchase money security interest, and the inventory consignment arrangement.

UCC-1 Financing Statement

If title retention is selected for risk reduction, the seller creates a security agreement between the buyer and seller that states the rights of each party in regard to the asset. The seller then files a UCC-1 financing statement with the required government office (usually the secretary of state) to publicly reveal the presence of a lien on the asset. Doing so gives the seller seniority over other creditors who might also file liens against the asset at a later date; this is known as *perfecting* the lien.

The seller should have a procedure in place to terminate each security agreement as the underlying assets are paid by their purchasers.

There should also be a standard practice in place for how assets are to be repossessed under a security agreement. The most efficient approach from the seller's perspective is to notify the buyer and reach a mutual agreement for the seller to retrieve the goods. The seller is also entitled to repossess goods without the cooperation of the buyer, as long as the seller does not illegally break into any structures while doing so, or cause a public disturbance. The seller can obtain a court order to have the goods returned by the buyer, in which case a deputy sheriff is entitled to use force to obtain the goods. The use of a court order is usually considered a last resort if no other method of recovery will work.

> **Tip:** The UCC-1 financing statement will expire after five years. Therefore, track all unexpired financing statements to see which ones will expire soon, to ensure that all related payments have been received from customers, or to file continuation statements to extend the liens.

Given the time and expense of creating security agreements and financing statements, this approach may only be used for those customers deemed at most risk of non-payment. However, if there is a notable risk of customer bankruptcy, placing a lien on goods sold is nearly mandatory, since it positions the seller ahead of unsecured creditors.

The title retention concept may not be a good alternative in situations where the perceived value of re-sold goods is significantly lower than that of goods being sold for the first time. For example, the value of consumer electronics declines so fast that taking back goods after just one month may mean that they can only be re-sold at a substantial discount. In addition, state laws may require that these goods be labeled as having been refurbished, which tends to reduce their resale prices. Further, it may be necessary to offer an extended warranty to customers in order to convince them to buy these goods. Consequently, the option to re-sell goods taken back from a customer may not be a very profitable proposition.

Another situation in which liens are less useful is when customers of the seller are distributors or retailers. As soon as these entities sell goods to their customers, the original seller loses its lien on those goods. In a situation where the turnover of inventory at a distributor or retailer is rapid, and especially when the goods are sold prior to the date when the underlying invoice to the original seller is due, a lien on specific goods is essentially useless.

Tip: If the seller is forced to liquidate returned goods at a reduced price, the seller can pursue the original buyer for the difference between the original sale price and the amount eventually collected. However, the buyer can then claim that the seller did not maximize the price at which it sold off the goods, which can result in a reduced liability by the buyer.

Purchase Money Security Interest

When a seller files a UCC-1 financing statement, it may find that it has done so after several other creditors, which means that its claim is junior to the claims of those entities that preceded it in making their claims. It is possible to leapfrog ahead of these other creditors by obtaining a *purchase money security interest* (PMSI). Obtaining a PMSI is not simple. The seller must send notice of the arrangement to all other secured parties, so that they are fully briefed on the proposed PMSI arrangement. A PMSI statement and UCC-1 must then be filed at the office of the secretary of state for the state in which the company's primary office is located. Also, the customer should sign the PMSI. The PMSI is only available to those sellers whose goods are readily identifiable in the buyer's inventory.

Tip: The seller can identify its goods with a unique label or radio frequency identification tag, so that its goods are readily identifiable and can therefore be considered allowable under the requirements of a purchase money security interest.

Inventory Consignment

There may be situations where a distributor or retailer wants to sell a company's products, but does not have sufficiently robust finances to purchase the goods outright. If so, the distributor or retailer can act as an agent for the seller, rather than a buyer, and hold the goods on behalf of the seller. Under this consignment arrangement, the "seller" retains ownership of the goods and cannot recognize a sale until the distributor or retailer actually sells the goods to a third party. At that point, the agent notifies the seller of the sale transaction, and remits payment to the seller, while retaining its profit.

This arrangement is outlined in a consignment agreement that states the responsibilities of both parties, insurance coverage for the goods, the terms under which third party purchases are remitted to the seller by the agent, procedures for the retrieval of goods by the seller, and so forth. The seller should also establish a purchase money security interest in the inventory, as just described in the preceding sub-section.

Tip: The seller should periodically inspect a selection of consigned inventory to see if any inventory shrinkage has occurred, and to verify quantities for its own inventory tracking system.

A large amount of ongoing paperwork is required for a consignment arrangement, since funds are regularly being remitted back to the seller, while both parties must keep track of the remaining inventory. Accordingly, this risk reduction method should only be used if it appears that the two parties will maintain the arrangement for a long period of time.

Collateral

A rarely-used option for a seller of goods and services is to obtain collateral from a buyer. Collateral involves a situation where the seller is given the specific right to seize an asset and sell it if the buyer cannot fulfill its payment obligations. Few buyers have assets available for use as collateral, and those assets are usually already spoken for under the collateral requirements of their lines of credit.

There may be rare instances where a customer actually has assets available that could be used as a valid form of collateral, and is desperate enough to offer it to mitigate the credit manager's concerns about the extension of credit. If the offer is made and the proffered assets are free of any other encumbrances, then this can be a valid option. The situation is most likely to arise when a buyer is asset-rich and is in great need of the seller's products or services.

Credit Insurance

A seller may find that it can shift some of the risk associated with its accounts receivable to a firm that provides credit insurance. Under a credit insurance policy, the insurer protects the seller against customer nonpayment. The insurer should be willing to provide coverage against customer nonpayment if a proposed customer clears its internal review process. Credit insurance offers the following benefits:

- *Increased credit.* A company may be able to increase the credit levels offered to its customers, thereby potentially increasing revenue.
- *Faster international deals.* An international sale might normally be delayed while the parties arrange a letter of credit, but can be completed faster with credit insurance.
- *Custom product coverage.* The insurance can cover the shipment of custom-made products, in case customers cancel their orders prior to delivery.
- *Reduced credit staff.* Credit insurance essentially shifts risk away from a business, so it is especially beneficial in companies that have an under-staffed credit department that cannot adequately keep track of customer credit levels.
- *Knowledge.* A credit insurance firm specializes in the risk characteristics of various industries, and so may have deep knowledge about the risk profiles of individual customers, as well as aggregations of customers by region. This information is a useful supplement to other sources of information about customers.

- *Tax deductibility.* Credit insurance premiums are immediately deductible for tax purposes, whereas the allowance for doubtful accounts is only deductible when specific bad debts are recognized.

As is the case with all insurance policies, be sure to examine the terms of a credit insurance agreement for exclusions, to see what the insurer will not cover. In particular, coverage should include the receivables of customers that file for bankruptcy protection or simply go out of business.

Insurers will only provide coverage for legally sustainable debts, which are those receivables that are not disputed by the customer. If there is a dispute, the insurer will only provide coverage after the company has won a court judgment against the customer. The issue of a legally sustainable debt can be a serious one if a company has a track record of disputes with its customers over product quality, damaged goods, returns, and so forth.

Tip: It may be possible to offload the cost of credit insurance to customers by adding it to customer invoices. This is most likely to be acceptable for international deals, where a customer would otherwise be forced to obtain a letter of credit to pay for a transaction.

Insurers are more willing to provide coverage of accounts receivable if the seller is willing to take on a small part of the bad debt risk itself. This typically means that a customer default will result in the insurer reimbursing the seller, minus the amount of a 5% to 20% deductible. There may also be an annual aggregate deductible that requires the company to absorb a certain fixed amount of losses in a year before the insurer begins to pay reimbursements. Requiring a deductible means that the company continues to have an interest in only selling to credit-worthy customers.

EXAMPLE

Micron Metallic sells stamping machines to a variety of industrial customers. The company's credit insurance policy states that Micron will absorb the first $200,000 of bad debt losses in each calendar year, after which the insurer will pay 85% of all bad debts incurred, other than for invoices related to international sales, which are not covered by the policy. The policy also specifically excludes receivables related to ABC Company, which the insurer considers to be at an excessively high risk of default.

For some customers, or geographic regions subject to considerable political risk, a credit insurer may consider the risk to be so great that it will not provide coverage, or only at a high premium. If so, the credit manager must decide whether it is better for the company to assume the risk of these sales, or to pay the cost of the insurance to obtain coverage. Also, if the insurer discovers that the company's historical loss experience with its customers has been excessively high, it may require such a large premium that the company may conclude that insurance coverage is not a cost-effective form of risk reduction.

Insurers may only be willing to insure a certain amount of receivables per year with some customers. If the company chooses to sell additional amounts on credit to these designated customers, the company will sustain the entire incremental amount of credit risk. To avoid the additional risk, it is necessary to track the cumulative amount of credit sales to these customers on an ongoing basis.

Factoring

Under a factoring arrangement, a finance company agrees to take over a company's accounts receivable collections and keep the money from these collections in exchange for an immediate cash payment to the company. This process typically involves having customers mail their payments to a lockbox that appears to be operated by the company, but which is actually controlled by the finance company. Under a true factoring arrangement, the finance company takes over the risk of loss on any bad debts, though it will have the right to pick which types of receivables it will accept in order to reduce its risk of loss. A finance company is more interested in this type of deal when the size of each receivable is fairly large, since this reduces its per-transaction cost of collection.

If each receivable is quite small, the finance company may still be interested in a factoring arrangement, but it will charge the company extra for its increased processing work. The lender charges an interest rate, as well as a transaction fee for the processing of each invoice it receives. A company working under this arrangement can be paid by the factor at once, or can wait until the invoice due date before payment is sent. The latter arrangement reduces the interest expense that the company pays to the factor, but tends to go against the reason why the factoring arrangement was established, which is to get money back to the company as rapidly as possible.

Factoring can be considered a form of financing, since it accelerates the receipt of cash, but it is also a form of risk reduction, since the risk of nonpayment is accepted by the factor. However, the cost of factoring is quite high, making this a less cost-effective option, and probably not a practical one for a business whose margins are already small.

Letters of Credit

A letter of credit is a useful tool for essentially eliminating credit risk, by having the buyer escrow funds in advance of a sale with a reliable third party (its bank). Doing so ensures that the funds will be available when payment is due. The letter of credit is most commonly used for international trade, where the importer's bank (known as the issuing bank) recognizes an obligation to pay the bank of the exporter, which in turn credits the funds to the account of the exporter. To obtain these funds, the exporter must present an invoice and proof of delivery to one of the banks (depending on the circumstances), sometimes accompanied by a certificate of insurance.

The issuing bank guarantees payment under a letter of credit arrangement, and so bears the risk of payment. The issuing bank offsets this risk by either paying the funds from the line of credit of the importer, or by blocking a sufficient amount of funds in the importer's bank account. In effect, this means that the importer is paying in advance for an order, even though the exporter will not receive the funds until all terms and conditions of the letter of credit arrangement have been met.

An alternative to the letter of credit is the standby letter of credit, which guarantees that the exporter will be paid if the importer is unable to pay. This instrument can be expensive if there is a high perceived risk that the importer may default on its obligations.

Either the regular or standby letter of credit can be used to reduce risk for transactions that are not international. The credit manager can insist on their use for entirely new customers, or for those whose financial statements are not especially robust, or because the underlying goods are custom made, and so cannot be re-sold if the buyer defaults. However, this means that the buyer must have the financial wherewithal at the start of the transaction to pay for the goods; if not, the letter of credit approach will probably not work.

Export-Import Guarantees

If it is not possible or practical to obtain a letter of credit for an international sale, an alternative may be to obtain a credit guarantee from the Export-Import Bank (Ex-Im Bank) of the United States. This guarantee is available to any entity shipping domestic goods to a customer in a foreign location. The Ex-Im Bank offers guarantees for a variety of situations, including:

- Preshipment coverage, to protect against the cancellation of an order for customized goods
- Coverage of sales to multiple buyers on open account terms
- Sales to individual customers

It is not always easy to obtain a guarantee from the Ex-Im Bank. Depending on the size of the proposed sale transaction, it may be necessary to submit the audited financial statements of the buyer, a credit report, and trade references. Further, the customer must have at least a three-year history of being in the same line of business. Also, it may be necessary to meet certain minimum financial ratios.

If a proposed guarantee is accepted by the Ex-Im Bank, the seller must pay the entire amount of the coverage premium in advance. Also, the seller must still retain some risk, since the Bank will not cover more than 90% of the net contract value. Further, because the Bank is an extension of the United States government, and follows the policies mandated by the government, it does not provide guarantees for sales to those countries not approved by the government.

In short, the Ex-Im Bank provides an alternative way to reduce credit risk. It is not an automatic provider of last resort; instead, it is a prudently-run financial institution that can be expected to turn away riskier deals.

Outside Financing

When the goods being sold are high-cost fixed assets, it may be possible to arrange with a third-party lender to provide financing to the buyer to either buy or lease the items being sold. This type of arrangement shifts the credit risk to the lender. Of course, the lender will apply its own credit granting standards to buyers, and may not provide financing to those customers it considers being at an elevated risk of default.

Distributor Sales

When the credit department decides not to extend credit to a prospective customer, it may still be possible to refer the proposed transaction to a distributor of the company's products. If the distributor has more relaxed credit standards, the sale may still go through, and the distributor takes on the risk of the deal. However, if the customer reneges on payment to the distributor, the distributor may have trouble paying the seller for the goods that the distributor is reselling. Consequently, this type of arrangement does not entirely eliminate credit risk – it only means that the distributor is now liable to the seller for payment, rather than the ultimate customer.

A further consideration when shifting customer orders to a distributor is that the seller is giving up what may be a substantial margin on the sale of its goods, since the distributor is buying from the company at a reduced price.

EXAMPLE

Luminescence Corporation sells a variety of LED lights, both directly to a variety of end customers and through a group of distributors. A large home construction company contacts Luminescence about a possible sale of LED lights that would generate $100,000 of revenue for Luminescence. The credit department is uncomfortable with the sale, given the highly leveraged condition of the customer. The alternative is to direct the customer to one of the distributors.

The problem is that the distributors buy lights from Luminescence at a 30% discount. Consequently, by shifting the prospective deal to a distributor, the company is automatically reducing its margins by $30,000, and may still retain some credit risk in the event that the distributor cannot pay Luminescence.

Adjustment of Days to Pay

A customer may request credit for an amount that the credit department decides is too risky for the company to allow, based on the normal number of days during which the receivable will be outstanding. However, the risk profile of the situation can be improved upon by shortening the number of days over which the customer is allowed to have credit.

EXAMPLE

The Hegemony Toy Company receives a $20,000 order for a large number of its action figurines from a new retailer. The credit manager concludes that the retailer's net worth warrants the extension of only $10,000 in credit. To meet the retailer's request, the credit manager proposes the initial sale of $10,000 of action figurines on 15-day payment terms, rather than the company's usual 30-day terms, with shipment of the next $10,000 of figurines to be completed as soon as payment is received for the first delivery. By taking this approach, Hegemony is never at risk for more than $10,000, and still sells the entire amount of the initial customer order.

This approach only works when a customer order can be subdivided into several pieces, and the customer has sufficient cash on hand to pay on shorter terms.

Cross-Selling Risk

When a company has multiple lines of business, there is a natural temptation to try to cross-sell the customers of one set of products on the other lines of business. After all, the company has already expended a substantial amount to acquire the customers, and cross-selling is considered to be a relatively inexpensive way to generate additional sales. The trouble with this approach is that a portion of the customers subjected to cross-selling were not good customers to begin with, and their negative impact on the company is now multiplied by their additional purchases. This can have a profound impact on credit risk and company profitability.

Credit risk increases for this subset of customers if they are permitted additional credit. This is a common occurrence that is driven by the sales staff, under the obvious logic that cross-selling will not work unless sales are allowed to increase by providing more credit. The trouble is that the financial position of these customers does not permit them to make additional purchases, resulting in an inevitable increase in payment defaults.

In addition to this credit problem, the expansion of sales to these more difficult customers will also result in more returned goods and more administrative staff time to service their needs. These factors add up to an increase in expenses that, in total, completely offsets any increase in revenues.

The clear answer to the cross-selling conundrum is to carefully analyze all customers prior to initiating a cross-selling campaign, and to exclude the more problematic customers from the campaign. The analysis may even result in the termination of *all* business with these marginal customers.

Treatment of Customized Goods

When a customer orders customized goods, this presents a special problem from a credit risk perspective, because the company may be unable to resell the goods elsewhere in the event of a customer payment default. In this case, the best form of risk reduction is to require a series of payments from the customer to ensure that all costs incurred to construct the goods are paid for as incurred. This means that both a down payment and a series of progress payments should be required of the customer. These payments also mean that the customer is less likely to cancel the order, since it already has so much cash invested in the order.

An alternative treatment for customized goods is to build the added credit risk into the price of the product, so that the higher price will deter customers from placing orders for these types of goods. In essence, the company decides not to incur this type of risk by pricing itself out of the market for all but the most price-insensitive customers.

Portfolio Approach to Risk

Thus far, we have discussed a variety of separate methods that can be used to reduce credit risk. Another option is to summarize the total credit risk to which the business is exposed, and make a determination regarding how much risk to retain. For example, receivables can be categorized into some variation on low, medium, and high risk of nonpayment, and the estimated bad debt percentage calculated for each of these categories. If the total amount of expected bad debt is equal to or less than the amount that management considers to be acceptable, then the current portfolio of risk reduction techniques may be considered acceptable. This means that the credit manager may allow a certain number of higher-risk sales to proceed without risk reduction, as long as there are a large number of extremely low-risk transactions that sufficiently reduce the total credit risk for the company.

EXAMPLE

The credit manager of Laid Back Corporation (which sells business chairs) constructs the following table of estimated bad debts for the company's current portfolio of receivables. The management team has decided that bad debts can reach as much as 1½% of sales. Since the table indicates an expected bad debt percentage of 1.4%, the credit manager has a small amount of room to offer somewhat more credit to higher-risk customers and still remain within the guideline set by management.

Risk Category	Current Receivable Balance	Historical Bad Debt Percentage	Estimated Bad Debt by Risk Category
Low risk	$10,425,000	0.4%	$41,700
Medium low	6,100,000	1.3%	79,300
Medium high	2,350,000	3.8%	89,300
High risk	630,000	10.5%	66,150
Totals	$19,505,000	1.4%	$276,450

The portfolio approach to risk tends to increase earnings, as long as it is used judiciously, since the credit risk associated with customer orders is no longer assessed on an individual basis, but rather as a group of orders where some orders have a higher risk than others.

Alteration of Credit Terms

An analysis of a customer's existing credit terms may indicate the need for some fine tuning to more closely align the terms with the seller's overall policy regarding credit risk reduction. However, doing so on a continual basis can annoy customers, especially when the changes routinely impact their ability to purchase goods and services from the seller under reasonable terms. Accordingly, it may be better to avoid continual terms alterations within a certain percentage of variability, in favor of making a much smaller number of larger changes at longer intervals.

EXAMPLE

A customer's latest financial statements reveal a slight reduction in net worth that would normally call for a reduction of 10% in its credit limit. Previous financial statements submitted by the customer have revealed a modest level of both positive and negative changes in net worth over the past few years, and the most recent decline in net worth is well within the range of previously-reported changes. If the credit limit were to be reduced by 10%, this would result in a decline of $25,000 in the seller's credit risk, which is considered immaterial. Consequently, no action is taken.

A material credit loss is considered to be $50,000, so the seller sets a minimum change threshold of $50,000 on the account. A change in the credit limit for the customer will only be enacted if subsequent changes in its net worth indicate that a credit limit reduction of $50,000 is warranted.

Summary

The risk reduction techniques described in this chapter do not entirely eliminate risk, and may even introduce additional costs and delays. For example, the use of a personal guarantee to mitigate risk may result in a lengthy lawsuit against the guarantor, only to find that the guarantor does not have sufficient assets to pay the guaranteed amount. Similarly, a credit insurance policy may be invalid for a specific claim because the customer disputes the invoice. Consequently, do not assume that risk reduction strategies will always work. It may be necessary to instead adopt layers of risk reduction strategies, so that a backup strategy will still provide protection if the primary approach fails. Also, there will still be bad debts even if all of the strategies noted in this chapter are employed; the amounts will be reduced, but be prepared to incur some losses on an ongoing basis.

Chapter 12
Customer Billings

Introduction

The key document used by the collection staff is the invoice. The timing and process flow of invoice generation are useful for collectors to understand, possibly resulting in a variety of improvement suggestions to the billing manager. In this chapter, we address the basic process flow for billings, and then state a number of techniques for enhancing both the efficiency and effectiveness of billings. These changes can be of use to the collection staff, since the result may be faster customer payments and fewer issues caused by billing errors.

> **Related Podcast Episode:** Episode 73 of the Accounting Best Practices Podcast discusses billing best practices. The episode is available at:
> **www.accountingtools.com/podcasts** or **iTunes**

Billing Processing

In this section, we present the outlines of a billing system that requires the manual creation of an invoice, which is still the predominant approach in most businesses. We then follow the outline with a discussion of the problems with such a system.

Billing Processing

The following steps show the basic transaction flow for the creation of a customer invoice. The steps are:

1. *Access shipping documents.* This is a document sent from the shipping department that states what has been shipped to a customer. It is frequently a copy of the bill of lading or packing slip.
2. *Access customer order.* Locate the sales order, of which a copy should have been sent from the order entry department to the accounting department when the customer originally placed an order.
3. *Verify prices (optional).* Compare the prices listed on the sales order to the standard price list, and flag any items that vary from the standard rates for additional review.
4. *Calculate shipping.* Determine the shipping charge to add to the invoice.
5. *Charge sales tax.* Charge the sales tax rate for the government entity in which the customer is receiving the goods.
6. *Print invoice.* If a pre-printed invoice form is used, make sure that it is positioned properly in the printer, conduct a test print if necessary, and print

the invoice. Otherwise, simply print all invoices and verify that they have printed correctly.

7. *Mail invoice.* Stuff the completed invoices into envelopes and mail them.

8. *Retain extra sales order copy (optional).* If a sales order has not been entirely fulfilled, make a copy of it, circle the remaining items that have not yet been shipped, and store it in a pending file. This is eventually matched to the shipping documents for the backordered items when they are shipped.

9. *File documents.* File an invoice copy in the customer's file, along with the sales order and proof of shipment.

The billing process is approximately the same if the company is providing services, rather than delivering products. There are two possible process flows for service billings:

- *Service order.* Employees may be called upon to complete a specific one-time service, after which they indicate the number of hours worked and other charges on a service order, which they submit to the billing clerk. The service order is treated as a notification to invoice the customer.
- *Project based.* Employees may be working for a customer on an hourly or fixed-fee basis, in which case their efforts are usually compiled at the end of each month and converted into an invoice.

Analysis of Billing Processing

The billing process flow requires that information be successfully transmitted from the order entry and shipping departments to the billing clerk, transformed into an accurate invoice, and forwarded to the customer. The timing and nature of these information flows can result in a convoluted billing process. The following bullet points explain these issues:

- *Bottlenecks.* In many businesses, there is a surge of shipping at month-end. Since the billing function is not typically staffed to handle this jump in transaction volume, it may require several days to complete all invoicing for the month, which can delay payment by customers.
- *Distance.* The customer order must be transferred to the billing clerk from the order entry staff, while the shipping notification must be delivered from the shipping department. The inter-departmental transfer of these documents can occasionally result in the delay or loss of documents.
- *Controls.* There is a considerable risk that the billing clerk will not always be notified that an order has shipped, which means that *no* invoice is sent to the customer.
- *Error rates.* One of the key problem areas with billings is issuing incorrect invoices, since customers then hold up payment until a correction can be made. This also typically calls for the issuance of a credit memo to cancel or adjust the original invoice, which creates additional work for the accounting

staff. The collection staff must also sort through the array of invoices and offsetting credits.

In short, the billing function relies upon the accurate and timely flow of information from two other departments in order to initiate an invoice, after which the billing staff may have trouble issuing an accurate invoice in a timely manner. These issues can cause problems with the ultimate goal of customer billing, which is to be paid in a timely manner. In the next section, we will examine a number of improvement options that can increase the ability of a business to be paid on time, as well as avoid the involvement of the collection staff.

Billing of Change Orders

A change order is an authorization issued by the customer to alter the specifications of goods to be delivered by the seller. Change orders most commonly apply to construction projects, but can also apply to goods that are being custom-designed or modified for a customer. Change orders can represent a collection problem if there is any disagreement between the parties concerning which orders were approved, the agreed-upon price, and whether the changes were implemented. When an invoice is issued that includes change order billings, the duration of the collection effort is likely to be extensive. Here are several ways to improve upon the situation:

- *Dual sign-off.* Representatives of both the customer and seller should sign off on each change order, including a statement that the requested change has been completed to the satisfaction of the customer.
- *Change order document coordination.* The project manager for a customer's project is likely responsible for maintaining the official file of change orders. If so, the billing clerk should meet with the project manager prior to issuing a billing, to ensure that all authorized change orders are included in the invoice.
- *Separate billing.* Where possible, bill change orders separately from the main invoice. By doing so, any issues that the customer may have with a change order will not impact the speed of payment for the main invoice.
- *Incomplete change orders notification.* Some change orders may linger for a long time for a number of reasons. If so, and the company has performed some or all of the work related to these change orders, management needs to understand the amount of funds tied up in these unbilled items. Consequently, it makes sense to maintain a database of unbilled change orders and to discuss it regularly with those responsible for completing customer projects.

Efficient and Effective Billing

It may be possible for a business to enhance the efficiency and effectiveness of its billing operation by enacting one or more of the upgrades noted in this section. The collection staff should be mindful of these opportunities, and bring them to the attention of the billing manager if they have not yet been implemented.

Payment in Advance

The key issues for a billing system are to ensure that there are no invoicing errors, and that the customer's accounts payable staff receives the invoice, with the eventual goal of being paid in full and on time. What if we can eliminate both problems by obtaining payment in advance from customers? This can be accomplished by offering a small discount for payment in advance, and may also be encouraged by offering a somewhat higher commission to the sales staff if they can obtain these kinds of sales. Once the cash is in hand, the billing staff can create an invoice at its leisure, stamp it "paid," and forward a copy to the customer. The only problem with this approach is that the accounting staff must initially spend the time to record the payment as a liability, and then shift the liability into a sale transaction once the goods have been shipped or services provided.

Bank Account Debits

In a few industries, the amount that a company bills to its customers is unchanged from month to month, and continues over many periods. Examples of such situations are health club memberships and monthly parking fees. In these cases, consider requiring all customers to have funds automatically deducted from their bank accounts with debit transactions that are initiated by the company. This approach requires more authorization work up front, but virtually eliminates the need for any subsequent collections work (unless a debit transaction fails).

There are only a few business models under which this approach works. Also, even where it is applicable, there will still be situations, such as the first month of a membership or a partial month, where direct payment by the customer may be required, and which will therefore still call for some collection activity. Nonetheless, the long-term convenience of this option makes it nearly mandatory in those rare cases where it can be used.

Systems Integration

A significant problem with the billing function is that the billing clerk must assemble information from multiple departments in order to generate an invoice – the sales order from the order entry staff, and the shipping notification from the shipping department. Given the need to transfer documents across the company, sometimes over long distances, there is a strong likelihood that some of this information will be lost in transit, resulting in no invoices being generated.

The issue can be rectified by installing a computer system where the transactions generated by the order entry, shipping, and accounting departments are fully integrated. Under such a system, the billing clerk is notified by the system as soon as a shipment has been made, and can generate an invoice from an on-line copy of the sales order. An integrated system mitigates the risk of not issuing invoices, while also requiring minimal re-typing of information for each billing – which reduces the incidence of invoice errors.

The downside of having integrated systems is the cost of installing and maintaining them. In particular, the shipping department in some heavy industries can be considered a hostile environment for computer equipment, so that the manual transfer of shipping information may still be needed when the computer system is not functioning.

Buffer Staff

If the billing staff is overwhelmed at month-end by the volume of deliveries that must be invoiced, consider training additional staff to shift into the billing function during this time period. The solution is not without risk, since part-time billing clerks are less practiced in issuing invoices, and so will probably generate more errors. However, it may be possible to use these extra staff in a supporting (administrative) role, where they increase the overall capacity of the function without causing more errors.

Tip: Installing an integrated billing system eliminates much of the billing bottleneck, since the system allows the billing staff to generate invoices much more quickly than would be the case if invoices were being individually prepared by hand.

Contract Terms Verification

If there is a large invoice with unusual payment terms, verify the accuracy of the terms before creating the invoice. Otherwise, customers may refuse to pay until a replacement invoice is issued. This step usually only applies when there is a contractual arrangement underlying a billing.

Funding Verification

If an invoice is based on a multi-period contract with a customer, verify that there is sufficient funding left on the contract before issuing the invoice. A more comprehensive version of this approach is to monitor available funding throughout the month and stop any additional work on a contract once the funding limit has been reached. If funding verification is not done, customers may reject invoices because the amounts billed exceed the amount approved.

Update Customer File

When an invoice is sent to an old or incorrect customer address, it can take several weeks for the invoice to be marked as undeliverable by the postal service and returned to the company. This inherent delay increases the required collection period, even though it is not the fault of the collection staff.

Whenever an invoice is returned in the mail, investigate why the wrong address was used, identify the underlying problem, and create a procedure to prevent the issue from occurring again. Another option is to have the mailroom staff route all customer change-of-address notices to the controller, who presumably can ensure that the address changes are input into the customer master file as soon as possible.

In those cases where the bulk of all invoices are issued at the end of the month, it may make sense to give the list of prospective invoices, with associated addresses, to the sales staff. The salespeople, who have the best knowledge of customer contact information, can then inform the billing manager of any addresses that should be changed prior to issuing the invoices. This approach works best when there is a substantial sales commission, since the sales staff is then more inclined to assist with billings in order to receive customer payments in a timely manner. If there are many invoices to be reviewed, it may be more cost-effective to only issue information about the largest invoices to the sales staff, on the grounds that their time is more valuable than the potential delay of a small amount of cash flows related to the multitude of smaller invoices.

From the collection perspective, it is useful to use an overnight delivery service for the re-issuance of any invoice that was returned due to an incorrect address. By doing so (and despite the delivery expense), it is possible that customers will still have sufficient time to schedule these invoices to be paid as of their original due dates.

Invoice Layout Improvement

It may be possible to make several modifications to the invoice template to reduce the time required to receive payments from customers, as well as to reduce the number of customer payment errors. Consider implementing the adjustments noted in the following table.

Invoice Format Changes

Credit card contact information	If customers want to pay with a credit card, include a telephone number to call to pay by this means.
Early payment discount	State the exact amount of the early payment discount and the exact date by which the customer must pay in order to qualify for the discount.
General contact information	If customers have a question about the invoice, there should be a contact information block that states the telephone number and e-mail address they should contact.
Payment due date	Rather than entering payment terms on the invoice (such as "net 30"), state the exact date on which payment is due. This should be stated prominently.

The goal in creating an invoice format is to present the minimum amount of information to the customer in order to prevent confusion, while presenting the required information as clearly as possible. The following sample invoice template incorporates the invoice format changes that we just addressed.

Sample Enhanced Invoice Template

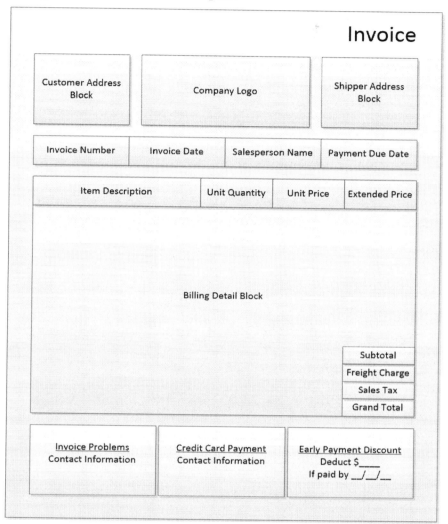

Complex Invoice Separation

When a company issues a complex, multi-line invoice, there is an increased risk that the customer will find issue with some portion of the invoice and refuse to pay it. The billing staff can mitigate this risk by separating the invoice into a larger number of invoices, each containing one or just a few line items. This approach involves more work by the billing staff, but increases the odds of immediate payment for the bulk of the line items being billed.

This recommendation should only be used for those customers that have a history of arguing over the details of invoices. Splitting apart invoices is not productive when there is a low risk of customer non-payment.

Invoice Proofreading

Some billings are extremely complicated. The billing clerk must assemble many line items of information, as well as account for an array of adjustments and discounts. These invoices will also be reviewed intensively by the customer's accounts payable staff, especially if the company has a reputation for issuing incorrect invoices. There is a strong likelihood that these invoices will be rejected due to errors, which means that even more time must then be spent to create a revised invoice.

The possible payment delay associated with invoice errors makes it nearly mandatory to have an experienced person review these more complex invoices before they are sent to the customer. The best reviewer is usually the person in charge of the business relationship with a specific customer, since they are deeply involved in the work being done for the customer. In addition, it may make sense to have an experienced clerk review these invoices for clerical-level errors that might also lead to invoice rejection.

> **Tip:** The key issue with proofreading invoices is deciding which invoices to proofread, since the process is time-consuming. Possible options are to require an invoice review for all invoices issued to the more picky customers, or to only require reviews when the number of invoice line items exceeds a certain amount, or when only a certain amount of funding remains available for a customer project.

Invoice Creation at Delivery Point

One of the ways in which an invoice can be considered in error is when the customer disputes the quantity delivered or the nature of the services provided. In these cases, it may be possible to sidestep the error by having the delivery person or service provider generate the invoice on the customer's premises. This can be done with a simple handwritten form, or through a tablet or smartphone app that creates and e-mails the invoice to the customer.

Once created, the delivery person sends a copy of each invoice to the billing clerk, who enters it into the accounting system. Since the invoice has already been delivered to the customer, there is no rush to input these invoices into the accounting system, which eliminates any bottleneck in the billing function.

There are three issues with creating invoices at the delivery point that may limit its effectiveness:

- *Employee only.* This option is not available when deliveries are made by a third-party freight carrier. Only an employee can generate invoices on-site.
- *Sales taxes.* The person creating the invoice must have access to the correct sales tax percentages to compile the invoice.
- *Training.* Employees must be well-trained in the creation of invoices, since there would otherwise be a risk that they might create incorrect invoices.

Invoice Creation at Shipping Dock

A variation on invoice creation at the delivery point is to do so at the shipping point. In essence, the invoice is automatically printed at the same time as the packing slip, and is included on the outside of the shipment. This approach eliminates the risk of not having the billing clerk create an invoice. However, it requires some customization of the accounting software to ensure that an invoice is automatically generated when the packing slip is printed. Another issue is that the customer's receiving staff may not forward the invoice to their own accounting department. Also, this method is limited to physical deliveries; it is useless for the billing of services. In summary, this approach eliminates the risk of not issuing an invoice, but introduces the risk that the invoice will not be sent to the appropriate party within the customer's organization.

Electronic Invoice Delivery

One way to eliminate the delay associated with mailing an invoice to a customer is to e-mail it to them. The transmission has the advantage of being essentially instantaneous. However, it suffers from several possible problems. First, the e-mail may be shunted into a junk e-mail folder or rejected by the customer's e-mail server. Second, it may be read by the recipient but not acted upon. Third, the recipient may no longer work for the customer, and his or her e-mail account is no longer being monitored. Finally, the subsequent print-out of the invoice may not be considered an "original" by the customer, and is rejected. These concerns can be resolved or mitigated in three ways:

- Install an electronic data interchange (EDI) connection between the computer systems of the two companies, which essentially transfers the invoice directly into the customer's computer system. While ideal, EDI connections are mostly used among large companies that are frequent business partners.
- Send an invoice both by e-mail and regular mail. By doing so, an invoice will hopefully find its way into the accounting system of a customer before the printed version arrives in the mail. However, this also results in multiple copies of the same invoice being sent to customers, which they may not appreciate.
- Manually enter the invoice into the customer's accounting system via a form on an Internet page. This approach is increasingly common, but suffers from a notable amount of manual labor. See the next sub-section for additional discussion of this item.

Of these options, the most likely one for a smaller business is the manual entry of an invoice through an on-line form operated by a customer. If there is a considerable amount of transaction volume between two business partners, the most cost-effective route is to pursue an EDI solution.

On-line Invoice Entry

Whenever a customer creates an on-line form for the entry of invoices by suppliers into its accounts payable system, the billing department should embrace the form with enthusiasm. There are two reasons why on-line forms are useful:

- *On-line error checking.* Most on-line forms contain error-checking routines that ensure that all required fields are completed, that an authorizing purchase order number (if any) is referenced, and that sufficient funding has been reserved to pay the invoice. Some of these routines are so comprehensive that customer accounting staffs conduct no further invoice reviews. Thus, if the system accepts an invoice, it is more likely to be paid without further examination by the customer.
- *Delivery confirmation.* Once an invoice has been entered in the system, an acceptance message should be issued. This gives the billing staff confirmation that its invoice has been delivered. The company no longer has to worry that an invoice might be lost in transit to the customer.

The downside of on-line invoice entry is that these forms are not known for being quick and efficient methods of data entry. Instead, each form has its own quirks that make it time-consuming to enter invoices.

> **Tip:** Since there is no standard format for the layout of on-line forms, consider creating a standard data entry procedure for each customer's on-line form. The billing staff will likely be more efficient in entering information using these procedures.

Shipping Log Exception Tracking

The shipping manager always maintains a shipping log, in which are summarized the dates and times of shipments, the name of the carrier, and the name of the customer. As a last line of defense in detecting missing invoices, it is useful to have an accounting clerk compare the month-end invoice register to the shipping log to see if any shipped items were not billed. There will be a few normal exceptions, such as the shipment of marketing samples for which no billing is intended, but this examination may bring up a small number of additional items that should be billed at once. This issue is not of great importance to the collection staff, since customers will simply pay as of the new (and later) due dates listed on any additional invoices resulting from the review. The one exception is if the billing manager requires that these invoices be backdated to the original delivery date, in which case the collection staff may be called upon to collect payment on invoices that customers may have only just received.

Practices to Avoid

From the perspective of having a truly efficient accounting system, we advise against the use of any practices that complicate the billing process flow. For example, there may be a temptation to provide an overwhelming amount of evidence to customers that the goods they ordered have arrived, in which case a company could wait several days to obtain proof of delivery from its freight carrier, and attach this information to its invoices. However, doing so delays the invoicing process by multiple days (especially if a customer elects to pay for the slowest form of delivery), and so may also delay customer payment.

Analysis of Efficient Billing

The one systems improvement having the most profound impact on the billing process is the use of systems integration. It eliminates all billing bottlenecks, eliminates all distance considerations between the various departments, and reduces the risk that an invoice will not be issued. However, the remaining recommendations in this section were largely targeted at the goal of obtaining payments from customers, and so generally added to the work load of the billing department, so that prompt payment could be achieved.

The following flowchart reveals the altered process flow for the customer billing function, assuming the use of systems integration, occasional invoice proofreading, and the on-line entry of invoices into customer systems. To improve the clarity of the flowchart, minor recommendations and alternative forms of invoice preparation are not included. Process improvements are noted in bold.

Efficient Billing Process Flow

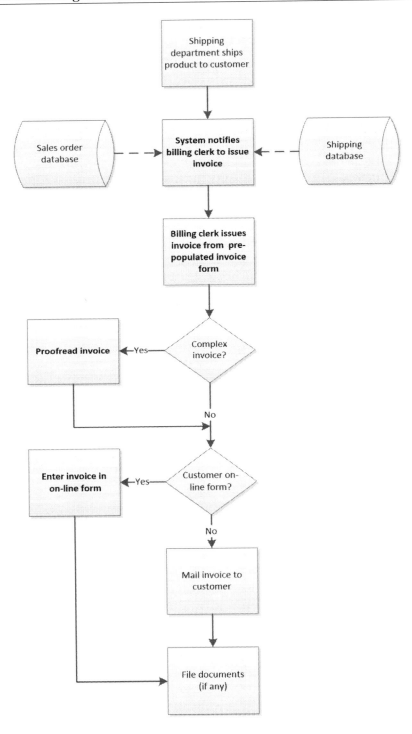

Statements of Account

The statement of account is a report sent periodically to customers, noting those invoices that remain unpaid, and any credit memos that have not yet been used. The intent of this report is to notify customers of the presence of any invoices that do not appear in the accounting records of the customers. Hopefully, receipt of a statement of account will trigger an inquiry from customers, asking for more detail about missing documents. The statement should be formatted to include all of the information that a customer needs to make such an inquiry or to make a payment, including company contact and pay-to information. A sample of a properly formatted statement of account is shown below. Note that the top part of the form is designed to be torn off by the customer and used as a remittance advice.

Sample Statement of Account Template

Company Logo		Statement of Account

Shipper Address Block	Customer Address Block	Statement Date / Customer Name / Customer Number

Company Contact Information

Amount Due

Amount Paid

— — — — — — — — — — — Tear Here — — — — — — — — — — —

Invoice Date	Invoice Amount	Payment Date	Payment Number	Payment Amount	Balance Due

Statement of Account Detail Block

Payment Status

Current	31-60 Days	61-90 Days	90+ Days		Total Due

The billing manager may be inclined not to issue statements of account, since this is simply an additional chore for the billing staff. Consequently, the collection manager may have to push hard to ensure that the statements are issued in a timely manner. It may even be necessary for the collections staff to issue statements, if the billing staff will not do so.

The statement of account is not cost-effective in all circumstances. The cost of forms, printing, mailing, and staff time may be offset by a relatively small amount of related collections. Consequently, monitor the situation and terminate use of the statements if the cost-benefit analysis is not favorable for the company.

Summary

It is critical for the collection department to understand the process by which customer billings are created, since this process directly impacts the work of each collection employee. It is particularly useful to understand which step in the billing process may have created an invoice error or payment delay, so that collection personnel can go straight to the person responsible for that step in order to have an issue corrected.

We reviewed a number of possible methods for improving the billing process, in hopes that the collection manager can suggest them to the billings manager. The result should be the faster delivery of more error-free invoices to customers, which in turn reduces the workload of the collection department.

Chapter 13
Payment Handling

Introduction

The task of the collections staff is influenced by how customer payments are handled by the accounting department. A payment made by a customer can be delayed by a company's in-house payment processing systems, which means that it still appears in the accounting system as unpaid. Consequently, the collections staff continues to take various actions to obtain customer payment when the payment may already be within the company. In this chapter, we describe the basic process for handling incoming check payments, and how this process can be improved upon. The result should be faster recognition of received checks within the accounting system.

> **Related Podcast Episodes:** Episodes 38, 41 and 137 of the Accounting Best Practices Podcast discuss automatic cash application, remote deposit capture, and a lean system for cash receipts, respectively. They are available at: **www.accountingtools.com/podcasts** or **iTunes**

Check Receipts

The primary form of payment to many businesses remains the check. The basic process flow for the handling of received checks involves the receipt, recordation, and depositing of checks by different people, where there are controls in place to monitor the checks at each transfer from one person to the next. This process is designed to mitigate the risk of loss, but does so at the price of being extremely inefficient.

The processing of check receipts involves the transfer of incoming payments from the mailroom to the cashier, then to a bank courier, and finally to a person who reconciles received to deposited cash. The following steps show the basic transaction flow.

1. *Record incoming checks.* The mailroom staff opens incoming mail, records all checks received, and stamps checks "for deposit only," before forwarding payments to the cashier. This step is a control point, designed to keep a second record of check receipts in case the cashier attempts to abscond with any funds.
2. *Transfer checks.* The mailroom uses a locked pouch to transfer checks to the cashier, along with a copy of their record of checks received.
3. *Apply checks.* The cashier records the received checks, either directly to sales or as reductions of specific accounts receivable. The amount of the

checks recorded by the cashier should match the amount of the checks recorded by the mailroom staff.

4. *Deposit checks*. The cashier creates a deposit slip for the checks. A courier takes the deposit to the bank, where a bank teller tallies the deposit and issues a receipt.

5. *Match to bank receipt*. The cashier matches the company's record of checks transferred to the bank to the bank's record of the amount received. This step is a control point that can detect checks removed from the deposit by the courier, or a recordation difference between the cashier and the bank teller.

There are two key bottlenecks in check receipts processing. The first resides in the mailroom, where the mail may not arrive until late in the day, and the mailroom staff may not assign much priority to tabulating check receipts. The cashier is another bottleneck, since this person may have difficulty ascertaining how some payments are to be applied. Further, the company has no control over bank teller availability, which can extend the time period required to deposit funds. The net result is a possible overnight delay before payments can be forwarded to the bank and accepted for deposit. In some businesses where payment processing is given a low priority, multiple days may pass before checks are applied to open accounts receivable and sent to the bank.

> **Tip:** A simple way to ensure that cash application is not delaying the daily bank deposit is to have the accounting staff record all unapplied payments in a suspense account, and keep copies of the related payments. The originals can then be deposited at once.

The check receipts process is laced with controls, since a business wants to ensure that no payments are lost or stolen. This means that payments are recorded at each step of the process and reconciled to the information recorded in the preceding step, which slows down the entire transaction. Errors are most likely to arise because check totals were incorrectly recorded during one processing step, requiring a reconciliation at the next processing step. Thus, the system of controls is itself causing errors that must be reviewed and corrected.

Check Receipt Improvements

There are several excellent techniques available that can truncate most or a portion of the check receipts process, or introduce automation that improves processing speed. These techniques are noted in the remainder of this section.

The Bank Lockbox

The cash receipts process and related controls can be vastly reduced by having customers send their payments to a bank lockbox. Under this approach, the bank manages the mailbox address to which payments are sent, so that the company is taken out of the business of handling checks. Instead, the bank deposits all checks received, and posts scanned images of all receipts on its website. The cashier then accesses the check images on this secure site, which are then used to record the payments against open accounts receivable. This approach has the added advantage of posting cash to the company's bank account somewhat sooner, so that the company can take advantage of additional interest income on its invested funds. The cash receipts process flow when a lockbox is used is compressed to the following steps:

1. The bank processes receipts that arrive at the lockbox. This involves depositing payments into the company's bank account, as well as storing digital images of checks and remittances on-line.
2. The cashier accesses the bank's website each day to view the images of scanned payments from the preceding day. The cashier uses this information to apply the payments to open accounts receivable.
3. The cashier reconciles the applied amount of cash to the amount reported by the bank.

It is possible to expand upon the lockbox concept by opening a *lockbox network*. The larger banks now offer lockboxes throughout the country that are linked to a single bank account, so that customers can be instructed to send payments to the lockbox located closest to them, thereby reducing the amount of mail float. The lockbox network is especially useful for those companies that cater to many customers throughout a large geographic region. Conversely, a company with a regional presence may find that a single lockbox is sufficient for its needs.

> **Tip:** The bank offering lockbox network services should periodically include a free analysis of the most cost-effective locations in which to have lockboxes.

The downside of the bank lockbox is a combination of fixed monthly fees and per-receipt fees charged by the bank, which makes this alternative cost-effective only for medium to larger-size companies that receive large numbers of checks. If this method does not appear to be cost-effective, then consider the later discussion of remote deposit capture, which may be available for free, and which can accelerate the speed with which cash becomes available to earn interest.

It can be quite a chore to convince customers to route their payments to a lockbox. Schedule several reminder messages to customers, as well as a number of follow-up phone calls, and even then there will still probably be a few intransigent customers who persist in mailing their payments to the company. If so, have the mailroom staff immediately mail these payments to the lockbox. Doing so eliminates the need for in-house cash controls.

> **Tip:** Include in customer billings a return envelope that is stamped with the lockbox address. Also, make sure that all billing documents sent to customers only include the lockbox address; there should be no reference to the company's normal mailing address.

If the company does not want to use a lockbox, an alternative that can speed the collection of cash is to rent a post office box in or near the primary mail processing facility for the local area, and then have an employee or courier pick up the mail as soon as it is made available at the post office box. The primary mail processing facility should receive cash several hours prior to the local branch offices, so this approach can shave hours from the time required to process payments, apply them against open accounts receivable, and deposit them at the local bank.

The use of a lockbox is the key enhancement of the cash receipts process, since the only person directly involved in check receipts is now the cashier; the bottlenecks related to the mailroom staff, courier, and bank teller are eliminated. If a lockbox is implemented, there is no need for any of the other improvements noted through the remainder of this section, with the exception of automatic cash application.

Automatic Cash Application

When a company receives a large number of customer payments every day, it can be quite difficult for the cashier to apply the receipts against open accounts receivable in a timely manner. If so, deposits may be delayed. The cash application process can be substantially compressed through the use of automatic cash application.

Automatic cash application requires that the lockbox operator use a data feed to forward to the company the magnetic ink character recognition (MICR) information from each check received at the lockbox, as well as the total payment amount. The cash application software uses a decision table to decide how to apply these payments to open accounts receivable. The automated decision process generally follows these steps:

1. Match the bank account number shown in each check's MICR information to the correct customer. This accesses the correct customer record of open accounts receivable.
2. Only match payments to invoices where the payment amount exactly matches the invoice amount.
3. Of the remaining payments, only match cash to invoices where the cash amount matches the exact amount of several invoices that have just come due for payment.
4. Kick out all remaining payments for manual review.

The decision table can contain more sophisticated rules, such as applying cash if payment amounts do not include the freight and/or sales tax elements of an invoice. As a company examines the payments kicked out by the system, it can gradually adjust the decision table to increase the number of automatic cash applications.

However, the variety of deductions taken makes it unlikely that it will ever be possible to completely automate the cash application process. Nonetheless, automatic cash application can greatly improve the speed with which cash is applied to open accounts receivable.

Mailstop Number

A potential delay in cash processing is when the mailroom sorts through all of the day's mail, opens those items containing cash or checks, and forwards them to the accounting department as part of its general distribution of mail. A faster approach is to have all customers incorporate a mailstop number into the address to which they mail funds. When the mailroom employees see these addresses, they immediately forward them to the accounting department without opening the envelopes. To encourage the use of a mailstop number, include it in all invoices, and also consider sending a separate mailing to customers that announces the change.

A potential problem is that payments will no longer be recorded by the mailroom staff, which reduces the level of control over cash. There are two ways to deal with this concern:

- Have someone in the accounting department who is not involved with cash receipts record all incoming checks to replace the work done in the mailroom.
- Instead of making a separate list of incoming checks against which receipts are later reconciled, have the accounting person handling the incoming checks make two complete photocopies of all payments made, and then immediately prepare the original checks for deposit. One of the photocopies goes to the cash application staff, to be used as the source document for cash applications, while the other copy is used as a control document that can be reconciled to the register of cash receipts.

Remote Deposit Capture

A remote deposit capture system involves the use of a check scanner and bank-provided scanning software that creates an electronic image of each check to be deposited. The accounting staff then sends the scanned check information in an electronic message to the bank, rather than making a physical deposit. The bank accepts the deposit information directly into its database, posts the related funds to the company's account, and assigns funds availability based on a predetermined schedule. This approach is useful from a cash application perspective, for there is no need to send a courier to the bank each day, leaving more time for the studied application of payments to open accounts receivable.

Remote deposit capture requires slightly more time by the accounting staff to prepare a deposit (by scanning checks) than by the traditional approach of preparing a deposit slip. However, it completely eliminates the time required to make a physical deposit at the bank, as well as the control point of matching the bank's receipt to the deposit slip.

Remote deposit capture will require the inclusion of new steps in the check processing work flow, which are:

1. Derive the batch total for all checks to be scanned.
2. Scan all checks in the batch.
3. Match the scanned total to the batch total and adjust as necessary.
4. Transmit the batch to the bank.
5. Print and retain a deposit slip.

There may also need to be an additional step to retain the scanned checks for a short time to ensure that they have been accepted by the bank, after which they should be shredded or perforated with a "deposited" stamp. The check destruction or mutilation is required to ensure that they are not inadvertently deposited again.

Special Check Endorsement Language

A customer may send a check that contains the words "paid in full" (or some variation thereof) in either the memo section on the face of the check or in the endorsement section on the back of the check. By including this language on the check, the customer is attempting to make a legal claim that it is not required to pay any additional money to the company. For example, if a customer owes $600 on an invoice and sends in a partial payment of $400 with "paid in full" text on the check, the customer intends to avoid paying the remaining $200.

The exact placement of this text on the check makes a substantial difference in its legality. If the text in written in the memo section on the face of the check, this is *generally* considered to have no legal significance; however, check local laws to see if there is some variation away from the general rule. If the text is written in the endorsement section on the back of the check, this is *generally* considered to be legally binding (again, check local laws).

Consequently, if the "paid in full" text appears in the endorsement area on the back of the check and the company cashes the check, the customer can make a reasonable case that the company accepted the money as final payment, and agrees that no further payment is required. This may actually be a reasonable decision, if the collector concludes that it will take an inordinate amount of effort to obtain any additional payment.

The best way to sidestep the issue is to not cash a check that contains such language, no matter where the text is located. Instead, contact the customer and request a replacement check that does not contain any special language on it. In addition, a customer who includes such text on a check is clearly not dealing fairly with the company, and so should be stricken from the list of acceptable customers with which the company wants to do business.

Summary

In this chapter, we have described the basic process flow for payments made by check, as well as several techniques for improving the process. Most of these processes are inherently inefficient or expensive, and can delay the application of cash to open accounts receivable. To ensure that the collections staff has access to the most recent customer payment information, it is therefore useful to focus on restructuring how customer payments are handled. Of particular importance is the use of a lockbox to receive check payments, since it eliminates a number of processing steps and controls.

Chapter 14
Collection Tactics

Introduction

When a customer is having cash flow problems, the easiest loan it can obtain is from its suppliers, by not paying them. This is not acceptable to the seller, who has only agreed to a small loan in the amount of the credit it is granting to the customer, and only for the number of days stated in the payment terms. There may be other cases where a customer's procedures or the lack of information are preventing the release of a payment. These scenarios are the primary reasons for delayed payments.

In this chapter, we describe a number of techniques for accelerating payments that are being delayed for either of these reasons, as well as discussions of how a collection call should be conducted and whether on-site collection visits may be warranted.

Overview of Collection Tactics

There is no tried-and-true collection methodology that works for all overdue invoices, all of the time. Instead, the collection staff must choose from an array of collection tactics, depending on such issues as the amount of the invoice, the intransigence of the customer, and common collection practice in the industry. Accordingly, we do not present a collection methodology in this chapter, but rather a series of possible collection options. These options are listed in order from the most innocuous to the most severe. The following table shows the tactics, along with a brief statement of when they should be used.

Collection Tactic	When to be Used
Courtesy calls	For larger invoices where the customer historically has payment issues
Grace period reduction	For customers who always pay late
Dunning letters	For all sizes of invoices, to be issued shortly after due dates have passed
Check payment by e-mail	For customers who repeatedly delay payment
NSF check resubmission	When a check has bounced, and there is a chance to obtain funds with a second attempt
Pay undisputed line items	For customers who are using disputed invoice line items to delay payment
Confirm payment date	For customers who have committed to pay as of a certain date

Collection Tactic	When to be Used
In-person check pickup	When it is possible to route a person to the customer to collect a payment
Take back merchandise	For sales of goods where customers cannot pay
Hold orders	When there are orders from a customer that have not yet shipped
ACH debits	For customers with little cash on hand
Split payments	For customers able to pay in small increments
Postdated checks	For customers able to pay as of a specific future date or dates
Interest and penalties	For customers who deliberately delay payment
Promissory note	For customers without sufficient cash to pay in the short term
Salesperson assistance	When a salesperson is assigned to the customer
COD roll	For customers with unpaid balances who now pay on COD terms
Barter	For customers who are completely unable to pay by other means
Arbitration	When customers may have legitimate claims relating to a sale
Attorney letters	For somewhat larger invoices, where dunning letters have not triggered payment
Final demand letter	When all other normal collection efforts have been attempted
Small claims court complaint	When on the verge of filing a lawsuit

The collection manager is responsible for training the collections staff in the use of the various collection tactics, as well as setting expectations for how collectors should spend their time. For example, the primary goal of the collections manager is obviously to collect cash as soon as possible. Since the amount of staff time and other resources available to the collections manager is limited, the manager will likely have to communicate to the staff the need to stratify accounts receivable, so that larger invoices receive a considerable amount of hands-on attention, while smaller amounts are targeted by more cost-effective methods, such as automated dunning letters. The manager then monitors actual collector activity to see if they are achieving the stated goal, and adjusts their activities as needed to maximize the amount of cash collected.

Collection Tactics

In this section, we list a number of collection tactics, sorted in order from the most innocuous to the most aggressive. The items early in this list are intended for those customers who will likely continue to be granted credit by the seller, while the more "scorched earth" items near the end of the list are intended for those customers with whom the seller has no intention of doing business again. The collections manager should be consulted before embarking on the more aggressive tactics, since they will certainly have a deadening impact on customer relations.

Courtesy Calls

Many customers do not pay their suppliers because of administrative issues, rather than a focused intent not to pay on time. For example, any of the following issues could be delaying payment:

- Invoice not received
- Invoice out for approval
- Error on invoice being investigated
- Cannot locate receiving documentation
- Cannot locate authorizing purchase order

Many of these issues can be resolved by the seller, since it has nearly the same packet of information pertaining to the sale transaction as the information being collected by the customer's accounts payable department.

A reasonable approach to collecting the larger invoices is to make a courtesy call some days before the invoices are due for payment, just to see if they are scheduled for timely payment. If not, the caller can offer to assist by providing any needed information, such as clarification of the invoiced amount, documentation of delivery, and a copy of the customer's authorizing purchase order.

These courtesy calls can be assigned to someone other than the normal collection staff, since the intent of the calls is to provide information, rather than demand payment. Given that the mindset of a courtesy call is completely different from a collection call, it makes sense to separate the two types of calls among different staff. By doing so, those assigned to courtesy calls can be trained in an entirely different method of customer contact that focuses on servicing the needs of the customers.

> **Tip:** If someone makes a courtesy call to a customer and then suspects that payment of an invoice will be deliberately delayed, contact the regular collections staff at once, so that they can begin collection activities sooner than would normally be the case.

The use of courtesy calls is only cost-effective for the larger accounts or those accounts that have a history of being flummoxed by payables paperwork. If a customer has a proven history of reliably paying on time, there may be no point in annoying them with courtesy calls.

Grace Period Reduction

It is customary for a collections department to not begin collection activities until a number of days have passed in addition to the payment terms stated on an invoice. By doing so, collectors do not waste time contacting customers whose payments are already in transit. This is a simple cost-benefit calculation for the collections manager, who can roughly estimate the amount of time that must pass before it is reasonable to assume that there are problems with all remaining invoices that have not yet been paid.

The trouble with the grace period is that some customers abuse it. They know that no collector will contact them for a certain number of days past normal terms, so they always delay their payments through the grace period. If so, the pattern of late payments will be recurring, and so can be easily identified. The collections staff should make note of these customers in the customer master file, so that they can begin calling these customers as soon as payment dates are exceeded. In short, the grace period is ignored for certain customers who do not deserve the privilege of having a grace period.

Dunning Letters

A dunning letter is a notification sent to a customer, stating that the customer is overdue in paying an account receivable to the sender. Dunning letters typically follow a progression from polite reminders to more strident demands for payment, if the customer continues to be non-responsive in paying. The first few letters that are sent should be polite, on the theory that the customer has simply overlooked payment, and the company wants to retain its goodwill for future business.

However, as more time passes, the company begins to change its assumption of doing further business with the customer, and so tends to downplay the amount of customer goodwill that it wants to retain in favor of being paid now. Irrespective of the tone of the letter, it always states the amount due, the date of the unpaid invoice, the number of the invoice, and any late payment fines or interest penalties.

> **Tip:** If there has been no response to the first few dunning letters, send a copy of the next letter to someone more senior in the organization, such as the CFO or president, and note that this has been done on the copy going to the accounts payable department.

At some point following the normal payment date, the effectiveness of issuing dunning letters will decline, so that a company discontinues their use and relies upon personal contacts, attorneys, and collection agencies instead.

A dunning letter can take a variety of physical forms. It was originally a letter that might be sent by regular mail, registered mail, or overnight delivery in order to convey the increasing urgency of the request, as well as to create a record of receipt (in the case of registered mail or overnight delivery). However, a dunning letter can also be sent as an e-mail or text message. These electronic delivery methods can go astray, and may not be as effective as the more traditional paper-based method.

> **Tip:** The final dunning letter sent should be by overnight delivery or certified mail, to reinforce the point that the seller is about to shift to a more aggressive form of collection.

Dunning letters are frequently generated by a computer, with no human input at all. The system is configured to use a particular text if payment has not been made within a certain number of days, and to then use a different text for letters generated after a longer time period has passed without payment.

The collections staff may periodically change the timing or content of these automatically-generated letters, if they feel that some variation will improve the rate of collection. This can be accomplished with *A-B testing*, where two versions of a dunning letter are issued, and the effectiveness of each one monitored; if one version results in more customer payments, that version becomes the new default letter format to be used.

There are rules governing the level of threat that can be included in a dunning letter, depending upon the government jurisdiction in which a customer resides, so avoid excessively strident letters.

A dunning letter is not the same as a month-end statement. A statement is sent to all customers having unpaid invoices at the end of the month. The statement includes all invoices that have not yet been paid, even if they are not yet due for payment. The statement is not considered to be harassment, but rather a simple statement of account as of a point in time. However, it is still considered a collection tool, since it may result in customer inquiries about invoices that they do not have in their records, and which they therefore would not have paid.

> **Tip:** A simple variation on the dunning letter is to mail customers a copy of overdue invoices, with a collection sticker on each invoice. The wording on the collection stickers can vary, depending on how long invoices have been overdue.

> **Tip:** If the party issuing dunning letters is a government entity, an interesting technique is to appeal to the sense of civic duty of customers, pointing out that the cash is needed to provide services to them.

Check Payment by Fax or E-mail

It can be extremely difficult to extract a check payment from a customer, especially if you want an immediate delivery that will cost the customer an overnight delivery charge. An alternative is to have the customer fax or e-mail a scanned image of a completed and signed check to the seller, and then follow these steps:

1. Obtain check printing software, which is available from many companies (search for "check by fax software" on an Internet search engine).
2. Enter the information from the check into the software.

3. Print the check using check security paper, which can be obtained from a local office supply store. Use standard printer ink, not the special magnetic ink character recognition (MICR) ink used by banks. The check printing software will include the following text in place of the signature line:

> SIGNATURE NOT REQUIRED
> Payee to hold you harmless for
> payment of this document
> Absence of endorsement is guaranteed
> by payee's bank

4. Deposit the check at the company's bank. This may require manual processing by a bank teller, since the bank's check scanners will not detect any MICR encoding on the check.
5. Retain a copy of the faxed or e-mailed check, as proof that the customer authorized payment.

An alternative is to obtain the required information for a check payment over the phone, but doing so provides no evidence that the customer agreed to make the payment. Also, it is easier to make a mistake when writing down information obtained over the phone. Consequently, this approach is not recommended.

Yet another option is to send the customer a form to fill out that includes all of the information normally found on a check, as well as an authorizing signature line. This should be accompanied by a voided check, so the seller can reference a check number.

The end result of this process is the complete elimination of the mail float from the collections process. This approach is time-consuming, but is at no cost to the customer, who may find it an appealing alternative compared to paying for an overnight delivery.

NSF Check Resubmission

When a customer's check payment is rejected by the bank, this is because there is not a sufficient amount of funds in the customer's bank account to pay the amount stated on the check. This "not sufficient funds" check is a major indicator that a customer is having cash flow difficulties. However, rather than simply fuming and badgering the customer for a replacement check, consider resubmitting the NSF check to the bank. It is possible that the cash flows of the customer will have increased the cash balance in the account since the date on which the check was originally rejected, so that the check will be accepted on the next submission.

> **Tip:** When a check is declared NSF, this can be treated as a criminal violation in some jurisdictions. If so, the collector may be able to use the threat of prosecution to obtain a replacement payment.

Pay Undisputed Line Items

When a customer has a reasonable issue with a small number of line items on an invoice, the most efficient practice for them is to not pay the entire invoice until those line items have been resolved, since a single payment will then settle the entire invoice. The reasoning is different for a customer that actively wants to delay payment; they simply pick a line item on an invoice and actively dispute it, thereby delaying payment of the entire invoice. The latter tactic is most evident when a customer only questions line items on larger-value invoices.

It might initially seem obvious to always have collectors demand that all undisputed line items be paid at once. This approach should certainly be used when a customer has a history of using disputes to delay payment. However, the demand should not be made in the first case, where a customer really does have an issue, and may resent having to make an additional payment – one for all other line items right now, and one at a later date for the disputed item. This is an inconvenience for the customer, so if the seller wants to maintain good relations, it may not want to demand immediate payment of undisputed line items.

Confirm Payment Date

A common part of a collection call is when the collector asks for a date by which payment can be expected, and the customer's accounts payable person states a certain date. It is customary for the collector to write down this date and contact the customer again if payment was not received by that date. The trouble is that the payables clerk accords much less importance to this date than the collector, may not write it down, and so may not pay by the designated date.

The collector needs to give the payables clerk a strong sense of just how important the payment date is, so the collector should document the conversation with the payables clerk and send it in a letter to the clerk. Depending on the level of urgency, this letter can be in the form of an e-mail, a regular letter, certified mail, or overnight delivery.

> **Tip:** Always keep a copy of all confirming letters sent, so there is evidence of the original conversation if the payables clerk later claims that either no letter was sent or that its contents are incorrect.

The confirmation letter approach is particularly valuable if a customer has agreed to a series of payments, since the receipt of an additional letter just prior to each scheduled payment date tells the customer that the seller is closely watching the timing of all promised payments.

In-Person Check Pickup

If a customer is located nearby, or is routinely visited by one of the company's salespeople, arrange to have an employee (possibly the salesperson) stop by to pick up a payment from the customer's accounts payable department. This approach has two benefits. First, it prevents a customer from claiming that a payment is in the mail. Second, it establishes a specific date and time on which a person will be arriving at the customer to collect payment, which forces the payables department to prepare a check by the designated time. A possible further benefit that applies to larger payments is that it may be cost-effective to then take a check directly to the company's bank to be deposited, thereby eliminating some mail float.

Take Back Merchandise

If a company is selling goods, the buyer usually finds a use for or resells the goods in short order, leaving no asset that the company can take back in the event of nonpayment. This is particularly likely when the terms of payment are relatively long, giving the buyer more time in which to disposition the goods. However, if this is not the case and the customer still retains the goods in unused condition, a reasonable option is to take back the goods if the customer is unable to pay.

Taking back merchandise is a better option when the goods have long-term value and can be readily resold at roughly the same as the original price. If the goods decline rapidly in value, as is the case with fashion goods and some consumer electronics, the decision to cancel a receivable in exchange for taking back merchandise may be a more difficult one.

Hold Orders

A similar concept to taking back merchandise from a customer is blocking any additional shipments to the customer. To do so, the collections staff must have access to the customer orders database, and the authority to halt shipment of a pending customer order. This can be a highly effective way to dislodge a payment, especially if the seller is in the enviable position of selling goods that no other suppliers offer for sale. The company's computer system can even be set to trigger a warning message to the collections staff when a forthcoming customer order will cause a customer's actual receivable amount outstanding to exceed the amount of its credit limit.

While the order holding concept may initially sound ideal, here are two cautionary items to consider:

- When the goods on order can be commonly found elsewhere, a customer may simply cancel the order as soon as it receives an order hold notification, and take its business elsewhere.
- Holding an order may not be possible if the order is already in the production process, since doing so would throw the production schedule into disarray. If this is the case, the goods will have to be produced, and then a hold is placed on the shipment. This can be a problem when goods are customized, since the company may have no other way to dispose of the goods.

Tip: If an order hold is imposed, be sure to contact the responsible salesperson at the same time. Otherwise, the salesperson will first hear about it from an irate customer.

ACH Debits

A customer may prove to be completely unreliable in making payments, possibly because it is working with an extremely small amount of on-hand cash. If so, an option is to have the customer agree to small but very frequent ACH debits from its bank account. Under this approach, the seller sets up a recurring ACH debit transaction that withdraws the same amount of cash directly from the customer's bank account. The frequency of the withdrawals could be once a week, or even every business day. By keeping the amount of each individual debit low, the customer is less likely to resist this payment method.

For example, there may be a $1,000 invoice outstanding, which the customer is completely incapable of paying. However, if the payment method is presented as a $50 daily ACH debit for 20 business days (one calendar month), the seller will still be paid relatively soon, and the reduction in cash is less noticeable to the customer.

The only issue with the ACH debit is that the seller incurs a small fee for each transaction, so a large number of debits will cumulatively represent a fairly large bank fee.

Split Payments

If a customer claims that it cannot pay an invoice right now, offer to split the invoice into several payments over the short term. Better yet, ask for part of these split payments immediately over the phone, using a credit card. By doing so, a pattern of payment is immediately established, which the collector can follow up on at regular intervals. This may result in a series of credit card payments over the phone, but at least results in payments.

The split payments approach varies from the following promissory note concept in that split payments are intended to cover a relatively short period of time, and do not have an associated guarantee or assets used as collateral. There may or may not be an interest charge associated with split payments.

Postdated Checks

It may be possible to obtain from a customer one or more postdated checks, which the collector promises not to cash until the date listed on each check. If so, the collector notes on a calendar when each check is to be cashed, and does so on the specified date. If a postdated check is from a commercial customer, no further notifications to the customer need to be made. If a check is from an individual, the collector must send a written notification to the customer within three to ten business days of the date when the check will be cashed.

Interest and Penalties

Add interest charges and/or late fees to a customer's account once unpaid invoices exceed a predetermined threshold number of days late, and notify the customer that this is happening. The key point is to educate the customer that there are consequences to delaying payments.

If this tactic is to be used, be sure to state the seller's policy for imposing interest and penalties on unpaid invoices at the time when credit is granted to a customer. Also, verify that these fees are in accordance with any state laws regarding the amount of interest that can be charged.

> **Tip:** Customers frequently ignore interest and penalty charges. To make it clear that the company intends to collect these amounts, impose a hold on any customer orders until all interest and penalties have been paid.

Promissory Note

There will be times when a customer does not have sufficient cash to pay for an overdue invoice, but is willing to work with the seller to pay off the amount over a longer time period. If so, an option may be to convert the invoice into a promissory note that contains a series of specific payment dates, an interest component, and a guarantee or collateral. The key element of this note is that the company is either given a guarantee of payment by a third party, or collateral that can be accessed if the customer defaults on payments. This approach improves the ability of the seller to obtain some form of payment, even if it may take some time to do so.

> **Tip:** The key element in a promissory note is a guarantee or collateral; to obtain it, consider such inducements as a low interest rate, a slight reduction in principal, or allowing a restricted amount of credit for continuing purchases from the seller.

It is much easier to win a lawsuit over nonpayment of a promissory note than over nonpayment of an account receivable, since the customer has signed the note, and therefore has agreed to its specific terms.

Be sure to assign the promissory note to a collector, so that payments are regularly monitored along with other accounts receivable. In addition, send out a statement to the customer at regular intervals, showing the original amount due, the amounts and dates of prior payments, and the next amount due, with a tear-away remittance advice they can use to remit the next payment. There is a certain amount of work required to formulate and issue these statements, but they are useful not only for reminding customers, but also for formalizing the system of payment.

> **Tip:** To make a customer more inclined to agree to a promissory note, keep its language as simple as possible, and keep the interest rate reasonable. Otherwise, the customer will be more likely to bring in an attorney to examine and negotiate the terms of the note.

If the seller proposes reasonable terms for a promissory note and the customer still persists in rejecting the offer, this is a clear signal that the customer has no intention of paying, in which case a more aggressive legal solution may be required.

Salesperson Assistance

The salesperson who originally made the sale that is now unpaid can be of use in obtaining payment. Salespeople have developed a completely different set of contacts at the customer, and so can work through different channels to obtain payment. Thus, with the collector working through the accounts payable staff and the salesperson working through the buyer, resistance to payment may crumble. Also, an effective salesperson can sometimes be seen as a relatively neutral party between the seller and the buyer, and so can adopt the role of mediator between the two parties.

Salesperson assistance can be remarkably effective, but we caution against overuse of this approach. The primary role of the salesperson is to sell, which requires all of their attention. If they are constantly being diverted by collection issues, revenues will suffer. Accordingly, the best approach is to make all reasonable attempts to collect without the sales staff, and then request their assistance only when other approaches have failed.

The only way that salespeople will be willing to assist the collections staff is by building relations with them. This can be accomplished by pairing up collectors with salespeople, running joint meetings, solving billing problems brought to the attention of the salespeople by customers, and so forth.

COD Roll

The typical approach that a seller uses to deny credit to its customers is to switch them to cash on delivery (COD) terms once they consistently fail to pay in a timely manner. However, taking this approach means that the seller no longer has any leverage over its COD customers in regard to their old outstanding invoices, which will continue to age and will probably be written off as bad debts.

A way to ensure that the oldest invoices are eventually paid is to require COD payment on new customer orders, but the seller applies the resulting payments to the oldest invoices outstanding, rather than the invoice that was actually paid. By doing so, the oldest invoices are gradually cleared from the seller's books. This approach means that only newer invoices remain in the seller's accounts receivable aging report, which can be used as collateral for short-term loans. An advantage to the buyer is that payments are being made against old invoices for which late payment penalties would otherwise be accrued, so the payments are also reducing the amount of finance charges that they may eventually have to pay.

There can be some confusion between the seller and its COD customers regarding how many invoices are still overdue, since the buyer will apply payments against new invoices, while the seller applies payments against old invoices. Also, the COD roll concept only works as long as COD customers continue to buy from the seller. If they stop, there will still be a significant number of unpaid invoices outstanding.

> **Tip:** An alternative to the COD roll is to add the entire overdue amount to a COD payment, which must be paid before an item will be delivered. This approach usually only works when a unique item is to be delivered that the customer cannot obtain anywhere else.

Barter

Some customers own assets or can provide services that may be of value to the seller. If so, a possible consideration is to accept these assets or services in exchange for an unpaid receivable. Doing so is not recommended unless all other collection alternatives have been attempted, for two reasons:

- If accepting assets, the seller now has the burden of converting the assets into cash.
- If accepting services, the seller must now badger the customer to provide the services (which may take as long as the collection efforts!)

Barter is a more common alternative for a small business where customers are located nearby, since proximity is required to obtain the assets or services.

Arbitration

There may be cases where the customer feels that it has a legitimate complaint against the seller. For example, the customer may believe that it ordered goods with certain specifications, and received goods that did not meet the specifications. If the seller is not willing to negotiate the issue, then consider shifting the claim to arbitration. Under arbitration, the parties select a presumably impartial third party to review the claims of both sides, and then issue a judgment that the parties agree to respect. The arbitration process tends to be fairly short, but it does require time to prepare a presentation to the arbitrator, and the arbitrator's fee must be paid. Also, the resulting decision may go against the seller.

Attorney Letters

It is entirely possible that a series of dunning letters will not convince a customer to make an overdue payment, possibly because a mere letter from the seller is not sufficient to provoke real action. A possible option at this point is to have an attorney send a letter, written on the attorney's letterhead and structured as a final reminder before legal action commences.

The fact that the matter has now been turned over to an attorney is a good way of telling a customer that the seller is now extremely serious about the unpaid receivable, and is not willing to tolerate any further delays. Consequently, the probability of payment is higher following an attorney letter than it is following a dunning letter. However, sending such a letter alters the relationship between the parties, since the seller is now making the assumption that it may not want to do business with the customer on an extended basis, and simply wants the account paid off now.

163

The least cost-effective way to issue an attorney letter is to refer each such matter individually to an attorney, who then crafts a unique letter for each customer. Doing so can be quite expensive, and so makes little sense for lower-value receivables. A better approach involves the following actions:

- *Pre-write letters.* Have an arrangement with the attorney, where the attorney and the collections staff mutually create a set of boilerplate letters to be issued. Thereafter, when an attorney letter must be issued, the attorney simply selects one of these pre-written letters, changes the names to the applicable parties, and issues it to the customer. This approach avoids a great deal of writing time.
- *Respond to company.* State in the letter that responses are to be made to the company, not the attorney. By doing so, the time of the collections staff will be used, rather than the attorney. This can greatly reduce legal bills.

An attorney is more likely to agree to this arrangement if the seller refers some proportion of its legal work to the attorney that relates to actual legal action against the more intransigent customers.

Final Demand Letter

At some point, the collections staff will have collectively exhausted every possibility in attempting to collect overdue funds. At this point, there are three remaining options:

- *Write off the receivable.* The most common option, especially if the amount is small or the customer does not appear to have sufficient assets to pursue a legal judgment.
- *Shift to a collection agency.* The second likeliest option, when the collection manager is not willing to pursue litigation, but is willing to shift the collection burden to a third party.
- *Litigation.* Reserved for large overdue amounts where the company has a strong case, and the customer has sufficient assets to pay any resulting judgment.

In the first case, the customer is not informed that the invoice has been written off. In the other two cases, however, it may make sense to issue a final demand letter, in which the collector states that the overdue amount must be paid by a specific date, or else the issue will be escalated to a collection agency or attorney. Doing so informs the customer that life is about to become more unpleasant, which can sometimes dislodge a payment.

Issue Small Claims Court Complaint

After all manner of threats have been exhausted, one last option that may result in payment from an intransigent customer is to fill out a small claims court complaint form and send a copy of it to the customer, with a note stating that the complaint form will be filed at a specific date and time, unless payment is received before then. Doing so makes it extremely clear that a judgment against the customer is likely to be made in the near future, and that the seller is willing to proceed down this path.

This option has the additional advantage of being inexpensive, since there are no attorney fees involved, nor any court costs. The only downside is that the seller clearly signals no further interest in an ongoing business relationship with the customer.

The Collection Reputation

Thus far, we have described a series of steps to be followed for collecting from customers. Unfortunately, customers are also aware of these steps, and can anticipate every move that a collector may take. If the customer is a hard-core nonpayer, this can mean that nothing a company attempts will work, and the customer can roughly estimate the time period over which collection contacts must be endured before the company ceases its efforts and goes away. Further, some companies develop a reputation for being unusually easy to deal with, offering long payment terms or writing off receivables after token recovery efforts. The end result is more difficulty for the collections staff, since everyone knows that the company is a pushover.

An alternative is to develop a reputation for pursuing debtors to the ends of the earth (figuratively speaking). This means engaging in ongoing pursuit, including litigation, to collect an overdue amount, and rarely negotiating down an outstanding balance. Doing so is not cost-effective from the perspective of an individual receivable, but can create a fearsome collection reputation that the company is not to be trifled with. Taking this path depends on the commitment of the entire company to create such a reputation, which includes a discussion of what this will do to ongoing relations with customers.

Credit Repayments

Occasionally, customers will overpay for an invoice or pay twice, possibly due to systemic problems in their accounts payable systems. Or, the seller may grant a credit on an invoice that has already been paid. In both cases, this results in a credit balance on a customer's account. While this may initially appear to be "free money" from the perspective of the seller, these credit balances must eventually be remitted to the state government as unclaimed property.

Rather than remitting the funds to the state government, consider having the collections staff periodically review the accounts receivable aging for unused credits and credit balances, and contact customers about these items. Doing so can create customer goodwill, might trigger additional sales, and will at least return the money to its rightful owner.

Contacting customers about credit balances can be conducted at fairly long intervals, since it takes time for a significant amount of these items to build up.

Consequently, conducting a review at quarterly or annual intervals should be sufficient.

The Collection Call

The core of many collection efforts is the telephone call by a collector. These calls can be highly effective if properly prepared for, scheduled, and conducted by properly trained professionals. The following sub-sections describe a variety of concepts that can result in more effective collection calls.

Preparation

The primary tool of the collector is the collection call. However, before making a call, consider a number of preparatory steps that will make the call more effective. Otherwise, the collector may find that the customer simply requests information that is not immediately at hand, which will require another call after the collector has found the information. Accordingly, consider collecting the following information in advance:

- *Billing packet*. The customer's authorizing purchase order, the resulting sales order (if any), any related shipping document(s), and the issued invoice.
- *Notes*. The complete set of notes from any prior conversations with the customer.
- *Proof of delivery*. A confirmation of receipt from the delivery company, preferably including the name of the person who signed for the delivered goods.
- *Statement of completion*. If the sale involved the provision of services, locate the customer approval document, including the name of the person who signed it.

In addition, have on hand a list of other contacts at the customer. If the primary contact is not answering his or her phone, consider immediately escalating to the next person on the list.

The amount of paperwork required to prepare for a collection call may appear considerable. To reduce the work load, consider using administrative staff to collect the paperwork, or use computerized collection software to automatically assemble much of this information from other databases around the company.

Scheduling

There is an optimum time at which customers are most likely to be available to answer a call. This is partially based on the time zone in which they are located, which can be included in any autodialing software that the collection staff may use. In addition, it may become apparent over time that a customer's accounts payable person is much more likely to answer the phone at a certain time of the day. If so, make note of this time, and try to call at or near the same time for all future calls.

> **Tip:** Schedule a large block of time at that point in the day when customers are most likely to be available, and conduct *all* collection calls, in continuous sequence, at that time. Doing so gets collectors in the flow of making collection calls, and so improves call efficiency.

Phone Skills

There are several skills a collector can use that will result in enhanced collection success. Here are a number of improvements to consider:

- *Scripting.* The content of a collection call should be approximately the same for every call made. It helps to practice with a prepared script in which you identify yourself and your company, and request payment. The actual conversation may vary somewhat from the script, but just be sure that the essentials are covered in every call.
- *Build a relationship.* Collection calls are not fun for the collector or the customer, and may even be considered repugnant by both parties. If a few moments of each call can be spent building even the smallest hint of a relationship, this will separate the seller from the pack of other collection calls that a payables clerk receives, and makes the clerk much more inclined to pay the company ahead of all the other sellers demanding payment.
- *Enunciate.* Do not speak so fast that the customer does not understand what is being said. Slow down and make sure that each word is clearly stated.
- *Wait for answer.* After asking when the customer will pay, wait for an answer – which may be a long time in coming. This can become a waiting game between the caller and the customer.
- *No waffling.* Have a confident and direct manner when stating the situation and asking for payment. Any waffling in the basic approach will result in delayed or no payments.
- *Empathy.* Keeping the preceding point in mind about not waffling, this must also be combined with a certain amount of empathy, to see the situation from the customer's perspective. If the collector does not at least attempt to empathize, the customer will perceive a rigid, unyielding caller and will be less inclined to pay.
- *Negotiate.* It may initially appear that the customer simply cannot pay, but if you work through a series of options, some form of payment may be forthcoming. This can include offering to split payments, delay payments, take back merchandise, and so forth.

> **Tip:** If it seems possible that a customer may be willing to negotiate, create a negotiation plan in advance of the call to establish your position. This could include the minimum acceptable offer, points that can be conceded, and any points that you are *not* willing to concede.

If a collector's phone skills have been properly honed, the result should be a much higher incidence of calls where the result is a documented commitment to pay a specific amount by a specific date.

Escalation

It is quite likely that someone higher in the customer's organization has decided to conserve cash by delaying payments to suppliers. If so, badgering the customer's accounts payable staff will not help. Instead, escalate subsequent calls higher in the organization until a position is reached that can impose payment instructions on the accounts payable staff. This may be the controller, CFO, president, or some other position. Engage in escalation as soon as it is evident that the person currently being contacted cannot authorize payment.

Documentation

Writing down the results of a discussion with a customer is critically important, since these notes are the basis for future contacts. The task is easier with an on-line note-taking function that stores notes by customer, and links to a calendar of activities for future calls.

Caller Personality

The personality of the person making collection calls can have a massive impact on the outcome of these calls. The person must have a calm demeanor that cannot be cracked, even in the face of the evasions, screaming, crying, and other non-standard behavior that may be evinced by a customer. There can be no display of temper, even in the face of outright lies, waffling, and any other technique a customer may attempt in order to delay or deny payment. Further, the collector must have a strong level of bulldog persistence in staying on topic, as well as in repetitively contacting the customer to ensure that the highest level of ongoing contact is maintained. And throughout every communication, the collector must behave in an absolutely professional manner. Conversely, anyone who is easily delayed by excuses, who has a need to please the other party, or who cannot reliably pursue a customer over time has no place in the collections function.

In-Person Visits

The assumption in most of this chapter has been that the collector does collections work at a distance, since doing so is more cost-effective than on-site visits. However, there are times when the overdue amount is so large, and the customer so intractable that an on-site visit is warranted. In this situation, there are three goals to be achieved through a visit:

- Establish relations with the accounts payable staff of the customer, which can be of immense use in future dealings

- Decide whether the customer is one with which the company should continue to do business
- Collect the overdue funds

Each of the preceding goals requires different tasks. Establishing relations calls for protracted (and preferably informal) discussions with the customer, while an on-site tour is useful for deciding whether the customer is a viable business. Collection of overdue funds calls for more detailed discussions about specific invoices. Given the different tasks involved, it may be necessary for several people to visit the customer, and for the visit to cover a full day. The following people could participate in the visit:

- *Collector.* The collector responsible for this account should attend, in order to establish relations with the accounts payable staff, as per the first goal.
- *Credit manager.* The credit manager should evaluate the business to see if it is worthy of the continuing grant of a credit limit, or whether the company should do business with this customer at all, as per the second goal.
- *Collection manager.* The senior collections person should attend, in order to authorize any payment deals reached as per the third goal. Alternatively, this authority can be given to the collector.
- *Salesman.* The salesperson responsible for the customer may also want to be present, to be fully briefed on any decisions reached.

Summary

When deciding upon the most appropriate set of collection tactics to use with a customer, the key issue is whether the seller wants to have an ongoing relationship with the customer. If so, then a number of the more aggressive collection tactics are probably not feasible, and should be avoided in order to keep from damaging the relationship. On the other hand, if the decision is made to terminate the relationship, the only remaining issue is how quickly the unpaid items can be collected; this decision may trigger a batch of considerably more aggressive collection techniques that would not normally be contemplated.

In general, the collector-to-customer relationship is somewhat similar to that of a parent to a child, where the collector has to be understanding, yet firm. This means working with the customer to resolve issues, while still following through to ensure that the customer does what it agrees to. Much as is the case with a child, if the collector does not follow through with any threatened actions, such as sending an invoice to a collection agency, the customer will be more difficult to deal with in the future. Consequently, consistent follow-through is perhaps the overriding principle of collection tactics.

Chapter 15
Payment Deductions

Introduction

The amount of deductions taken by customers from their payments to sellers can average several percent of the total sales of a seller. If the seller has relatively low profits, there could be an opportunity for a large profit increase by taking control of the deductions process. In addition, the resolution of deductions is extremely time-consuming, requiring a large amount of senior staff time, and issues may linger for months, thereby delaying the receipt of cash. Accordingly, we discuss a number of options for managing the payment deduction conundrum, with the dual objectives of increasing profits and accelerating cash flow.

Deduction Management

There are a number of ways to improve how payment deductions are managed. In this section, we address the use of subject matter experts, a team approach to handling deductions, the deduction process flow, how to reduce the deduction backlog, and similar issues.

Subject Matter Experts

Customers may take a number of different deductions from their payments, such as for damaged goods, marketing allowances, and volume discounts. Typically, these deductions are consolidated by customer and assigned to a single collections person. However, it can be difficult for one person to understand the details of a number of different kinds of deductions. An alternative is to route different types of deductions to subject matter experts (SMEs), each having deep experience with a specific type of deduction.

The use of a dedicated SME system requires that all customer deductions be coded by type when the related invoices arrive. A workflow management system is then used to route the deductions to the deduction SMEs. The workflow management system is also useful for monitoring the time required to resolve each deduction, which can be used to track efficiency levels and adjust work systems.

The main problem with the deduction SME system is that several deduction specialists may be involved with the resolution of a single customer invoice, so a customer may end up interfacing with a number of people. Also, deduction SMEs are highly specialized individuals with a great deal of knowledge about the areas for which they are responsible. It may be necessary to go to considerable lengths to retain these people, or at least document their knowledge.

In order to incrementally work your way into a deduction SME system, consider applying its concepts for a single type of deduction to one of the department's best deductions analysts, and work through any issues that arise with that person. Once any issues appear to have been resolved, gradually roll out the concept for other types of deductions. It is not usually necessary to have deduction SMEs for *all* types of deductions – only for the most difficult ones.

Team Approach

Deductions cannot always be resolved by handing them off to a single person, no matter how expert that person may be. Instead, it may be necessary to supplement the SMEs with teams whose members represent different parts of the company. For example, a SME could be the leader of a team that includes members of the production, materials handling, shipping, and billing departments, as needed. Doing so results in faster action from the various parts of the company that must be involved in resolving a deduction issue. The only problem with the team approach is that not everyone on a team will be as motivated to resolve a deduction as the SME; the result can be a certain amount of hounding of team members by the SME to have them fulfill their obligations.

> **Tip:** If a team approach is used, consider installing workflow management software. This software can be used to assign issues to different members of a team, route documents to them, and track the progress of their work. The team leader can use the software to spot where there are delays in the process, and take steps to route action items around anyone who is not dealing with an assigned task in a timely manner.

The Deductions Process Flow

Proper deduction management can also be achieved at a general level by ensuring that a standard process is used to handle every deduction. The steps in this process are:

1. *Compare to action threshold.* If the deduction is smaller than the company's minimum action threshold, write it off at once.
2. *Examine provided information.* Review the information provided by the customer to determine the nature of the deduction, and contact the customer if more information is needed.
3. *Forward to marketing.* If the deduction is a planned one, forward it to marketing for approval, or compare it to the marketing promotions database for approval.
4. *Examine remaining claims.* Apportion all remaining claims to the subject matter experts responsible for the various types of claims.
5. *Contact customers.* If deductions are rejected, contact customers with this information.
6. *Educate customers.* If it is apparent that certain customers are not providing sufficient information to support their payment deductions, contact these customers regarding the proper documentation that should be supplied.

7. *Terminate customers.* If ongoing deduction behavior indicates unwarranted usage on an ongoing basis, conduct a profitability analysis of the customer and stop accepting orders from it.

8. *Account for decisions.* Rebill deductions that are rejected, and generate credits for deductions that are accepted.

9. *Aggregate problems.* Periodically aggregate the reasons for deductions and discuss them with the management team, to address the underlying issues causing the deductions.

The primary management issue with this deduction process flow is to monitor every deduction to ensure that it does not stall somewhere in the system. Also, calculate the time required to deal with the average deduction, and apply more resources to the process if there is an increasing trend in this period of time. Further, the manager should look for outlier deductions that are requiring an exceptionally long time period to settle, and apply more resources to them to clear them from the system as soon as possible.

> **Tip:** Whenever a business acquires another entity, review the deduction management systems of the acquiree to see if it has a better process. If so, combine the best elements of both systems and implement them in all company locations.

Mitigating the Deductions Backlog

It is possible that the person responsible for deduction management inherits an overwhelming number of deductions that have not been resolved, and does not have sufficient staffing to deal with the problem. The solution is to reduce the incoming flow of deductions to the point where the available staffing is more than sufficient to deal with *new* deductions, and then conduct a "mopping up" operation to clear out the older deductions. To do so, it is necessary to examine the types of deductions being taken by customers, and eliminate the underlying reasons for the highest-volume deductions as soon as possible. The following issues may be considered when deciding which deduction problems to handle first:

- *Age of deductions.* Some deductions may be so old that there is little realistic chance of obtaining any payment owed to the company, and so can be written off.
- *Cash involved.* If a large amount of easily collectible cash is associated with a particular deduction type, that issue should be resolved first, if only to provide more cash to pay for additional staffing to address other deduction issues.
- *Customer-centric issues.* Some deductions may be taken in large volume by just a small number of customers, in which case serious consideration should be given to eliminating the customers, if they are not profitable.
- *Ease of improvement.* Some issues causing deductions, such as improper invoicing, may be relatively easy to correct, and so should be implemented

first. Others, such as a product design that must be corrected, may require so much time that they should be shifted lower in the list of priorities.

The following is a short list of some of the underlying problems that can cause deductions, and how they may be resolved:

- *Change orders*. Change orders have been billed for amounts that the customer did not approve. Can be resolved by instituting a detailed change management procedure that requires customer approval of all change orders prior to billing.
- *Defective merchandise*. The goods shipped to the customer do not meet the customer's quality expectations. Can be avoided with better internal quality assurance processes, a redesign of the product, or the use of higher-quality raw materials.
- *Disputed terms*. A customer may claim that a salesperson offered longer payment terms or other alterations to the seller's standard terms of sale. Can be avoided by having the customer sign a term sheet prior to the sale transaction.
- *Invoicing errors*. Errors in issued invoices cause the invoices to be rejected. Can be resolved by having a second clerk proofread all invoices prior to issuance, splitting complex invoices into several simplified invoices, creating an automated invoicing system, and so forth.
- *Prices charged*. Customers pay based on the price they stated in their purchase orders, not the prices listed on the seller's invoices. Can be resolved by having the order entry staff resolve these pricing issues before customer orders are fulfilled.
- *Shipping damage*. Products may be damaged during shipment to customers. Can be resolved by switching to a different third-party shipper, improving protective packaging or shipping containers, or by improving the robustness of the shipped goods with a product redesign.
- *Short shipments*. The unit quantity shipped is less than the amount billed on the invoice. Can be resolved by having the shipping department notify the billing clerk of changes in the quantities shipped from the amounts ordered.
- *Variance from contract*. The invoice does not reflect the amounts and terms stated in the contract that the customer agreed to with the seller. In particular, the amount billed is likely to be higher than the total funding permitted by the contract. Requires close comparison of both documents to avoid this problem.

Dealing with a staffing shortage by curtailing new deductions is the only possible solution to gaining control over a rampant deductions problem. However, it does not yield a quick solution. On the contrary, the deductions staff may spend many months using its limited resources to eliminate the residual backlog of deductions. The oldest deductions will be difficult to collect, which presents a reasonable argument in favor of obtaining more staff, at least until the deductions backlog can be eliminated.

Personal Visits

Some customers may have taken an enormous number of deductions, for a broad array of reasons. Though the normal flow of information for deductions involves on-line interaction and discussions over the phone, it may be necessary to visit these customers in person to resolve issues. Though these visits can require expensive travel and staff time, it may be better to do so if there is a reasonable prospect of recovering significant funds in the short term by accelerating the settlement process. It is likely that these visits will involve the same customers over a period of time, so it may be best to schedule an ongoing series of visits to settle deduction issues.

Personal visits are also useful for establishing relations with counterparts at the more important customer accounts. They can also be useful for obtaining first-hand experience of the issues that cause deductions, which can be used to convince company employees that their processes are responsible for deductions being taken by customers.

Salesperson Involvement

A number of deductions are caused by the customer, and do not relate to any internal seller problems. These deductions may relate to an excessively picky accounts payable department or receiving inspection team, or other factors that perhaps relate to a general corporate culture of avoiding every possible expenditure. In these cases, the accounting department can hardly be expected to conduct ongoing negotiations. Instead, have the responsible salesperson visit it to resolve outstanding issues. This person is in the best position to determine the reason for a deduction and resolve the issue on the spot, or at least coordinate resolution of the issue. Doing so requires the presence of a system for sending deduction-related information to the sales staff in the field.

If the salesperson finds that he or she is spending an inordinate amount of time settling deduction problems with an intransigent customer, a likely outcome is that the salesperson stops selling to that customer, and shifts to a different prospect that is less likely to take large numbers of deductions. This is a reasonable outcome from the perspective of the accounting department, which no longer has to deal with the customer.

> **Tip:** It is easier to obtain the cooperation of the sales staff in settling deduction issues when their commissions are not paid until the company is paid by its customers, since a delayed payment impacts the income of the sales staff.

Repairs Department Involvement

Some customer deductions are based on products that have been returned to the seller for repair work, after which they will be re-billed to the customer. In these instances, the repairs department may only be aware of its backlog of repair work, and not the amount of prospective revenue associated with each repair. The result may be a delay in rebilling, as repair jobs are assigned a normal level of priority and addressed in accordance with their assigned place in the work queue.

A better alternative is to make the repairs manager aware of the revenue associated with these repairs, and jointly determine a revised work queue that gives higher priority to high-revenue items, while still allowing for a reasonable completion date for lesser-priority repairs. This can be a difficult negotiation, since the repairs department may deal with requests from multiple sources, both internally and from outside the company, to assign higher priorities to certain orders.

Product Returns Management

When a seller deals with a distributor or retailer, a common occurrence is for these customers to routinely attempt to return all unsold merchandise to the seller, and then deduct the price of these returns from their payments to the seller. Unless such returns are allowed by the underlying sales agreements, the seller should not allow them. Otherwise, the seller could quite possibly experience such a massive and ongoing return of products that it is driven out of business.

A reasonable solution is to implement a return merchandise authorization (RMA) system, under which the seller rejects all attempts to return products unless they are marked with a pre-assigned and unique RMA number. The customer service department is in charge of reviewing all RMA requests and granting RMA numbers for all reasonable requests. The receiving department inspects the RMA numbers on deliveries from customers, and accepts them as long as the items received match the pre-assigned authorization number, and contain the correct number of authorized items. All other receipts or excess returns are rejected.

RMA numbers should be valid only for a specific period of time, after which they expire. Otherwise, customers might return goods so late that their market value has declined, and the seller can no longer obtain a reasonable price by reselling them to other customers.

Planned Deductions

Some payment deductions can be planned for in advance. These deductions are related to internal promotions by the marketing department, such as advertising allowances that can be deducted from their receivable payments. The following are all valid approaches to dealing with these planned deductions:

- *Price discounts.* Have the marketing department negotiate price discounts for their promotions in advance of customer billings, so the discounts can be incorporated into invoices. Doing so eliminates deductions. However, if there are many customers, the marketing staff may resist this request. It may not even be cost-effective if only a small percentage of customers are expected to take advantage of a promotion.

- *Promotions memo.* If marketing promotions are only offered on an occasional basis, it may be sufficient for the marketing staff to include the accounting department on its distribution of a memo that states the terms of each promotion and its duration.
- *Promotions database.* Have the marketing department share its database of which deals have been offered to which customers, including the termination date of each promotion. The collection staff can compare this database to deductions to see if the deductions are valid, or perhaps if they were taken for promotions that have expired.
- *Marketing approval.* If no database is available, meet with the marketing people responsible for promotions and have them approve each deduction. This is time-consuming, but does match the in-house expert on planned deductions with the deductions being taken.

The last alternative may be necessary under all circumstances where a planned deduction exceeds a certain threshold amount. Having the person in charge of a promotion specifically approve these deductions reduces the risk that an exceptionally large deduction will be incorrectly taken. A useful side benefit is that the marketing staff may gain insights into how customers are using their promotions, which may lead to altered promotional programs in the future.

Deduction Prevention

A large proportion of all payment deductions are taken because of errors within the seller's organization. For example, delivered goods may not match what was ordered in a purchase order, a sales tax exemption certificate was ignored, or goods were damaged in transit because of improper packaging. Proper prevention of the underlying issues can bring about a startling decline in deductions. However, doing so requires the use of a measurement system to track the types of problems causing deductions, assigning responsibility for corrective actions, and ensuring that the seller's processes are adjusted to reduce the risk of these issues recurring. The following steps are needed to prevent payment deductions:

1. *Collect information.* Collect information about each deduction taken, such as the name of the customer, the various reasons for the deduction, and the amount taken. Since the reason is not always stated in a customer payment, this information may require that you contact the customer, which is not cost-effective for smaller deductions. If so, initially ignore data gathering for the smaller deductions and focus on the larger amounts.
2. *Report information.* Assign a reason code to each deduction, based on the information collected in the first step. Then aggregate the deductions by reason code, and create a report that sorts deductions in declining order by reason code.
3. *Determine priorities.* Usually, the highest priority for reducing deductions is to tackle those that will immediately generate the largest decline in deduc-

tions if fixed. An alternative approach is to see if a set of smaller deductions can be jointly resolved with a small number of system fixes.

4. *Assign responsibility.* Assign responsibility to those employees responsible for the areas requiring improvement.

5. *Adjust systems.* Modify the underlying systems to ensure that the alterations are permanent. This may require changes in procedures, forms, compensation systems, and so forth.

6. *Monitor results.* On an ongoing basis, measure the percentage of perfect orders shipped, which are delivered on time, with all ordered items included, free of damage, and properly documented for the customer's payment system. Any exceptions should be included in the next iteration of deduction prevention activities.

Tip: Proper deduction prevention may require that a formal database of deduction issues be constructed. This database should be widely accessible throughout the company, and present information in a variety of formats, such as by customer, date, amount, and issue type, so that the information can be sifted to uncover patterns.

Customer Terminations

Certain customers may take an inordinate number of payment deductions, or may not provide justification for the deductions taken. If so, calculate the contribution margin generated by each of these customers, net of deductions taken, to see if it makes sense to continue doing business with them.

Contribution margin is calculated as revenues minus all direct costs associated with that customer, such as direct materials, direct labor, sales commissions, *and* deductions taken. The cost of accounting staff time may also be included in the calculation of contribution margin, but only if the company would actually reduce its labor costs if the deductions associated with a specific customer were not present.

An additional factor to include in contribution margin is the cost of any inventory that is held by the company for the specific use of a certain customer. For example, inventory may be held in a warehouse adjacent to the customer's facilities, or the company may own inventory located on-site at the customer. The cost of this inventory can be significant, since it can include the costs of obsolescence, damage, warehouse staff, insurance, leases, interest expense, and more.

If the contribution margin calculation reveals that a customer is not profitable, management should terminate the customer, thereby leaving more staff time to service those customers more deserving of the company's attention. It may be useful to first attempt a price increase or warning regarding the volume of deductions taken, or perhaps a switch to cash-in-advance terms. However, the best long-term decision is to terminate these more demanding customers that do not generate a profit.

EXAMPLE

Giro Cabinetry finds that one of its customers, Acme Construction, is routinely taking an inordinate number of deductions from its payments to the company, claiming that Giro's cabinets have been scratched or dented during delivery. Giro's president decides to conduct a contribution margin analysis of Acme, to see if the customer should be dropped.

In the past year, Giro recognized $100,000 of revenue from sales to Acme, and recognized $65,000 of direct labor and materials costs that would not have been incurred in the absence of this customer. There is also a 4% commission paid on all amounts invoiced to customers. Further, Acme took $18,000 of deductions during the year. There are no employees whose employment would be terminated if Acme were to be eliminated as a customer. Based on this information, the contribution margin earned from sales to Acme was:

Revenues	$100,000
Direct labor and materials	75,000
Commission	4,000
Deductions	18,000
Contribution margin	$3,000

The analysis reveals that Acme is still generating a small amount of positive contribution margin for Giro. The target contribution margin for all customers of Giro is 20%, as compared to the 3% being generated by sales to Acme. Rather than dropping the customer, it may make sense to work with Acme to see if the amount of deductions can be reduced, or prices increased somewhat, to bring the margin back up to the target level. If not, Giro's president could consider dropping Acme as a customer.

Small Discount Management

The earlier discussions of payment deductions might make it appear as though every possible deduction should be analyzed, no matter how low-value it may be. This is not the case, since it is not cost-effective to investigate miniscule deductions. In most cases, it is simpler to institute an automatic approval for all deductions below a certain threshold amount. By doing so, the accounting department avoids quite a large percentage of the total number of deductions, while incurring only a small deduction expense, in aggregate, for these items.

If the company does institute a fixed threshold for investigating deductions, it is possible that a customer will learn of this amount, and routinely take deductions just below the threshold. To spot this type of behavior, create a report that sorts all deductions below the threshold level by customer, and see if an inordinate number of deductions can be traced to certain customers. If so, the offending customers are singularly lacking in business ethics, and should be dropped.

Early Payment Discounts

A key question for the credit manager is whether to offer early payment terms to customers in order to accelerate the flow of inbound cash. This is a common ploy if the company is cash-strapped, or where there is no backup line of credit with the local bank to absorb any cash shortfalls.

The early payment terms offered to customers need to be sufficiently lucrative for them to want to pay their invoices early, but not have such egregious terms that the company is effectively paying an inordinately high interest rate for access to the funds that it is receiving early.

The term structure used for credit terms is to first state the number of days being given to customers from the invoice date in which to take advantage of the early payment credit terms. For example, if a customer is supposed to pay within 10 days without a discount, the terms are "net 10 days," whereas if the customer must pay within 10 days to qualify for a 2% discount, the terms are "2/10." Or, if the customer must pay within 10 days to obtain a 2% discount or can make a normal payment in 30 days, then the terms are stated as "2/10 net 30."

The table below shows some of the more common credit terms, explains what they mean, and also notes the effective interest rate being offered to customers with each one.

Sample Credit Terms

Credit Terms	Explanation	Effective Interest
Net 10	Pay in 10 days	None
Net 30	Pay in 30 days	None
Net EOM 10	Pay within 10 days of month-end	None
1/10 net 30	Take a 1% discount if pay in 10 days, otherwise pay in 30 days	18.2%
2/10 net 30	Take a 2% discount if pay in 10 days, otherwise pay in 30 days	36.7%
1/10 net 60	Take a 1% discount if pay in 10 days, otherwise pay in 60 days	7.3%
2/10 net 60	Take a 2% discount if pay in 10 days, otherwise pay in 60 days	14.7%

In case you are dealing with terms different from those shown in the preceding table, be aware of the formula for calculating the effective interest rate associated with early payment discount terms. The calculation steps are:

1. Calculate the difference between the payment date for those taking the early payment discount and the date when payment is normally due, and divide it into 360 days. For example, under "2/10 net 30" terms, you would divide 20 days into 360 to arrive at 18. Use this number to annualize the interest rate calculated in the next step.
2. Subtract the discount percentage from 100% and divide the result into the discount percentage. For example, under "2/10 net 30" terms, divide 2% by

98% to arrive at 0.0204. This is the interest rate being offered through the credit terms.

3. Multiply the result of both calculations together to obtain the annualized interest rate. To conclude the example, multiply 18 by 0.0204 to arrive at an effective annualized interest rate of 36.72%.

Thus, the full calculation for the cost of credit is:

$$(\text{Discount \%} \div (1 - \text{Discount \%})) \times (360 \div (\text{Allowed payment days} - \text{Discount days}))$$

Tip: It usually takes a hefty discount to persuade customers to pay early. Consequently, unless the company has a desperate need for cash, it is generally not worthwhile to offer a temptingly-high discount. However, consider offering a discount with a low effective interest rate on an ongoing basis; this might trigger a few early payments at little cost to the company.

There may be instances where a customer treats an early payment discount as a price reduction, and takes the discount without paying early. In this case, firmly point out that payment was not received in time to take the discount, and charge the customer back for the discount that should not have been taken. Also, if the billing software allows it, consider discontinuing the early payment discount offer on the invoices issued to that customer.

Tip: When denying a customer an early payment discount due to late payment, it may be easier to collect the discount by issuing a new invoice, on which is stated the reason for the billing. Otherwise, the customer's accounts payable staff can be hard to convince that the residual amount must still be paid.

Summary

Despite all of the deduction resolution options discussed in this chapter, it is entirely possible that most of the payment deductions taken by customers are, in fact, legitimate. More attention to deductions by the seller will simply clear these items from its accounting records more quickly, in the form of credits against accounts receivable. However, more attention to deductions also means that the seller is working to improve its processes, so that the reasons for deductions are eliminated. By doing so, customers will have fewer deduction claims to clog up their payment processes and delay payments. Thus, the end result of an effective deduction handling system may not be a large improvement in cash receipts from customers, but rather the acceleration of cash flows.

Chapter 16
Skip Tracing

Introduction

Some debtors are not interested in paying, and so will change addresses, cancel their phones, and generally try very hard not to be found. This is a particular problem when selling to individuals, or when a business has closed and you are pursuing a guarantee issued for that business by an individual. The solution is skip tracing, which is the art of locating a debtor who does not want to be found. In this chapter, we discuss a variety of methods for locating people who are trying very hard to cover their tracks.

Cost of Skip Tracing

A person who changes addresses without telling anyone could have done so inadvertently, simply by forgetting to leave forwarding information. If so, it is relatively easy to find them again and update their information. The real objective of skip tracing is to find those debtors who do not *want* to be found. Of this latter group, the most challenging of all are those individuals who have made a practice of hiding from creditors in the past, and who know how the game is played. This group makes use of fake addresses and routinely alters their publicly-available records to hide their locations; even if you can locate this latter group, doing so will take time, and it is entirely likely that the targets will have squirreled away assets where they cannot be found, making it even more difficult to generate a return from these efforts. Thus, the targets of skip traces lie along a broad continuum of effort that must be expended.

If there are a number of skip traces to be conducted on an ongoing basis, consider the extent of this time investment, and decide whether it is really cost-effective to engage in skip tracing activities. If the amount of debt being pursued is small, or if there is an indication that the targeted individual has few available assets, or if (as just noted) the target is a hard-core skip, then it may make more sense to write off the related debt after only a minimal search, and spend additional time on more promising opportunities. In particular, if a debt is owed by a corporation, there is little point in pursuing its officers unless they have personally guaranteed the liabilities of the corporation.

> **Tip:** It may be worth pursuing a corporation if the owners have commingled their personal assets with those of the corporation.

The ideal skip tracing scenario is one where the amount of assets that can potentially be recovered is substantial, and there are no liens on those assets by other creditors. If such is the case, an in-depth skip tracing effort may be justified.

Skip Tracing Information Sources

There are an enormous number of sources of information that a skip tracer can use. The following list includes the more traditional sources of information:

- *Acquaintances.* Any one of the friends, relatives, business associates, or neighbors may know the exact whereabouts of an individual. Though it can be difficult to extract information from this group, it can also lead you directly to the target.
- *Bank information.* Send an official-looking form to the person's bank, asking for the checking and savings account numbers of the individual.
- *Caller ID.* Send a mailing to all addresses at which the individual may live, stating that you need to contact the person, and leaving a phone number. If the person ever calls the number out of curiosity, your caller ID can capture the phone number, which can then be input into www.411.com as a reverse phone search to reveal the current address of the person.
- *Corporate filings.* The secretary of state may have corporate filings that reveal the locations of company officers.
- *Court records.* If a person has been involved in a lawsuit, the name of the representing attorney should be listed in the court documents. It may be worthwhile to contact the attorney for additional information. Conversely, contact the plaintiff's attorneys, who may be only too happy to assist in tracking down the target.
- *Criminal search.* A criminal search may reveal that the individual is incarcerated or on parole.
- *Department of motor vehicles (DMV).* For a small fee, the state departments of motor vehicles will issue basic information about a driver and any vehicles registered to that name. However, information requests may have to be made in person, and DMV responses may be quite late. Given the low cost-benefit of this approach, it could be limited to more protracted investigations where there is a need to determine the rightful owner of a vehicle to be repossessed.
- *Directory assistance.* Even if a phone line has been disconnected, contact directory assistance and ask for any phone numbers for other listings in the area that have the same last name.
- *Divorce filings.* Though not always available to the public, a divorce filing can be a treasure-trove of information, since it contains a net worth statement that describes all assets.
- *Driving records.* There may be accident reports or traffic fine information available that at least indicate where the traffic issues took place, which can be useful for establishing the general location of a debtor.

- *Fraternal organizations.* If the person is a long-standing member of a fraternal organization, he or she may not be willing to sever the relationship, and so will continue to provide updated contact information to the organization.
- *Insurance company.* If vehicle insurance information can be ascertained from a Department of Motor Vehicles search, contact the insurance company to obtain the last known address of the individual.
- *Judgments.* Court records can reveal whether any other parties have obtained judgments against the individual, which can be useful in deciding whether the person has any assets remaining after the judgments have been paid off.
- *Landlord.* Contact the individual's former landlord. When applying to rent an apartment, the landlord probably required the person to fill out a credit application, which could contain a variety of useful information.
- *Local merchants.* The person may have been granted credit by local merchants, in which case there may be credit applications on file with those merchants.
- *Postal service change of address.* Mail an empty envelope to the last known address of the target, with the following stamp on the outside: Do Not Forward – Address Correction Requested. The postal service will eventually return the envelope with a label on the outside that lists the forwarding address of the target. Of course, this approach only works if the individual supplied the postal service with a forwarding address.
- *Probate filings.* Probate court records can provide details about inheritances received, which can indicate the amount of assets available.
- *Professional licenses.* If the person is certified by a state organization, the certifying agency should have contact information, assuming that the person has an interest in continuing to use his or her certification. The following table contains a sampling of professions for which licenses may be required.

Architect	Dentist	Pharmacist
Barber	Doctor	Private investigator
Beautician	Engineer	Public accountant
Chiropractor	Financial planner	Real estate agent
Construction contractor	Insurance agent	Real estate appraiser
Cosmetologist	Nurse	Therapist

- *Real property.* A property record should contain contact information for the owner, though this information may be outdated.
- *Reverse address search.* Run a search on the last few known addresses of the individual to see if other names crop up, and then run searches on these other names.

- *Reverse telephone directories.* Enter a phone number in these directories and they return the address to which the phone number is linked. These directories do not provide information for unlisted numbers. An example of a reverse directory is www.411.com.
- *School records.* Local schools may have records of which parents have enrolled their children for classes.
- *Search engine.* Enter the name of the individual in a search engine, using quotes, and see if information about the person appears. General searches of this nature tend to contain relatively older information, so if the person has just skipped town, it is less likely that useful information will be obtained.
- *Securities and Exchange Commission* (SEC). The SEC monitors publicly-held companies, and posts all of their filings on its website at www.sec.gov. The site contains a vast amount of information, but only for companies that are current in their filings as publicly held companies.
- *Tax assessor.* The county tax assessor may have records of the owners of property that has been assessed. This information is not always available in on-line databases, and so may require more time-consuming on-site research to obtain.
- *Tax liens.* A tax lien on a property should state the owner of the property; this information may be stored at the county level, which is less likely to be available in an on-line database.
- *Telephone listing.* Both on-line and printed telephone directories may contain phone and address information, though this information is more likely to be available just for land lines.
- *Third party trace.* If the individual has lived with another person at some point in the recent past, conduct a trace on the other person. You may find that the target has moved back in with the third party.
- *Title company.* A title company may allow paid inquiries into the existence of property held by an individual, possibly for an entire state.
- *UCC filings.* These are claims filed against the assets of an individual or business. While these filings will not provide information about the whereabouts of a person, they will indicate if someone else has the rights to any remaining assets, which could impact the decision to proceed with a skip search.
- *Utility company.* A person changing to a new location is more likely to pay the local utility company in order to use it as a credit reference with the new utility where the person plans to reside. That being the case, contact the utility company to see if they kept a record of which other utilities have contacted them for a reference.
- *Vehicle registrations.* Registration information for vehicles and boats can be used to find the address of the owner, though the address information may be somewhat outdated, depending on how frequently the records are updated.

- *Voter registrations.* The local city government maintains a list of registered voters, stating names, addresses, and birth dates. It may be necessary to access this information in person.

Some of the information just described is available through commercial websites that aggregate the information for you. Using these sites is certainly efficient, but may not yield access to all possible information. In addition, it may be necessary to bookmark a lengthy list of websites maintained by local and state governments, and which should also be searched when a commercial site does not provide enough information. For example:

- *Local governments.* Records of judgments may be available through the local court system, as well as property tax rolls, real estate ownership records, and asset liens. This information is least likely to be available on-line.
- *State governments.* Incorporation information, vehicle registrations, criminal records, liens, and licenses can be found at the state level. Records may also be available for the state-level court systems. The availability of this information on-line is mixed, depending on state funding for on-line access and laws permitting access to the information.
- *Federal government.* The federal government provides less information about individuals than at the local and state levels, though federal, district, and bankruptcy court case information can be found through the Public Access to Court Electronic Records (PACER) system, at www.pacer.gov.

The preceding list makes it clear that there is an overwhelming amount of information available that can be used to track down a person and his or her assets. The trouble with much of this information is that it is outdated. Asset ownership records in particular are more likely to be old, since they only contain information that was correct when title to the asset was transferred; subsequent information changes may not be listed. Also, there is a risk of confusion because so many names are similar. For example, a plethora of information for John Smith may be for the wrong John Smith. Also, since much of this information was transcribed into databases, there is a risk that information was incorrectly entered as part of the data entry process. All of these factors make it difficult to wade through the sea of available information to find the necessary information.

Tip: Continually verify the information you have against all possible sources, to see if you are working with incorrect information.

Fee-based Search Tools

The Internet is full of search tools. A few are entirely free, in which case expect the amount of information provided to be more limited, and the sites to be full of ads. Better search information is available from a large number of on-line databases that charge fees on either a per-report or subscription basis. Here are some of the more popular sources of information:

accurint.com	experian.com	microbilt.com
cbcinnovis.com	inetcreditexchange.com	peoplefinders.com
dnb.com	intelius.com	transunion.com
equifax.com	lexisnexis.com	whitepages.com

Profile Reports

The best starting point for skip tracing is the profile report, which can be purchased from an investigative search firm. These reports are an assemblage of information garnered from a variety of databases, and include such information as a person's date of birth, social security number, known addresses, liens, judgments, bankruptcies, the names and locations of known relatives, bank accounts, and the locations of identified property holdings. These search firms pull in information from across the country, so their reports are particularly useful if the targeted individual has moved across state lines. Though not necessarily complete, a profile report contains sufficient information to form the basis for a more in-depth search.

Profile reports can be moderately expensive, and so may not be cost-effective if the amount being recovered is relatively small. However, in most cases the amount of information provided outweighs the cost of the report. Better yet, obtain a subscription to this service, which results in a lower price on a per-report basis.

Social Media

It is astonishing how people who do not want to be found by collectors are willing to divulge quantities of information about themselves on social media sites. It can be relatively easy to scan through Facebook, LinkedIn, and Twitter to find the latest updates about a supposedly missing person, who is actually quite active and appears willing to divulge all sorts of job-related and personal contact information.

The success of social media searches is so great for a skip tracer that it should be considered one of the top methods available for tracking down a missing person. However, it does not work for all demographics, for some people are completely inactive on the social media sites. In general, it is a worthwhile search for younger people, but may yield less success for older targets.

Pretexting

Pretexting is the practice of making inquiries about a person under false pretenses. Thus, you could pose as someone else and use this pretext to make inquiries regarding the location of the target. Examples of pretexting are:

- Posing as an employment agency to discuss background information for a possible employment offer
- Posing as a representative of a public opinion poll or research project
- Posing as a contest organizer, where certain information must be provided to collect a prize
- Posing as an employee of an insurance company, who is investigating a car accident
- Posing as the debtor and contacting a credit card company to verify the address they have on file, because the last statement did not arrive

This approach can be highly effective for extracting information from friends and co-workers, but is also considered a gray area from an ethical perspective. Pretexting is banned in some organizations, since it is misleading and can reflect poorly on the organization if publicized.

Location by Social Security Number

Certain ranges of social security numbers are assigned to each state. This is useful for identifying the state in which a person was born, which can be used for subsequent searches. The first three digits of the social security number are assigned by state, and are as follows:

Social Security Number Assignments by State

First Three Digits	Associated State	First Three Digits	Associated State
001-003	New Hampshire	440-448	Oklahoma
004-007	Maine	449-467 | 627-647	Texas
008-009	Vermont	468-477	Minnesota
010-034	Massachusetts	478-485	Iowa
035-039	Rhode Island	486-500	Missouri
040-049	Connecticut	501-502	North Dakota
050-134	New York	503-504	South Dakota
135-158	New Jersey	505-508	Nebraska
159-211	Pennsylvania	508-515	Kansas
212-220	Maryland	516-517	Montana
221-222	Delaware	518-519	Idaho
223-231 | 691-699	Virginia	520	Wyoming
232	West Virginia, N. Carolina	521-524 | 650-653	Colorado
233-236	West Virginia	525 | 585 | 648-649	New Mexico
237-246 | 681-690	North Carolina	526-527 |600-601 | 764-765	Arizona
247-251 | 654-658	South Carolina	528-529	Utah
252-260 | 667-675	Georgia	530 | 680	Nevada
261-267 | 589-595 |765-772	Florida	531-539	Washington
268-302	Ohio	540-544	Oregon
303-317	Indiana	545-573 | 602-626	California
318-361	Illinois	574	Alaska
362-386	Michigan	575-576 | 750-751	Hawaii
387-399	Wisconsin	577-579	District of Columbia
400-407	Kentucky	580	Virgin Islands
408-415 | 756-763	Tennessee	586	Guam, American Samoa
416-424	Alabama	596-599	Puerto Rico
425-428 | 587-588 | 752-755	Mississippi		
429-432 | 676-679	Arkansas	700-728	Railroad*
433-439 | 659-665	Louisiana	729-733	Enumeration of entry**

*   Prior to July 1, 1963, a separate set of social security numbers were reserved for use by members of the Railroad Retirement Board. The practice has since been stopped.

** Enumeration of entry refers to the assignment of social security numbers to noncitizens admitted for permanent residence.

Beginning in June 25, 2011, all new social security numbers are being assigned on a random basis. This means that the utility of the preceding assignment system will gradually decline over time, as the holders of these new social security numbers enter the work force. Also, a victim of identity theft or someone being harassed can request a new randomized social security number at once; this accelerates the decline in usefulness of the state-level assignments.

Outsourced Skip Tracing

If you do not want to invest any staff time conducting in-house skip tracing, then consider hiring a skip tracing specialist. These people have considerable experience in rooting through the various public databases, and can probably locate information about a debtor faster than an employee who only engages in this sort of work at infrequent intervals. Also, it is less expensive to employ an outside skip tracer if the company only has an occasional need for one, since doing so avoids the cost of a full-time paid employee.

The type of skip tracing services received will depend upon the pricing structure of the arrangement. If the specialist charges a fixed fee per search, this likely means that he or she will quickly run through a set number of databases and issue a report on the findings, without scanning any additional information sources. This may be sufficient for low-value debts. However, if the company can potentially recover a large amount, it should instead obtain the services of a specialist who charges by the hour. This person will dig for as long as you are willing to pay, and can come up with potentially much more information about a missing person. In short, higher-quality searches are usually associated with more expensive fee structures.

Another pricing issue is expediting fees. A specialist may charge a substantially higher price to provide information within the next few hours, since it interrupts their work flow to do so. If a wait of a few days is acceptable, then pricing may be substantially lower. However, avoid specialists who consider a response within several days to still be a rush order; these people are essentially structuring their pricing models to ensure that most customers pay a surcharge.

> **Tip:** Consider periodically hiring a professional skip tracer to review the company's records of unpaid accounts and determine which debtors are bankrupt, in prison, or have died, so that these records can be written off. Cleaning up the records in this manner avoids the waste of any additional collection effort on the indicated records.

Profile of a Skip Tracer

Many organizations do not have anyone in-house with the requisite skill set to be an effective skip tracer. Instead, they draw someone from the ranks of the collection staff and ask them to take over skip tracing. However, a collector has a significantly different skillset from a skip tracer. A collector has excellent phone skills and the ability to persuade someone to pay the company. The working hours tend to be tightly defined, since they must conform to the hours worked by customers. Given the amount of customer interaction, the collector is more likely to be an extrovert.

A skip tracer is more interested in research, and may delight in spending all day perusing abstruse databases for useful information. This person may work during all hours of the day or night, and so tends to be more self-directed than a collector. Given the research nature of the job, a skip tracer is more likely to be an introvert, but requires enough inquisitive skills to obtain information from the associates of people in hiding. Obtaining information in this manner requires that a skip tracer be good at posing the correct questions, listening carefully to answers, and interpreting this information "on the fly" to obtain additional information with just the right questions. In short, a skip tracer is essentially a detective.

In essence, a skip tracer has the skills to be an excellent collector, but a collector does not necessarily have the skills or desire to be a skip tracer. This means that quality skip tracers are a small subset of the population of collectors, and so are hard to find and retain. Given their rarity, they must also be paid more than collectors for their services.

Tip: Be aware that, if you have an employee who engages in skip tracing, it may be necessary to obtain a private investigator license, a collection agency license, or both, depending on the applicable state laws.

Skip Tracing Documentation

When engaged in a detailed skip tracing search, you may follow several dozen avenues of investigation. If so, be sure to fully document which steps were followed as you move through the process, as well as the results obtained. By doing so, you can monitor the documentation and stop the search when sufficient information has been accumulated. A high level of documentation is also useful for ensuring that a search step is not repeated, thereby avoiding whatever fees (and staff time) may be associated with that step (such as ordering the same credit report twice).

One way to document a skip trace is to begin with a standard template of the complete set of information that you ideally want to accumulate, a second page for unusual information items, and a check-off list on a third page that itemizes a standard set of search steps. Then incrementally fill in the form as you progress through the various searches, and add unusual items to the notes page.

Summary

There is an enormous amount of information available that can be used to track down a debtor and any related assets that can be recovered. However, doing so can require a fair amount of time, so you must balance the skip tracing effort with the amount of funds that can potentially be recovered. In many cases, even though the tools are available, it is simply not cost-effective to pursue certain debtors. If so, write off the related receivables or transfer them to a collection agency, and move on to the pursuit of other debts that are more likely to be realized. To make this decision consistently, calculate a threshold debt level below which outstanding debts are considered to *not* be cost effective for a skip trace, and only trace debtors above this level.

Chapter 17
The Collection Agency

Introduction

When a company's in-house collections program has difficulty collecting from an account, it can be worthwhile to shift the collection effort to a collection agency. This is an independent group of collection specialists who may succeed where the company has failed. Though their fees are high, paying the fee in exchange for collecting an invoice is much better than writing off the invoice. Thousands of collection managers have come to this conclusion, which is why there are so many collection agencies from which to choose. In this chapter, we address the nature of the collection agency, when to use it, how to manage the relationship, and the concept of the in-house collection agency.

The Collection Agency

A collection agency is a third party whose mission is to collect overdue receivables on behalf of a client. Their fee structure is usually performance-based, so they are only paid if they collect funds from a customer. The amount they charge may initially appear stratospheric, at 20% to 40% of the amount collected. Further, a collection agency is still entitled to its fee once an invoice has been referred to it, even if the customer pays the company directly, and not the agency. However, since the invoices usually referred to a collection agency are ones that a company has already given up on, any residual cash flow generated by the agency is essentially free money for the company.

The mechanics of a collection agency arrangement are that customers are supposed to send their payments to the agency, after which the agency subtracts its commission and forwards the remaining cash to the company. Doing so ensures that the agency will be paid its commission.

Having a collection agency can itself be used as a threat, somewhat like keeping an attack dog on a leash. In some cases, the mere threat of referring an invoice to a collection agency can be sufficient to cause a recalcitrant customer to issue a payment. This approach can even be used to save a relationship, where the in-house staff acts as the good cop and the collection agency as the bad cop, thereby shifting any customer anger to the agency and away from the company. Doing so may allow the customer and seller to continue doing business in the future on a reasonably cordial basis.

When to Use a Collection Agency

A collection agency is generally used as a collector of last resort, because of its high fee structure. However, this does not have to be the case. There may be a range of instances where it makes sense to shift a certain amount of collections work to a third party. Consider the following situations:

- *Seasonal collections.* A company may be highly seasonal (such as sales only during the summer months) and so experiences a large jump in receivables for just a few months of the year, after which there is essentially no collections work. Depending on the fees charged, a collection agency could take over a large part of this seasonal increase in receivables.
- *Small receivables.* Receivables may be comprised of a small number of very large receivables and a large number of very small receivables. If so, the collections manager may want to focus the collections staff on the large receivables, and shifts all of the small items to a collection agency.
- *Industry-specific expertise.* A company's collections staff may be quite good at collecting within a certain industry, but not from customers in another industry (such as the medical, auto, or insurance industries). If so, an option is to hire a collection agency that has specific collection expertise in the industry where the in-house staff has the least skill.
- *Specific customers.* A collection agency may have considerable experience in dealing with specific customers on behalf of their other clients. If so, the agency has established relationships in place, and so may be more effective than the company in collecting from these customers.
- *Consumer or commercial.* A collection agency may be specialized in collecting just on commercial accounts, or just on consumer accounts.
- *Types of receivables.* A collection agency may specialize in the collection of certain types of receivables, such as unauthorized deductions taken for un-earned cash discounts or allegedly damaged goods. A company may not be equipped to deal with these deductions, and so refers all of them to the agency.
- *NSF collections.* A collection agency can specialize in resubmitting checks rejected by the bank due to not sufficient funds (NSF), using the Automated Clearing House (ACH) system. These resubmissions can be timed to meet the periods when customers are expected to have more cash in their bank accounts.
- *Full service.* A collection agency is most useful when it is staffed with both collectors and a legal department that pursue judgments through the court system. Enrolling with such an agency allows a company to deal with fewer outside entities as it pursues customers for payment.
- *In-house incompetence.* In some organizations, the collections department is poorly managed, underfunded, or (more likely) only accorded part-time priority by a general purpose accounting staff. If so, customers are not given

sufficient collection attention, resulting in far more items being uncollected than should be the case.

In some of these situations, the fee structure will need to be reduced to make the situation economical for the company referring business to the agency. Also, the agency may need direct access to the company's accounts receivable computer system, so that it can immediately begin monitoring receivables as soon as they are generated. These arrangements will be needed if a large part of a company's collection activities are to be shifted to a collection agency.

A few collection agencies have built up alternative areas of expertise that do not relate to collection calls. These areas include:

- *Credit reviews.* Some specialize in conducting credit checks on behalf of their customers, for which they have established databases of payment information within certain industries. These agencies have detailed information about prospective customers, and so can provide quality information to their clients.
- *Dunning letters.* Both credit reporting agencies and collection agencies are willing to issue dunning letters to the customers of their clients. Since these letters are issued on agency letterhead, customers may assume that their accounts have already been referred for collection, which is more likely to trigger a payment.
- *Skip tracing.* This is the process of locating debtors who are no longer located at their original addresses. The concept is discussed in the Skip Tracing chapter. Many collection agencies provide this service.

When to Refer an Account to a Collection Agency

The decision to refer an account to a collection agency can be an excessively judgmental one, where the collections manager reviews collection progress and decides that no further progress is being made by the in-house collections staff. A better alternative is to formally review a list of referral triggers at regular intervals (such as weekly), to ensure that referrals are made as speedily as possible. Here are a number of triggering events to consider:

- *Commitments broken.* The collections staff no longer trusts the customer, because it has broken a payment promise at least once. Alternatively, a customer promises to pay a certain amount, and then pays a lesser amount without justification.
- *Communications halted.* The customer no longer returns calls, or decision makers are unwilling to talk.
- *Credit report downgrade.* The most recent credit report for the customer indicates a downgrade in its credit rating, and especially when the report reveals a major decline in the ability of the customer to pay on a timely basis.

- *Date threshold.* An invoice is now a certain number of days past due. Use this trigger with caution, since there may be genuine progress on an account that is taking time to resolve.
- *Disputes.* The customer is disputing a receivable and does not appear to have justification for doing so. This is a particularly strong trigger when a customer has made such claims repeatedly.
- *Economic downturn.* If the business environment is declining rapidly, this may have a powerful negative impact on the ability of customers to pay.
- *Lending requirements.* The company's lender does not want to see a large proportion of old accounts receivable as collateral for a loan.
- *No written commitment.* The customer is unwilling to commit to a payment plan in writing, or to sign a written plan.
- *NSF check.* When a customer has issued a not sufficient funds check without a reasonable excuse. Multiple NSF checks should be considered a strong trigger for referral to a collection agency.

If a number of these triggering events are present, it may even make sense to bypass referring an account to a collection agency, and instead send the issue straight to an attorney to initiate litigation activities. Doing so may allow the company to attach some assets of the customer before less proactive sellers have a chance to do so.

> **Tip:** Before referring an account to a collection agency, consider making a final notification to the purchasing department of the customer, and possibly its president as well, to let them know what is about to take place. Sometimes, these parties can resolve the issue.

Once an account has been referred to an agency, the company should engage in no further collection discussions with the customer. Otherwise, the customer may attempt to obfuscate who is handling collection activities in an effort to further delay payment.

Management of a Collection Agency

The person who manages relations with a collection agency is the collections manager. In this section, we address a variety of issues that this person must be aware of when dealing with collection agencies.

Selection Criteria

It is relatively common for a collection agency to repeatedly cold call a company's controller or president to pitch its services. The result may be a mandate from one of these individuals to the collections manager to give them a try. Cold calling skill is not an indicator of an agency's collection skill. Instead, consider the following factors when selecting a collection agency:

- *Time in business.* There are many collection agencies, but far fewer with the staying power to have remained in business for at least five years. Pick from this latter group, if only because they are least likely to shut down while holding the company's money.
- *Staff experience.* Discuss the collection experience of the agency's collectors.
- *Financial condition.* Ask for the financial statements of an agency and see if its financial results and cash flow indicate a reasonable amount of stability.
- *Specialization.* If the company sells in a specialized industry, give preference to any collection agencies that also work in that industry.
- *Licensing and bonding.* Verify that the agency is properly licensed for its line of work, and that it is bonded.
- *Collection techniques.* Interview the agency regarding the methods it uses to collect from customers, and decide whether these methods are acceptable to the company.
- *Payment.* Find out how long the agency holds funds before remitting them to its clients. There may be a delay of a few days, or (when collected amounts are small) cash could only be remitted once a month.
- *Invoices accepted.* Some collection agencies have a minimum threshold amount, below which they will not accept invoices. For example, a $250 invoice may be the smallest invoice amount they will accept.
- *Progress reports.* Does an agency report on its collection progress with a formal reporting system?
- *Attorney referral.* At what point will an agency refer an invoice back to the company, with a recommendation that it be sent to an attorney for legal action?

A collection agency may not score highly on all of the preceding points, and yet still be an acceptable candidate; the ranking depends upon the priorities assigned by the company to each of the selection criteria.

Pricing

The pricing structures charged by collection agencies are highly negotiable. Here are some of the factors that can influence pricing, all of which are under the control of the collections manager:

- *Volume.* There is definitely a tradeoff between spreading collections work among several collection agencies and concentrating most of it with a single agency. A high volume of collections work will lead to a reduced price, but does not allow the manager to compare the performance of different agencies.
- *Lateness.* It is more difficult to collect older invoices than newer ones, so an agreement to refer invoices sooner can impact pricing.

- *Invoice size.* A collection agency will certainly be interested in larger invoices, and is more likely to offer lower pricing for these items. Alternatively, arrange for a single price for all invoices referred, assuming a standard mix of invoice amounts.

Pricing could also be set up in tranches. For example, prices are higher if invoices are below a threshold amount, or invoices are older than a threshold date, or the total volume of invoices referred is below a threshold amount.

A major point with pricing is not to force down prices too much if a collection agency has proven to be effective. The agency must have an incentive to work aggressively on invoice collections, so give them a sufficient incentive to do so. Keep in mind that the best collectors charge the highest prices because they perform. Someone offering minimal prices may do little more than issue a few dunning letters, which will not yield an effective rate of return for the company.

Under no circumstances should the collections manager agree to any fee arrangement in which the company must pay in advance for the services of the collection agency, or be tied into a long-term arrangement. Instead, all arrangements should be based on pay for performance, with the company able to take its business elsewhere with little or no notice.

Contract Terms

Sign a contract with each collection agency that clearly defines those issues most important to the company. Of particular concern are the following:

- *Cash remittances.* State how long the agency is allowed to retain collected funds before remitting them, and how the funds are to be remitted.
- *Fees.* Clarify the entire fee structure that will be applicable to the company, such as the percentage fee for each collection, and any additional charges.
- *Termination.* The company should be able to terminate the services of the agency with minimal notice, though the agency may justifiably want to continue collecting on any invoices already referred to it.

The key clauses to avoid in a contract are a requirement to exclusively work with a single agency, and a minimum period over which the company must work with an agency.

Speed of Referral

One of the most important issues in dealing with collection agencies is to give them a fair chance of collection by referring accounts to them as soon as possible. It is much easier to achieve a collection when only a short period of time has passed since an invoice has been issued. This means that the collections manager should have a procedure in place for continually examining invoices to see if any additional in-house collection work can be done; once all reasonable collection steps have been taken, accounts should be *immediately* shifted to a collection agency.

Ideally, the collections department could be encouraged to identify those customers who are clearly going to be hard collection cases, and shift them to a collection agency right away. The result could be referrals of invoices to an agency that are only a few weeks past due.

A fast referral is quite different from the more common approach, where a collection agency calls to ask for business, and the collections manager scans through her aging report to see if any items in the 90+ days time bucket should be handed over. By the time this many days have passed, a customer may not even be in business any more, or have become so entrenched in its position that it is completely unwilling to pay.

Paperwork Support

Even the best collection agency cannot be expected to collect an account without a significant amount of support. This means it is not sufficient to just send an invoice copy to an agency and expect money to be collected. Instead, be prepared to provide a complete packet of information, including:

- *Authorization documents.* The customer's purchase order and any subsequent revisions to it. This should include fully-documented change orders, if any were used.
- *Billing documents.* The invoice issued to the customer, as well as any subsequent credit or debit memos that adjust the balance.
- *Evidence of receipt.* Any third party shipper documents showing that goods were received.
- *Contact information.* The name, address, phone numbers, and e-mail addresses of the debtor. If this debt is for a consumer, also note the same information for the spouse and any relatives that the company's research has uncovered.
- *Prior discussions.* Notes from all prior discussions with the customer concerning the debt, such as payment disputes and promises to pay.

This information should be provided up-front, so that the collection agency knows just as much about the receivable as the company. Doing so can greatly accelerate the speed with which funds are collected.

Effectiveness Issues

Some collection agencies are more effective than others, depending on their levels of expertise in collecting certain types of receivables and the quality of their collectors. Effectiveness can be measured by dividing the amount of cash remitted back from the agency by the dollar volume of receivables referred to them. By tracking this collection efficiency on a trend line, it is possible to determine whether a relationship should be continued with an agency, or shifted to a new agency. Another option is to retain the services of several collection agencies, and compare the effectiveness of their collections to see which ones should be assigned more receivables (though doing so requires that you track which agency has been assigned certain invoices).

Tip: When using several collection agencies, do not apportion overdue invoices from one customer to several collection agencies. If you do, a customer may be confused by calls from multiple agencies.

The collection efficiency measurement can be misleading, so use it to evaluate agencies only while also keeping in mind the following issues:

- The company must be consistent in *when* it refers receivables to a collection agency. If the company holds onto receivables longer, then the agency is bound to experience a lower collection success rate.
- The company should refer the same *mix* of receivables to a collection agency. If the proportion of receivables changes to include more small-dollar receivables, the agency must expend more collection effort to bring in cash, so the success rate will decline.

Both of these issues are the fault of the company, not the collection agency. Consequently, review the referred invoices first, before automatically assuming that an agency has become less productive.

From a management perspective, the important issue is the total amount of cash retrieved by a collection agency, not the fees that it charges. Typically, if an agency charges a lower percentage fee on receivables collected, it will only be willing to accept larger invoices that are potentially easier to collect. A higher fee structure may correspond to a greater willingness to take on a larger array of invoices. Thus, the fee structure is less important than the results achieved. It is not uncommon for a results-oriented company to retain the services of the most expensive collection agencies, since these agencies are more likely to employ the best collectors.

Fraudulent Customers

When the collections staff realizes that the company has been duped by a customer acting in a fraudulent manner, there is no point in sending the related invoices to a collection agency. The agency will have little chance of success, and these invoices will only reduce the effectiveness measurement for the agency. Instead, consider shifting these accounts directly to the company's fraud investigation or legal staff for further action.

Liability Issues

Since a collection agency is acting as the agent for any business that retains its services, the business could be held liable for the actions of the agency. There are two ways to mitigate this risk:

- *References.* The person selecting collection agencies can be especially careful about talking to their references, to evaluate their aggressiveness in pursuing payments within the limits of the law.
- *Collection practices.* Have any selected collection agency describe its collection practices, and settle upon an agreement that outlines which of the practices are allowed or not allowed when attempting to collect on invoices referred by the company.

Feedback Issues

The collections manager should regularly query all collection agencies being used regarding any information gleaned from customers about *why* they are paying late. In some cases, this may be caused by internal problems at the company that can be corrected.

Bonding

Collection agencies require the targets of their collection activities to send payments directly to them, after which they remit funds to their clients. This means that a collection agency could be holding a company's cash for some period of time, and could delay remittance if it were to experience cash flow difficulties.

To avoid this non-payment problem, require all collection agencies with which the company works to be bonded, so that the bonding agency will pay the company if the agency were to fail. Further, require an annual review of each collection agency's bonding arrangements, to ensure that they have renewed these contracts.

Payment Tracking

Collection agencies tend to be underfunded, and so may be tempted to use the cash from their collection activities too long before remitting them to clients. While the bonding concept just noted can prevent the catastrophic loss of cash, it does nothing to keep an agency from holding cash for an inordinate period of time.

To keep cash from being held for too long, the collections manager should monitor which invoices have been referred to agencies, when collections have been made by the agencies, and the date on which the resulting cash should be received by the company. If cash does not arrive in a timely manner, the collections manager should vigorously pursue the responsible agency for payment. Usually, an ongoing pattern of late payments will arise, which should lead the collections manager to shift to a different agency.

The In-House Collection Agency

A variation on the collection agency is to create such an agency in-house. Doing so solves two problems. First, it can avoid the significant fees charged by outside collection agencies. With a reduced cost, the collections staff is more likely to shift problem accounts to the collection agency sooner, which can improve the odds of collection. Second, it gives the collections manager better control over the collection activities conducted by the agency's staff, which can improve customer relations by avoiding the more annoying collection activities.

This in-house agency must appear to outsiders to be an independent collection agency, so it must be separately incorporated, have phone numbers different from those of the company, have mail sent to a different address, use different letterhead, and avoid routing calls through the company receptionist. From an administrative perspective, the in-house agency can share administrative services with the rest of the company, such as payroll and accounting, since these activities are invisible to customers.

The in-house agency concept is not perfect. The company may not be able to attract the best collectors for this group if they cannot share in the high fees that would normally be collected by an outside agency. Also, knowing that the parent company will fund the agency even in the absence of cash flows from collections may make the group somewhat less entrepreneurial in pursuing outdated invoices. These issues can be mitigated by allowing the in-house group to pursue business from outside parties at the industry-standard fee structure, though doing so may lead the in-house group to give less attention to invoices forwarded from the collections department.

Summary

The use of a collection agency is a viable option for selected situations. However, if used too much, it can result in a company losing sight of the underlying issues that caused an invoice to be late, such as improper credit granting or product quality issues. An in-house collections staff is more interested in correcting these issues in order to make their work easier, whereas a collection agency has no such incentive. On the contrary, a collection agency makes more money if a company continues to have problems with its internal systems that cause more invoices to be referred to the agency.

The use of a collection agency is usually reserved for those customers with whom a company no longer wants to conduct business, except for those rare cases where an agency is used in a good cop, bad cop collection routine. Consequently, it makes sense to bring together the credit manager, collections manager, and sales manager to mutually agree upon which accounts are to be sent to a collection agency; once the decision to do so is made, it is unlikely that the targeted customer will want to do business with the company again.

Chapter 18
Litigation and Bankruptcy Tactics

Introduction

In this chapter, we address the use of litigation as a collection tool. The discussion includes the various types of preparatory steps that a business can take to increase its odds of litigation success, as well as specific litigation methods, how to collect money judgments, and actions to take when a customer seeks bankruptcy protection.

The Litigation Process

Litigation involves a number of activities that require notifying the parties, exploring the evidence, conducting a trial, and obtaining payment. Since the full-length litigation process is both slow and expensive, many courts encourage litigants to reach out-of-court settlements. The result is that the parties typically re-evaluate their positions at each stage of the litigation process, and decide whether it is more cost-effective to continue or to reach a settlement. Consequently, few cases work their way through the entire litigation process.

The essential litigation steps, which involve the plaintiff (the party seeking a legal remedy) and the defendant (the party being sued), are:

1. Determine which court should hear the case, and file a lawsuit with that court.
2. Notify the defendant of the lawsuit via a summons and complaint document.
3. Set a court date for hearings.
4. Attorneys for both parties exchange requests for documents. Each party issues interrogatories to the other party, which are questions to which written answers must be made.
5. Take depositions, which are testimonies concerning the case made under oath but not within the court. The written results of depositions may then be used in court proceedings.
6. File motions in court, which are requests for the court to take certain actions. Sample motions are to switch the location where the lawsuit is filed (change of venue), to dismiss the lawsuit, and to render judgment immediately (summary judgment).
7. Conduct the trial and render a judgment. If the defendant does not choose to respond to the plaintiff in court, the court may enter a default judgment in favor of the plaintiff.

Many of these steps can be avoided by filing a request for *summary judgment*, where the filer asserts that the other party does not have a credible case, and asks for an immediate favorable ruling. The motion may be granted when it can be established that there is no credible defense against the evidence. If it appears possible to achieve a summary judgment, this request can be made early in the litigation process. Alternatively, the court may issue a partial summary judgment, in which case the liability of the defendant is established, and the trial is then intended to determine the amount of damages that will be paid.

Litigation Advance Preparation

A company should prepare well in advance for the possibility that a claim over a receivable will end up in court. To do so, the business should consistently point out several legal issues to its customers, thereby establishing the ground rules for litigation. These and other issues are:

- *Venue.* The credit application should list the state within which any litigation is to be conducted. The state should be the location most convenient for the company, not the customer. The customer must sign the credit application, thereby agreeing to the designated venue.
- *Notes and guarantees.* Whenever possible, obtain a signed note or personal guarantee to pay a debt. These documents establish the customer's commitment to pay the company.
- *Acknowledgments.* Whenever possible, collectors should attempt to obtain written acknowledgments from customers that a debt exists. These documents can be admitted as evidence in court.
- *Interest and penalty policy.* State on all credit applications, invoices, dunning letters, and other communications with customers that the company charges interest on overdue account balances. The attorney can use these documents as evidence that an interest charge is an integral part of the arrangement between the company and the customer, which makes it more likely that an interest charge can be added to the company's claim.
- *Proof of delivery.* Obtain from the freight carrier a proof of delivery, which can be used as evidence in court. Freight carriers may only issue such proof within a certain number of months of the delivery date, so be sure to obtain this evidence as soon as possible.
- *Security interest.* If the company has already filed a security interest in customer assets or goods shipped to a customer, it should periodically file continuation statements to ensure that the security interest is maintained.

By consistently addressing these issues, a business provides its attorneys with a better set of tools for pursuing claims against customers.

Litigation Prescreening

Pursuing litigation against a customer for an unpaid debt is both prolonged and expensive, and has an uncertain outcome. For these reasons, it is not a cost-effective option for most smaller receivables (with the possible exception of a small claims court filing, as noted in a later section). Litigation may not be a valid option even for larger receivables, since a customer may be in such deep financial trouble that it has few unencumbered assets that can be liquidated to pay the company.

For these reasons, it is eminently worthwhile to prescreen customers for possible litigation. Any of the following scenarios are ones for which litigation may not be cost-effective:

- There is sufficient uncertainty about the claim that the company may not win in court
- The litigation process is inordinately expensive
- The customer has a reputation for fighting litigation for as long as possible
- The customer is known to have few assets and/or large amounts of debt
- Tax liens or other judgments have already been filed against the customer
- There is existing litigation already pending against the customer
- There is a substantial cost associated with seizing, storing, and selling the assets of the customer
- The customer's assets will not fetch much money at auction

However righteous the collections manager may feel about pursuing a claim, doing so simply may not make sense if any of the preceding factors are present. Instead, it may be best to write off the debt and turn the company's attention to collecting other receivables.

Litigation Timing

Litigation has traditionally been considered the last possible option for collecting a debt, primarily because of its expense. However, being last on the list of collection activities does not mean that litigation should be excessively delayed. If a customer is in financial difficulties, its assets are dissipating by the day, so any delay reduces the chance of collection further. Consequently, as soon as all reasonable collection measures have been taken, turn an account over to an attorney.

One issue with litigation timing is the use of a collection agency. Many organizations want to use a collection agency *before* turning to an attorney. This is fine, but set a time limit on how long the agency is allowed to retain the account before shifting it to an attorney. In too many cases, accounts languish at a collection agency for far too long, reducing the chances of collection through subsequent litigation.

There may be cases where it makes more sense to bypass a collection agency and go straight to an attorney. For example, if there is a signed document from the customer supporting a claim, the odds of success in court will be much higher, and so may be worth pursuing at once. This scenario arises when there is a promissory note, personal guarantee, or written acknowledgment of a debt. Conversely, when there is a valid dispute over an amount due that makes a favorable outcome in court less likely, it may make more sense to first route the account through a collection agency.

To ensure that accounts are referred to an attorney as expeditiously as possible, set up a weekly status review of all receivables that are above a certain threshold dollar amount, and review them to see if litigation is now the best option for obtaining payment.

Collection Trigger Points

One other factor may influence the use of the litigation prescreening that was described earlier, which is to first employ several methods through an attorney that may result in payment before the trial date. Consider the following options:

1. *Attorney letter.* Have the attorney send a final demand letter, noting exactly when a lawsuit will be filed, and stating that the company will request payment of attorney's fees and all litigation expenses from the customer.
2. *File lawsuit.* File the lawsuit and ensure that notice of the lawsuit is served upon the defendant. Be sure to name as defendants everyone who could be responsible for payment, including guarantors, company owners, and any successor companies; doing so may increase pressure from someone in this group to settle. Only name defendants for which you have a reasonable determination of liability.
3. *Enter discovery phase.* Send interrogatories to the customer, demanding information related to the lawsuit.
4. *Writ of attachment.* If there is a reasonable basis to believe that the defendant may be disposing of assets in order to make any judgment worthless, the plaintiff can request that a writ of attachment be issued. This writ gives the court jurisdiction over certain assets of the defendant before the trial date. There are risks and costs to this step, but it can be effective in scaring the defendant into reaching a settlement.

> **Tip:** It is not usually possible to recover attorney's fees in a lawsuit if the fees are contingent on the outcome of the lawsuit. It may therefore be more cost-effective to pay attorneys on an hourly basis.

At each of these steps, the increasing severity of the situation may trigger a decision by the customer to contact the company regarding settlement of the claim. These steps in the process are not especially expensive, and so may be considered worthwhile steps to pursue if there is a belief that the customer may react with an out-of-court settlement. If the customer proves to be intransigent after these steps have been completed, it is still possible to back out of the lawsuit and avoid any additional cost.

Attorney Selection

When pursuing claims that involve accounts receivable, do not hire attorneys who lack specific expertise in this area. Though they may be able to competently move through the general litigation process, they do not have expertise in the collection of cash from the defendant after a favorable settlement.

Instead, use attorneys who have significant experience in all three of the following areas that will lead to the collection of cash:

- Locating customer assets
- Filing the necessary paperwork to attach these assets
- Liquidating the assets

If the company has a large number of claims that require money judgment collection expertise, it may make sense to bring attorneys with proven skill in-house, to form an internal department that is specifically targeted at this aspect of collections.

Small Claims Court

The least expensive form of litigation is through small claims court. This court is designed to handle small-dollar claims on an accelerated basis, with trials typically lasting only a few minutes. In essence, the plaintiff needs to prove that there was an agreement to deliver goods or services, that the delivery was made, and that the defendant defaulted on payment. If there are witnesses, they must appear in court to give testimony. If properly documented, the odds of success are high.

Depending on local requirements, it is usually necessary to file the claim in a court in the county in which the customer resides. Many small claims courts maintain websites, from which complaint forms can be downloaded.

A key issue when using a small claims court is the maximum amount of any awards that the court will grant. If the amount you are seeking to collect is higher, either turn to more traditional litigation, or write off the amount of the debt that is in excess of the maximum court award, and just pursue payment of the maximum allowable amount. The amount of the write-off should be stated on the complaint form sent to the court.

There are a few administrative issues to deal with when using a small claims court. Consider the following:

- *Legal name*. Purchase a credit report on the customer to ensure that you are entering the correct legal name of the customer on the complaint form.
- *Attorney*. Hire a local attorney to represent the company in court. The fee paid could be a combination of a flat fee and a percentage of any proceeds. Since claims must be filed where customers reside, the company may have to create a pool of local attorneys from which to draw.

Tip: If a small claims court prohibits attorneys, someone from the company must attend the court in person. If so, the cost to travel to a distant court may make this option a less effective one.

Small claims court is an excellent way to obtain a low-cost judgment against a creditor, and within a short period of time. The relatively small value of awards granted makes this the obvious litigation path to pursue for the large number of smaller invoice amounts that companies have.

> **Tip:** To save money, wait until just before the trial date to see if the defendant wants to settle the case, and *then* hire an attorney to represent you in court.

Money Judgment Collection Tactics

If the company obtains a favorable judgment in court, it still faces the task of obtaining payment from the debtor. The court is not responsible for obtaining payment from the debtor – the company must do so.

Obtaining payment may require seizing debtor assets in payment of the debt, so the first task is to determine where the assets are located. One option is to conduct a *judgment debtor examination*, where the debtor is asked under oath about the locations and amounts of all assets. Debtors must appear in court for this examination, or else the court will issue a warrant for their arrest.

Once the company knows where personal property assets are located, it can contact the sheriff having jurisdiction over the county in which the assets are located, and request that they be seized and sold at a public auction.

> **Tip:** When seizing assets, be aware that other entities may have senior claims on those assets. A lien search will uncover these claims.

In some cases, and especially in family-run businesses, the debtor may attempt to shift its assets away from the corporate shell, where they are more difficult to locate. If you suspect that this is a possibility, ask the court to issue a restraining notice to the customer, prohibiting it from disposing of any assets. An asset restraining order is particularly effective when it targets a debtor's bank accounts. Unfortunately, an asset restraining order can only be requested after the company has obtained a favorable judgment against a debtor. It may have taken many months of effort to obtain the judgment, so the debtor will have had that entire period in which to move assets. Consequently, there may be few assets to which the restraining order can be applied.

If not sufficient funds have been raised through the seizure of personal property, another option is to place a lien on the real property of the debtor, which can be accomplished with a notice of judgment filing through the secretary of state. *Real property* is defined as land and any property attached to the land (such as buildings). This approach does not result in immediate payment, but makes it more difficult for the debtor to sell its assets to third parties, since clear title cannot be transferred until the lien is settled. It may be possible to request a judicial foreclosure of the property, in which case the company can be paid from the proceeds of the asset sale (assuming there are no senior liens on the property that must be settled first).

> **Tip:** A money judgment continues to accumulate interest at the legal rate of interest mandated by the state government, so be sure to add it to the amount of the judgment when collecting payment.

Never agree to set aside a money judgment in favor of an agreement by the debtor to pay under a promissory note. The debtor should have agreed to this before the company pursued litigation. The only reason a debtor wants to introduce the possibility of a promissory note is to have the judgment set aside, after which payment can be prolonged yet again.

In cases where the company is pursuing payment from an individual, it can apply to the court to issue a garnishment. A garnishment requires the employer of an individual to withhold a portion of the person's wages and remit them to the company. Wage garnishments may yield little cash if the company has a low priority after other garnishment claims on the person's wages, such as for child support payments and tax liens. A garnishment can also be repeatedly applied to the bank account of a debtor, which can be used to extract any funds that have been deposited into the account.

Tip: Be careful not to over-collect funds. If this happens, immediately remit the difference back to the debtor.

Finally, be sure to keep track of the original money judgment, any allowable fees or interest charges that can be legally added to the judgment, and any subtractions for payments made by the debtor. This is useful not only for dealing with the debtor, but also for responding to any inquiries from the court regarding the status of the judgment. Once the full amount of the judgment has been collected, file a *satisfaction of judgment* notice with the court, which closes the case. It may also be necessary to release any garnishments and property liens that are still outstanding.

Bankruptcy Activities

An individual or business may claim bankruptcy protection from creditors. There are several types of bankruptcy protection, of which we will focus here on the Chapter 7 liquidation. In essence, a Chapter 7 liquidation means that all debtor assets are placed under the control of a court-appointed trustee, which sells these assets and then distributes the proceeds to creditors. An individual is allowed to retain certain assets that are beyond the reach of creditors. The amounts retained fall into the categories of the home, personal property, automobile, trade tools, jewelry, pensions, life insurance, alimony, and social security payments. There is no asset retention when the entity seeking bankruptcy protection is a business.

The order in which distributions are made to creditors depends on the order of priority, which is set forth in the bankruptcy code. Under the *absolute priority rule*, certain classes of creditor must be paid in full before other creditors are paid. A common result is that some creditors eventually receive significant payouts, while general creditors receive little or nothing. In many cases, taxing entities, secured creditors, and former employees are paid most or all of the available funds.

While it is certainly undesirable for a seller to be caught in a bankruptcy situation, there are a number of actions that can be taken to mitigate the amount of the loss. These actions are:

- *Stop goods in transit*. If there are any goods in transit to the customer that have not yet been delivered, contact the freight carrier and have them return the goods to the company.
- *Stop orders in process*. If there are any orders from the customer that have not yet been shipped, halt them at once.
- *Terminate credit*. The credit department immediately sets the customer's credit limit to zero, so the system flags any new orders placed as requiring payment in cash.
- *Preference claim defenses*. If the customer has paid the company within the last 90 days, consult with an attorney regarding the company's defenses against a claim that a preferential transfer was made.
- *Proof of delivery*. Request proof of delivery for all unpaid items from freight carriers, since this information will be needed when filing a claim for payment.
- *File a claim*. Be sure to file a proof of claim form for all amounts owed, and do so promptly, so the claim is recorded with the trustee. Also, obtain a written confirmation of receipt of these documents from the court. If any claims are disputed, address the issues aggressively in order to resolve them as soon as possible. Disputes may be in regard to the amount of the claim or its order of priority for payment. Any claims filed after the *bar date* set by the court will be rejected. The bar date is the date by which claims must be received.
- *Report fraudulent conveyances*. If the company has a large claim and so stands to recover a significant amount, it may be worthwhile to engage in research to find any customer assets that may have been illegally transferred to a third party. If located, report these assets to the trustee.
- *Pursue third parties*. If the bankrupt entity is a sole proprietorship or a general partnership, pursue the personal assets of the owners of the entity, since there is no corporate protection afforded to the owners of these types of entities. Also, pursue any third party that issued a personal guarantee to pay the debts of the customer. However, be aware that an individual may also claim personal bankruptcy protection in order to eliminate the liability represented by a guarantee.

Tip: Do not send original documents to the court as part of a proof of claim, since they may be lost. Instead, photocopies are a sufficient form of evidence.

In addition, we cover asset reclamation and the sale of a creditor claim later in this section.

Tip: All collection activities against a debtor must cease as soon as the company receives notice that the debtor has filed for bankruptcy protection. To ensure that the filing is real, obtain the case number and confirm it with the court.

Asset Reclamation

If a customer declares bankruptcy, it may still be possible to reclaim goods sold to that customer, rather than filing a claim with the bankruptcy court. To do so, the following conditions must be present:

- The sale was made on credit
- The customer was already insolvent when it received the goods
- The demand for return of the goods is made within 10 business days of the date when the customer received them
- The customer still has possession of the goods

If all of these conditions can be met, then make the claim in writing, and send the claim via an overnight delivery service that obtains a receipt signature from the customer. This signature provides legal evidence of receipt.

If the asset reclamation claim is upheld by the bankruptcy court, the company may be paid back in one of the following ways:

- The goods are returned
- Cash payment of the full claim is made
- The company is granted a security interest in the goods

Sell a Creditor Claim

When a customer goes bankrupt, the seller can file a claim with the bankruptcy court to be paid for any related outstanding receivables. Though the seller may eventually receive compensation, it may not be for a long time, and for much less than the billed amount. Alternatively, and possibly worse, the seller may be paid with ownership shares in the customer, which can be quite difficult to liquidate.

To avoid the prolonged process of being paid through a bankruptcy court, it may instead be possible to sell the claim to a third party investor immediately, for cash. The investor takes over responsibility for pursuing the claim, hoping to eventually earn a reasonable return on the initial investment, as paid to the seller. Alternatively, the investor may collect a number of these claims and use them to:

- Gain control over the customer; or
- Block reorganization plans; or
- Resell the combined claims for a higher price to another investor

In order to sell a claim to an investor, the seller must verify with the customer that the claim for payment is not disputed. If so, the investor is much more willing to buy the claim. The investor then estimates the amount of the claim that will eventually be paid, discounts the result for the estimated amount of time that will pass before payment is made, and factors in a profit to arrive at an amount to offer the seller for the claim.

As part of the sale, the seller and investor must agree upon the terms of an *assignment of claim* agreement. The investor then notifies the bankruptcy court of the sale, which forwards the notification to the customer. If the customer has no objection, the bankruptcy court substitutes the name of the investor for the name of the original seller as the owner of the claim.

The seller should be wary of a number of terms on an assignment of claim agreement that are intended to shift the risk of bankruptcy court nonpayment from the investor to the seller. These issues include:

- The seller is required to repurchase the claim from the investor if the claim is not made
- The seller must pay the investor interest charges if the claim is not paid
- The seller must repurchase all claims subsequently disputed
- The investor is allowed to delay payment to the seller

If these terms are excessively onerous, the seller should strongly consider retaining its claim and waiting for a payout from the bankruptcy court, or at least finding a different investor that is willing to pay under more reasonable terms.

Chapter 11 Bankruptcy

Thus far, we have addressed bankruptcy claims from the perspective of a Chapter 7 liquidation. It is also possible that a person or business may file for protection under Chapter 11 of the bankruptcy code. Chapter 11 is intended for situations where the entity wants to reorganize its operations and then emerge from bankruptcy and continue in business. In this section, we will deal with a Chapter 11 filing only for a business.

When a business files for Chapter 11 protection, it has 120 days in which to create a plan for repaying its debts; this period may be extended by the court. In essence, the plan categorizes all creditors of the business and states how each category will be paid, if at all. The creditors then vote to accept or reject the plan. If a category of creditors refuses to accept the plan, the bankruptcy court can either have the business revise its reorganization plan for another vote or force the dissenting creditors to accept the plan.

If the creditors believe that the management of the bankrupt entity is incompetent or dishonest, it can petition the court to impose a trustee on the business, who is then empowered to run the business until it can be sold or its assets liquidated. The trustee may also review transactions taking place prior to the bankruptcy date to see if they were preferential or fraudulent transfers of assets; if so, the court can demand that these assets be returned to the entity. A *preferential transfer* can involve payments made to any third party within 90 days of the bankruptcy filing date or a payment to a corporate insider within one year of the filing date. A *fraudulent transfer* is when an asset is sold for less than its fair market value.

As part of the bankruptcy process, an unsecured creditor's committee is selected from the largest creditors. The role of this committee is to monitor the condition of the bankrupt entity, represent creditors at large to the court, and recommend to creditors whether they should accept a plan of reorganization. A place on this committee is a voluntary position. It may be useful to be a committee member if the seller plans to continue doing business with the bankrupt entity, in order to more closely monitor its financial condition. However, the commitment can be a lengthy one that takes up a significant amount of time.

The Involuntary Bankruptcy Petition

An aggressive collection tactic is for at least three creditors to file a petition for involuntary bankruptcy against a debtor. This approach is allowable when the creditors have, in aggregate, at least $10,000 of unpaid and undisputed trade debts with the debtor.

An involuntary bankruptcy petition is served to the debtor, along with a summons. The debtor can consent to the petition or elect to fight it in court. If the court decides in favor of the creditors, an order for relief is entered and the debtor is placed in bankruptcy proceedings. If the court decides in favor of the debtor, the creditors may be liable for the debtor's court costs.

Once in bankruptcy, the creditors may not have a greater chance of obtaining funds in the near future, given the time it takes to administer a bankruptcy and the presence of competing creditor claims. Thus, the involuntary bankruptcy option is typically only applied to a deeply resistant debtor that has refused to make payment under all other forms of pressure. It may also be a choice when it appears that preferential transfers of assets are being made out of the debtor entity, leaving fewer assets for the creditors to claim.

Summary

The litigation concepts and tactics discussed in this chapter are those you would expect to use with a customer that the company has no intention of doing business with again. The sole intent is to collect as much cash as possible, after which the company and customer go their separate ways. If a company wants to pursue ongoing business relations with a customer, it probably should not engage in litigation at all, given the more confrontational nature of this form of collection.

When a customer seeks bankruptcy protection, there are a number of steps that the collection staff can take as soon as it receives notification of the bankruptcy. After those steps are taken, the ability to obtain payment is no longer under the control of the company, in which case the issue is either parked until the trustee pays out funds, or the collection manager elects to sell the company's claim to an investor.

Chapter 19
The Allowance for Doubtful Accounts

Introduction

The credit and collection function is responsible for issuing credit and collecting receivables – not accounting for these items. However, accounting staff will likely call upon the collections manager for input regarding the allowance for doubtful accounts (also known as the bad debt allowance). This allowance is based on an estimate of future bad debts that will fall out of the current accounts receivable. Accordingly, we include in this chapter a discussion of how the allowance is constructed, how to calculate the amount stored in the allowance, and how to account for the allowance.

Estimation of the Allowance for Doubtful Accounts

The allowance for doubtful accounts is a reduction of the total amount of accounts receivable appearing on a company's balance sheet, and is listed as a deduction immediately below the accounts receivable line item. Technically, the allowance is called a contra asset account, because it offsets the account with which it is paired, which is accounts receivable.

The allowance for doubtful accounts represents management's best estimate of the amount of accounts receivable that will not be paid by customers. The amount is recognized within the same reporting period as the revenues to which the allowance is related, so that the financial statements reflect all expenses associated with those revenues. The allowance is usually reviewed and updated as part of the month-end closing process, to ensure that the balance is reasonable in comparison to the latest bad debt forecast. For companies having minimal bad debt activity, a quarterly update may be sufficient.

There are several possible ways to estimate the allowance for doubtful accounts, which are:

- *Historical percentage.* If a certain percentage of accounts receivable became bad debts in the past, then use the same percentage in the future to estimate bad debts. This method works best for large numbers of small account balances.
- *Pareto analysis.* Individually review the largest accounts receivable that make up 80% of the total receivable balance, and estimate which specific customers are most likely to default. Then use the preceding historical percentage method for the remaining smaller accounts. This method works best if there are a small number of large account balances.

- *Risk classification.* Assign a risk score to each customer, and assume a higher risk of default for those having a higher risk score.

EXAMPLE

Kelvin Corporation, maker of glass thermometers, periodically obtains new risk scores from a credit agency for all of its customers, and loads them into the customer master file. The accounting system's report writing software incorporates this information to create the following report that aggregates the current accounts receivable balance for several categories of risk, to which the historical bad debt percentage for each class of receivables is applied:

Risk Category	Current Receivable Balance	Historical Bad Debt Percentage	Estimate Bad Debt by Risk Category
Low risk	$10,425,000	0.4%	$41,700
Medium low	6,100,000	1.3%	79,300
Medium high	2,350,000	3.8%	89,300
High risk	630,000	10.5%	66,150
Totals	$19,505,000	1.4%	$276,450

The result of this largely automated analysis is an estimated bad debt total that can be used to populate the allowance for doubtful accounts.

You can also evaluate the reasonableness of an allowance for doubtful accounts by comparing it to the total amount of seriously overdue accounts receivable, which are presumably not going to be collected. If the allowance is less than the amount of these overdue accounts, the allowance is probably insufficient.

Accounting for the Allowance for Doubtful Accounts

A person involved in credit and collections does not normally need a detailed knowledge of accounting transactions. However, since the credit and collections function is largely responsible for the allowance for doubtful accounts, we include a discussion of the accounting for just this one line item on the balance sheet.

   If a company is using the accrual basis of accounting, it should record an allowance for doubtful accounts, which provides an estimate of future bad debts that improves the accuracy of the company's financial statements. Also, by recording the allowance for doubtful accounts at the same time it records a sale, the company is properly matching the projected bad debt expense against the related sales item in the same period, which provides an accurate view of the true profitability of a sale.

EXAMPLE

A company records $10,000,000 of sales to several hundred customers, and projects (based on historical experience) that it will incur 1% of this amount as bad debts, though it does not know exactly which customers will default. It records the 1% of projected bad debts as a $100,000 debit to the bad debt expense account and a $100,000 credit to the allowance for doubtful accounts. The bad debt expense is charged to expense right away, and the allowance for doubtful accounts becomes a reserve account that offsets the account receivable of $10,000,000 (for a net receivable outstanding of $9,900,000). The entry is:

	Debit	Credit
Bad debt expense	100,000	
Allowance for doubtful accounts		100,000

Later, several customers default on payments totaling $40,000. Accordingly, the company credits the accounts receivable account by $40,000 to reduce the amount of outstanding accounts receivable, and debits the allowance for doubtful accounts by $40,000. This entry reduces the balance in the allowance account to $60,000. The entry does not impact earnings in the current period. The entry is:

	Debit	Credit
Allowance for doubtful accounts	40,000	
Accounts receivable		40,000

A few months later, a collection agency succeeds in collecting $15,000 of the funds that the company had already written off. The company can now reverse part of the previous entry, thereby increasing the balances of both accounts receivable and the allowance for doubtful accounts. The entry is:

	Debit	Credit
Accounts receivable	15,000	
Allowance for doubtful accounts		15,000

The only impact that the allowance for doubtful accounts has on the income statement is the initial charge to bad debt expense when the allowance is initially created. Any subsequent write-offs of accounts receivable against the allowance only impact the balance sheet.

The Direct Write-off Method

A less-used method than the allowance method just described is the direct write-off method. The direct write off method is the practice of charging bad debts to expense in the period when individual invoices have been clearly identified as bad debts. The specific activity needed to write off an account receivable under this method is to create a credit memo for the customer in question, which exactly offsets the amount of the bad debt. Creating the credit memo requires a debit to the bad debt expense account and a credit to the accounts receivable account.

This method does not involve a reduction of the amount of recorded sales, only an increase in the bad debt expense. For example, a business records a sale on credit of $10,000, and records it with a debit to the accounts receivable account and a credit to the sales account. After two months, the customer is only able to pay $8,000 of the open balance, so the seller must write off $2,000. It does so with a $2,000 credit to the accounts receivable account and an offsetting debit to the bad debt expense account. Thus, the revenue amount remains the same, the remaining receivable is eliminated, and an expense is created in the amount of the bad debt.

This approach violates the matching principle, under which all costs related to revenue are charged to expense in the same period in which you recognize the revenue, so that the financial results of an entity reveal the entire extent of a revenue-generating transaction in a single accounting period.

The direct write-off method delays the recognition of expenses related to a revenue-generating transaction, and so is considered an excessively aggressive accounting method, since it delays some expense recognition, making a reporting entity appear more profitable in the short term than it really is. For example, a company may recognize $1,000,000 in sales in one period, and then wait three or four months to collect all of the related accounts receivable, before finally charging some items off to expense. This creates a lengthy delay between revenue recognition and the recognition of expenses that are directly related to that revenue. Thus, the profit in the initial month is overstated, while profit is understated in the month when the bad debts are charged to expense.

The direct write-off method can be considered a reasonable accounting method if the amount that is written off is an immaterial amount, since doing so has minimal impact on an entity's reported financial results.

The direct write-off method is required for the reporting of taxable income in the United States, since the Internal Revenue Service believes (possibly correctly) that companies would otherwise be tempted to inflate their bad debt reserves in order to report a smaller amount of taxable income.

Negative Bad Debt Expense

If uncollectible accounts receivable are being written off as they occur (the direct charge-off method), there will be times when a customer unexpectedly pays an invoice after it has been written off. In such a case the write-off should be reversed, which will yield a negative bad debt expense if the original write-off occurred in a reporting period earlier than the reversal. This transaction creates a larger profit in the current income statement, which offsets the lower profit from the previous period in which the bad debt expense was originally recognized.

Conversely, if you are using the allowance method and are charging an estimated amount to bad debt expense each month, an unexpected customer payment against a written-off receivable does not result in the reversal of the original bad debt expense. Instead, the balance in the allowance account is increased by the amount of the unexpected payment. This transaction does not impact the income statement at all; instead, the amount of the allowance is increased in the balance sheet.

Thus, the method used to record bad debts is the key determining factor in whether or not a business can experience a negative bad debt expense.

Summary

The collections manager is likely to be deeply involved in the ongoing calculation of the allowance for doubtful accounts. The crucial factor for the collections manager is to be extremely consistent in the method used to determine the amount of the allowance. By doing so, the current allowance should be comparable to the allowance reported in prior periods. It is permissible to change the method used to determine the allowance, but only if doing so results in an improved methodology that will provide better information. Under no circumstances should the method be altered just to provide a short-term boost to reported earnings.

Chapter 20
Credit and Collection Technology

Introduction

The credit and collection functions can be adequately handled with entirely manual systems and a bank of telephones. However, doing so ignores a number of technologies that can greatly improve the efficiency of these functions, while also reducing the rate of processing errors, and which may even allow employees to work off-site. In this chapter, we address several innovations that can significantly enhance the capabilities of a company's credit and collection activities.

> **Related Podcast Episode:** Episode 237 of the Accounting Best Practices Podcast discusses how artificial intelligence might be used in the collections area. It is available at: **www.accountingtools.com/podcasts** or **iTunes**

Collection Software

When collectors work with just a phone and no other technology, they must rely upon a printout of the latest accounts receivable aging report and their handwritten notes regarding prior conversations with customers. This primitive (and common) approach to collections uses old information, while the efficiency of collectors is closely associated with their ability to interpret their own notes. A better alternative is to purchase collection software to improve the efficiency of collection operations. Collection software includes the following features:

- *Receivables integration.* There is a direct data feed from the accounts receivable file in the accounting software to the collection software, so all customer payments received are immediately apparent to collectors.
- *Contact information.* The software contains a listing of all customer contacts, and the time zones in which they are located. An auto dialer can then be used to contact each customer at the optimal time of day.
- *Contact scheduling.* The system brings to the attention of collectors those customers whose payments are overdue, and may assign priority to those for which promised payment dates have passed without the receipt of any payment.
- *Management oversight.* The collections manager can view the activities of each collector, as well as their notes regarding the latest conversations with customers.
- *Note storage.* All notes regarding customer conversations are stored on-line, and are immediately accessible whenever a customer is contacted again.

- *Dunning letters.* The system can print, fax, or e-mail dunning letters in a variety of formats, in accordance with a pre-set schedule of activities.

Collection software is the single most important technology concept in the credit and collections area. However, it is also expensive, since it includes not only the cost of the software, but also installation, training, and maintenance fees. Nonetheless, a company that employs even a modest number of collections personnel will find that collection software is well worth the cost.

Document Imaging

Much of the information collected about a customer is manually completed and then stored in a customer folder. This may include credit applications filled out by customers, personal guarantees, and notes taken concerning trade reference calls. Whenever someone needs this information, they must retrieve the folder and later return it. During that time, the folder is not available for anyone else's use, and may not be put back in the correct order. In addition, there is a risk that the contents of these folders will be lost. And finally, the use of these manual records makes it imperative that the credit and collections staff be located near the files.

All of these issues can be eliminated by installing a document management system (DMS). With a DMS, documents are scanned and stored in a server, from which they can be readily accessed at the workstations of anyone allowed access to this information. The paper documents are still available, but are more likely to be shifted to a more distant location, since there is no longer a need to access them.

There are many advantages to a DMS system. Employees do not spend any time walking to and from the file storage area, multiple people can access the same document at the same time, and there is minimal risk of document loss. In addition, it now becomes possible for employees to work from remote locations, as long as they have a reasonable Internet connection. Also, the documents can more easily be shared with collection agencies and attorneys. And finally, since all of these documents are digitized, they can easily be attached to an e-mail and sent to dilatory customers.

The main issue with a DMS is its cost. The software and associated hardware are moderately expensive, and there is an ongoing labor cost associated with scanning documents into the system. Consequently, it is most cost-effective in large credit and collection departments, and less so when there are just a few employees involved in these areas.

Payment Deduction Database

In some organizations, there is a blizzard of payment deductions taken by customers, and for all sorts of reasons – marketing programs, damaged goods, inaccurate invoices, and so forth. Usually, the sole intent of the collections staff is to wade through this information and clear it from the accounts receivable records as soon as possible – without looking at the underlying reasons for the deductions. However, management must understand *why* deductions are being taken in order to stem the flow of deductions. Obtaining this knowledge calls for a payment deduction database.

A deduction database is intended to store all pertinent information about deductions taken and then aggregate it in a variety of ways, so that management can use it to determine such points as which customers are taking certain types of deductions, what complaints are causing the most deductions, and even which geographical regions appear to be generating the most deductions. The system should have a drill-down capability, so that managers can focus on a specific issue and then access the detailed deduction transactions relating to just that issue.

A deduction database can be built in-house using any number of database systems, so it is not especially difficult or expensive to create. The real cost of the system lies in the labor required to load the information for all deductions into the database – and especially if management wants to load historical records to gain some perspective on the extent of deduction problems over time.

An extension of this system is to integrate it into a workflow management system, where specific deduction issues can be electronically routed to individuals throughout the company for resolution. Managers can monitor the system to see if actions are being taken in a timely manner to resolve deduction problems. However, a workflow management system is more difficult to install than a deduction database. Also, the intent of the system is to mitigate specific problems within a short period of time, which differs from the reporting and analysis role for which a deduction database is used.

Enterprise Resource Planning Systems

Enterprise resource planning (ERP) refers to an integrated software package that supports all of a company's functional areas. Thus, it can handle the transactional requirements of the accounting, customer service, manufacturing, sales, warehousing, and other departments. Many ERP systems also accept data from a company's customers and suppliers for supply chain management purposes, so that the system essentially exceeds the traditional boundaries of a corporation.

The great advantage of an ERP system is that all corporate information is integrated, so that data is only entered into the system once. With a fully-integrated ERP system, companies find that their transaction error rates decline, while many tasks that formerly required manual effort are now entirely automated. Also, subject to confidentiality issues, employees can access information in other departments that was previously difficult to obtain, or only with the help of special programming by the information technology department. Further, it may be possible to install a single ERP system that stores information for all of a company's locations and subsidiaries, making it much easier to aggregate information.

These features of an ERP system are quite useful from the perspective of the credit and collection functions. Consider the following possibilities:

- *Information aggregation.* Combine the order entry and receivables systems of all locations and subsidiaries to determine the total consolidated credit exposure to the parent entity of a customer. Doing so may highlight unacceptable risks, and at least reduces the number of customer credit limits to be tracked.

- *Customer orders.* If the collections staff wants to apply pressure to a customer, they have complete visibility into the outstanding orders of the customer, and so will know when placing a hold on unshipped orders will be particularly effective.
- *Collection call module.* Some ERP systems contain a module that integrates all receivables information with a database of customer contacts, a note-taking function, and an auto dialer. This module massively improves the efficiency of the collectors, who have all of the information they need for collections work at their computer terminals.

However, this level of functionality comes at a price. ERP systems are very complex, and so require lengthy installation times. Also, because ERP systems can only be configured in a limited number of ways, most companies will find that they must alter their operating procedures to fit the software, rather than altering the software to fit their procedures. These changes call for a large training expenditure, which brings the total cost of the system into the millions of dollars. Consequently, an ERP system provides numerous benefits to the credit and collection functions, but must present similar improvements to other parts of the company in order to make it a cost-effective concept.

Miscellaneous Technology Concepts

There are several additional concepts where technology can be used to improve the efficiency and/or effectiveness of the credit and collection functions. For example:

- *Access to collection agency database.* Occasionally, a collection agency will allow its clients direct access to the agency's internal database of collection records concerning accounts forwarded to it. The collections manager can peruse these records to see if any accounts are nearing collection, and can make more informed decisions about when accounts should be shifted to a collections attorney for legal action.
- *Automated credit references.* Most companies assign a clerk to the task of responding to occasional requests for trade credit information. This clerk must research the payment history of the customers in question and communicate the information back to each inquirer. Though labor-intensive, this is a relatively minor task in most organizations. However, a larger company may find that entire positions are devoted to this task. These businesses can reduce their costs by installing an automated voice response system that asks callers for the name of the customer in question, and responds with a basic set of information, such as payment terms, average credit, high credit, the total amount currently owed, and the number of years that the company has done business with the customer. This approach has the advantages of

providing an immediate response to callers, cutting labor costs, and keeping callers from badgering the staff for additional insights into customer payment histories.

- *Automated late fees.* Many accounting systems can be set to automatically apply late fees to customer invoices that pass a certain age. However, this option can be considered more of a curse than a blessing, since many customers refuse to pay late fees. The result is additional effort by the accounting staff to reverse these charges from the receivable records.
- *Contacts database.* It is useful for the accounting and sales departments to jointly maintain a database of customer names and contact information for all customers. By doing so, collectors have the option to bypass their usual accounts payable contacts and talk to other people regarding overdue payments. If created, collectors should not use the additional names in this database too much, since these contacts should be intended just for emergency use. It may also be useful to store personal information about contacts in this database, such as birthdays, sports followed, and the names of children. Using this information during collection calls can make a collector stand out from the crowd and appear more human to an overburdened contact person.
- *On-line credit applications.* Create an on-line credit application that customers can access through the company website. Doing so has the advantage of dropping the resulting application directly into the company's computer system, for automatic routing to a credit analyst. Also, this approach means that an application can be configured to match the type of entity applying for credit, so that the form will ask different questions for a corporation than it does for an individual.
- *Receivables bidding platform.* There are a small number of on-line bidding platforms, on which a company can auction its accounts receivable. This is more of a financing alternative than a credit or collection solution, since the concept is designed to accelerate the receipt of cash in exchange for a financing fee.

Summary

Technology can play a substantial role in improving the operation of the credit and collection functions. However, always analyze the costs and benefits of each type of technology before acquiring a new system; in many cases, an expensive technology may not provide much of an advantage, especially in a smaller company. In many cases, the benefits of technology only work if its cost can be spread over a large department.

We have excluded from this discussion several types of technology that can be used to accelerate the receipt of cash, and which therefore indirectly impacts the collection function. For more information about bank lockboxes, remote deposit capture and automatic cash application, see the Payment Handling chapter.

Chapter 21
Product and Service Improvements

Introduction

In a great many cases, the credit and collection functions may be doing a fine job, and yet the incidence of customer late payments is inordinately high. If so, a possible culprit is the company itself. There are many ways in which the products, services, and processes of a company can lead to a sufficient degree of customer dissatisfaction that they refuse to pay invoices in a timely manner. In this chapter, we delve into a broad array of areas in which a company's own actions result in collection problems.

Pricing

There is an increased risk of pricing errors on invoices if the system used to derive prices is complex. Pricing complexity can arise not only from an overly enthusiastic sales manager, but also from selling products and services in an enormous number of configurations. Customers can be further confused if the pricing system results in their being charged with a number of unexpected additional fees.

If management can be persuaded to simplify the pricing and/or product structure, there will be a reduced risk of invoicing errors. The issue is not quite that simple, for management may be relying upon complex pricing to generate higher profits. For example, the pricing system may allow a customer to purchase a basic installation for a low price that is essentially a loss leader, while a number of upgrade options allow the company to recoup the initial loss. If these upgrade options were to be bundled into the basic product price, the product may no longer compare so well to the offerings of other companies.

This concept requires the cooperation of people outside of the accounting department, and over whom the controller and CFO have no control, so it is a difficult practice to implement.

Incorrect Order

A customer may rightfully complain that the item shipped was not the one ordered. This can be caused by a number of internal issues. For example:

- *Backorder replacement.* It may be considered a best practice to convince a customer to accept a related product if the original item ordered is currently on backorder status. While doing so increases revenue, there is a higher likelihood that the customer will not be pleased with the resulting product. If there is a demonstrable increase in bad debts resulting from this practice, consider reducing the use of backorder replacements.

- *Incorrect picking.* An inventory picker is given a pick list, on which are stated the items to be shipped with an order. The incorrect items could be picked for a multitude of reasons, such as mislabeled products, products stored in the wrong bin, an incorrect picking ticket, and picker indifference. Each reason requires a separate resolution. For example, product mislabeling may require a more automated bar code labeling system. If inventory is stored in the wrong location, an ongoing cycle counting program can be used to correct these errors. Incorrect picking tickets can be avoided by not using manual tickets. Employee indifference can be rectified through better working conditions, a different compensation plan, enhanced training, or employee terminations.
- *Product replacements.* The company may have eliminated a product and replaced it with an "improved" version. Alternatively, an engineering change order may have been implemented that slightly alters the configuration of a product. In either case, these changes may make a product unusable for a customer. The best approach to reducing this issue is to be very clear with customers about differences between the specifications of what they ordered and what they received.

Product Quality

In some industries, product quality can be the chief cause of collection difficulties, especially if product failure is so prevalent that a recall is warranted. Product quality is caused by a number of issues, including the following:

- *Flawed design.* A product may have been designed with a weakness that causes product failure after minimal usage, or when a modest amount of stress is placed on it. This issue is most likely to arise when inadequate resources are allocated to the testing of products prior to their release. In other cases, a flaw could not reasonably have been detected in-house, so the best alternative is to conduct a product recall.
- *Low quality materials.* A company can tread a fine line between using materials that are of excessively high quality or low quality. If it buys excessively high quality materials, customers may not notice the difference or be indifferent to the change. However, reducing the cost of materials means being extremely careful about avoiding low quality perceptions by customers. The result tends to be an ongoing process of attempting to use lower-cost materials without impacting customers and therefore their willingness to pay. Only a company with large profit margins can afford to ignore this issue entirely and just buy the highest quality materials, all of the time.
- *Production issues.* A section of the production process may not be producing parts within the predetermined specification level, which results in product failure in the field. Alternatively, production may simply leave dents or scratches on products that customers find unacceptable. These issues can be resolved most expensively by installing quality assurance checkpoints

throughout the production process. A better approach is to install production cells where batch sizes are minimized, so that issues of this kind are spotted at once and rectified before any additional units are manufactured.

Shipping Damage

Customers are obviously going to be less willing to pay if goods are damaged in transit, so finding the source of damage can be a key element in the effort to reduce the amount of delayed payments. There are a number of issues that can contribute to this problem:

- *Product design.* The flawed design problem noted under the Product Quality section extends to the shipping damage area as well. Some products are not designed to withstand the stress of transport. This may call for a product redesign, or perhaps a different mode of transport.
- *Packaging design.* The packaging for a product may not be sufficiently robust to withstand the stresses of transport, which may call for a package redesign. Another possibility for larger products is that the shipping department is doing an inadequate job of constructing custom pallets for these items, and/or not providing a sufficient amount of cushioning.
- *Mode of delivery.* There may be a higher incidence of damage associated with certain types of delivery, such as by train, ship, airplane, or truck. If a certain mode of delivery is clearly causing more damage, warn customers of this issue if they insist on using it, and possibly also have these customers sign a waiver that absolves the company from liability for damage claims.
- *Shipper used.* Some shippers have a reputation for damaging goods while loading, unloading, and storing them that is significantly higher than for other shippers. Tracing damage claims back to the responsible shippers is a good way to determine whether a new transport company is needed.
- *Customer inspection.* It is possible that a customer is causing damage, due to its processes for examining received goods. If proper care is not used in opening packages and testing goods, damage can be caused, which the receiving staff may ascribe to the seller. This is a very difficult issue for the seller to detect, and may only be traceable once every other shipping damage issue has been investigated and discounted as a likely cause.

Field Servicing

Customers may not pay their invoices because the company is not providing adequate servicing in the field. This is most likely to occur when there is a product installation problem that becomes apparent before the customer has paid its invoice for delivered goods. If the company's field servicing team is experiencing substantial delays in its service calls, the customer is more likely to delay payment.

Solving this issue involves close coordination between the collection staff and the field service coordinator, to ensure that service calls are scheduled as soon as possible for those cases where customer payment is contingent upon the resolution of an installation issue.

The Improvement System

The best way to trace customer payment issues back to the product and service problems described in this chapter is to develop a database that lists all of the issues noted by customers during collection calls. A report is generated from this database at regular intervals and aggregated by type of problem, to show which issues are causing the most collection delays.

A group of employees should be assembled from all of the areas impacting collections, and peruse this aggregated report on a regular basis. The group should focus on the higher-volume issues, drill down to the underlying causes, and work through solutions. Once an issue has been corrected, the team moves on to the next highest-volume issue, and so forth.

The use of this resolution team must be driven by a high-level executive within the company, since the collections manager probably does not have sufficient clout to enforce its use. The chief financial officer or controller would be a good choice for leading this effort, since its use directly impacts their areas of responsibility.

Summary

The main point of this chapter has been to show that a large proportion of collection issues are not the customer's fault. It is entirely possible that a company has a large number of internal problems that are causing its customers to rightfully rebel. If so, the collections manager must communicate to management that any number of issues must be resolved in order to reduce the investment in accounts receivable. This is not always an easy task, since the collections manager may be viewed as simply laying the blame on other department managers for his or her own collection inadequacies. Consequently, it is critical to obtain the support of a senior manager who understands that the business has serious internal issues that must be fixed.

Chapter 22
Credit and Collection Measurements

Introduction

The credit and collection functions deal with large numbers of customers and invoices on an ongoing basis. Given the high volume, this environment is suitable for a variety of measurements that can be used to monitor and manage the credit and collection functions. In this chapter, we begin with discussions of measurements related to collections, since most measurements are concentrated in this area, and not in the credit area.

Overview of Credit and Collection Measurements

The credit and collection functions deal with very large numbers of customers and their invoices. On a day to day basis, it is easy to be lost in the minutiae of granting credit and collecting receivables, without giving consideration to the overall result of these efforts. The measurements described in this chapter can be used to monitor performance, which is useful for deciding whether sufficient resources are being allocated to the department, or if action should be taken to improve efficiency. Some of the measurements can also be used to drill down to the specific issues causing certain types of collection problems.

At a minimum, there must be a measurement that compares the amount of accounts receivable to credit sales, so that you can roughly estimate the average period over which receivables are outstanding. The classic measure of this type is days sales outstanding (DSO), as described in a later section. In addition, consider using other measurements to obtain additional information about different aspects of the credit and collection functions. Ideally, such a system begins with a high-level DSO measurement and then drills down into the various components of the credit and collection functions to give the user additional information about why receivables are not being collected. For example, a manager may have an interest in the following additional measurements:

- The gross amount of receivables in each time bucket on the aged accounts receivable report, to determine the age range in which most overdue receivables are clustered
- The average number of days to pay, sorted by collector, which can be used to identify the most effective collectors
- The time required to settle payment disputes, which can be used to improve the deduction management process

When reviewing the results of a measurement system, keep in mind that the liquidity of customers, and therefore their ability to pay, varies somewhat from month to month, in a recurring cycle. For example, a partnership may pay out cash to its partners at the end of the calendar year, and so may delay some payments at the end of the year. Similarly, corporations may make estimated tax payments on a quarterly basis, which may impinge upon their accounts payable at the times when these payments are made. Further, there is a certain amount of seasonality in many industries, which can impact cash flows. For all of these reasons, a system of measurements will likely reveal that collection results differ from month to month, and quite possibly through no fault of the credit and collection employees. To filter out the effects of customers' ability to pay, compare the results of a particular month with the same month in the preceding year. For example, the DSO for this February may bear more resemblance to the DSO for the preceding February than to the DSO calculations for the adjacent January period in the current year.

The end result of a credit and collection measurement system should be specific actions to reduce the amount of overdue accounts receivable, such as:

- Adding credit and/or collection staff
- Adjusting the method for dealing with payment deductions
- Altering the policy for granting credit
- Altering the procedure for contacting customers
- Curtailing management overrides of credit decisions

In short, a system of measurements is only as good as the actions that result from its use. If a set of measurements are routinely calculated and no action results from these measurements, then the measurement system has failed.

Days Sales Outstanding

When evaluating the amount of accounts receivable outstanding, it is best to compare the receivables to the sales activity of the business, in order to see the proportion of receivables to sales. This proportion can be expressed as the average number of days over which receivables are outstanding before they are paid, which is called *days sales outstanding*, or DSO. DSO is the most popular of all collection measurements.

Days sales outstanding is most useful when compared to the standard number of days that customers are allowed before payment is due. Thus, a DSO figure of 40 days might initially appear excellent, until you realize that the standard payment terms are only five days. A combination of prudent credit granting and robust collections activity is the likely cause when the DSO figure is only a few days longer than the standard payment terms. From a management perspective, it is easiest to spot collection problems at a gross level by tracking DSO on a trend line, and watching for a sudden spike in the measurement in comparison to what was reported in prior periods.

To calculate DSO, divide 365 days into the amount of annual credit sales to arrive at credit sales per day, and then divide this figure into the average accounts receivable for the measurement period. Thus, the formula is:

$$\frac{\text{Average accounts receivable}}{\text{Annual sales} \div 365 \text{ days}}$$

EXAMPLE

The controller of Oberlin Acoustics, maker of the famous Rhino brand of electric guitars, wants to derive the days sales outstanding for the company for the April reporting period. In April, the beginning and ending accounts receivable balances were $420,000 and $540,000 respectively. The total credit sales for the 12 months ended April 30 were $4,000,000. The controller derives the following DSO calculation from this information:

$$\frac{(\$420,000 \text{ Beginning receivables} + \$540,000 \text{ Ending receivables}) \div 2}{\$4,000,000 \text{ Credit sales} \div 365 \text{ Days}}$$

$$=$$

$$\frac{\$480,000 \text{ Average accounts receivable}}{\$10,959 \text{ Credit sales per day}}$$

$$= 43.8 \text{ Days}$$

The correlation between the annual sales figure used in the calculation and the average accounts receivable figure may not be close, resulting in a misleading DSO number. For example, if a company has seasonal sales, the average receivable figure may be unusually high or low on the measurement date, depending on where the company is in its seasonal billings. Thus, if receivables are unusually low when the measurement is taken, the DSO days will appear unusually low, and vice versa if the receivables are unusually high. There are two ways to eliminate this problem:

- *Annualize receivables*. Generate an average accounts receivable figure that spans the entire, full-year measurement period.
- *Measure a shorter period*. Adopt a rolling quarterly DSO calculation, so that sales for the past three months are compared to average receivables for the past three months. This approach is most useful when sales are highly variable throughout the year.

Whatever measurement methodology is adopted for DSO, be sure to use it consistently from period to period, so that the results will be comparable on a trend line.

Tip: If DSO is increasing, the problem may be that the processing of credit memos has been delayed. If there is a processing backlog, at least have the largest ones processed first, which may reduce the amount of receivables outstanding by a noticeable amount.

Best Possible DSO

After running the DSO calculation, it may be useful to establish a benchmark against which to compare the DSO. This benchmark is the *best possible DSO*, which is the best collection performance to be expected, given the existing payment terms given to customers. The calculation is:

$$\frac{\text{Current receivables}}{\text{Annual credit sales}} \times 365$$

The key element in this formula is the *current* receivables. The calculation is essentially designed to show the best possible level of receivables, based on the assumption that DSO is only based on current receivables (i.e., there are no delinquent invoices present in the calculation).

EXAMPLE

The collections manager of the Red Herring Fish Company has established that the company's DSO is 22 days. Since the company requires short payment terms on its short-lived products, the question arises – is 22 days good or bad? At the end of the current period, Red Herring's current receivables were $30,000, and its trailing 12-month credit sales were $1,000,000. Based on this information, the best possible DSO is:

$$\frac{\$30,000 \text{ Current receivables}}{\$1,000,000 \text{ Credit sales}} \times 365$$

$$= 11 \text{ Days}$$

In short, actual DSO is running at a rate double that of the company's best possible DSO, and so should be considered an opportunity for improvement.

Collection Effectiveness Index

The days sales outstanding measurement operates at a relatively high level, and only gives a general indication of the state of receivables in comparison to sales over a fairly long period of time. An alternative that yields a somewhat higher level of precision is the collection effectiveness index (CEI). This measurement compares the amount that was collected in a given time period to the amount of receivables that were available for collection in that time period. A result near 100% indicates that a collection department has been very effective in collecting from customers.

The formula for the CEI is to combine the beginning receivables for the measurement period with the credit sales for that period, less the amount of ending receivables, and then divide this number by the sum of the beginning receivables for the measurement period and the credit sales for that period, less the amount of ending *current* receivables. Then multiply the result by 100 to arrive at a CEI percentage. Thus, the formula is stated as:

$$\frac{\text{Beginning receivables} + \text{Credit sales for the period} - \text{Ending total receivables}}{\text{Beginning receivables} + \text{Credit sales for the period} - \text{Ending current receivables}} \times 100$$

A collections manager can attain a high CEI number by focusing on the collection of the largest receivables. This means that a favorable CEI can be generated, even if there are a number of smaller receivables that are very overdue.

The CEI figure can be calculated for a period of any duration, such as a single month. Conversely, the DSO calculation tends to be less accurate for very short periods of time, since it includes receivables from prior periods that do not directly relate to the credit sales figure in that calculation.

EXAMPLE

Milagro Corporation, maker of espresso coffee machines, has been relying on DSO to measure its collection effectiveness, but wants to supplement it with a measurement designed for a shorter period of time. The collection effectiveness index is selected as that measure. For the most recent month, the company had $400,000 of beginning receivables, $350,000 of credit sales, $425,000 of ending total receivables, and $300,000 of ending current receivables. The calculation of its CEI reveals the following information:

$$\frac{\$400,000 \text{ Beginning receivables} + \$350,000 \text{ Credit sales for the period} - \$425,00 \text{ Ending total receivables}}{\$400,000 \text{ Beginning receivables} + \$350,000 \text{ Credit sales for the period} - \$300,000 \text{ Ending current receivables}} \times 100$$

$$= 72\% \text{ Collection effectiveness index}$$

Thus, Milagro was able to collect 72% of the receivables that were available for collection in that month.

Measurements Based on Time Buckets

After calculating total collection effectiveness, it is useful to drill down at the time bucket level to see how old the clusters of overdue receivables are that are impacting collection effectiveness. A time bucket is a time period listed on the aged accounts

Credit and Collection Measurements

receivables report, where each time bucket is in 30-day increments. Thus, the usual increments are:

- 0 to 30 days
- 31 to 60 days
- 61 to 90 days
- 90+ days

Many reporting packages allow you to alter the duration of time buckets, so these standard periods may not be reflected in all aging reports. For example, a company that has 15-day payment terms may set its first time bucket to be 0 to 15 days, the next time bucket at 16 to 45 days, and so on.

Usually, the amount of receivables in a time bucket is relatively consistent from period to period, unless a disproportionately large receivable is creating a bulge in a certain time bucket. Consequently, it is useful to calculate the percentage of total receivables in each time bucket, and monitor these percentages on a trend line. The following trend analysis for a six-month period illustrates the concept.

Sample Time Bucket Analysis

	January	February	March	April	May	June
0 to 30 days	58%	53%	49%	47%	45%	43%
31 to 60 days	30%	35%	34%	27%	29%	30%
61 to 90 days	10%	10%	15%	19%	10%	11%
90+ days	2%	2%	2%	7%	16%	16%
Totals	100%	100%	100%	100%	100%	100%

The sample time bucket analysis reveals a disturbing trend, where one or more large receivables have shifted out of the shortest time bucket near the beginning of the period, and gradually worked their way through the time buckets until they are now firmly parked in the oldest bucket. In short, there appears to be a cluster of uncollectible receivables burdening the aging report.

Some collection managers prefer to focus particular attention on the 90+ day time bucket, since it contains the most intractable collection problems. The formula for calculating the percent of receivables over 90 days past due is:

$$\frac{\text{Receivables} > 90 \text{ days past due}}{\text{Total receivables}}$$

We do not advocate focusing on the 90+ day time bucket to the detriment of the earlier time buckets, since receivables are much more likely to be collected during the earlier stages of their existence. Once a receivable reaches the 90+ time bucket, the probability of its collection, simply due to the passage of time, has declined. If anything, the collection manager should focus on the 31-60 time bucket, where collection problems first make their appearance and are most likely to be resolved.

232

Days Delinquent Sales Outstanding

Rather than focusing on the entire set of accounts receivable, consider focusing the measurement only on those receivables that are overdue, and ignoring those invoices that are currently within terms. This measurement is called the *days delinquent sales outstanding* (DDSO), for which the measurement is:

$$\frac{365}{(\text{Annualized credit sales from delinquent customers} \div \text{Average delinquent receivables})}$$

When deriving this calculation, the main factor is defining at what point a receivable is considered delinquent. Setting the threshold at 30 days when the payment terms are net 30 days will likely catch a large proportion of customers that pay on time, but whose payments have not yet arrived in the mail. Consequently, a somewhat higher threshold should be set, such as 10 days past terms.

EXAMPLE

New Centurion Corporation translates Latin texts for a variety of educational institutions. Most customers pay on time or early, but a small number of underfunded colleges pay quite late. The collections manager of New Centurion decides to focus attention on this small group by implementing the measurement of DDSO. She sets the delinquent account threshold at 40 days, and finds that the annualized credit sales to the resulting group of customers is $600,000, and the related average receivables are $150,000. The DDSO calculation is:

$$\frac{365}{(\$600,000 \text{ Annual credit sales} \div \$150,000 \text{ Average receivables})}$$

$$= 91 \text{ Days delinquent sales outstanding}$$

Average Days to Pay per Collector

When investigating the reasons for a lengthy DSO, one possibility is to subdivide the measurement by collector, to see if any collectors are unusually efficient or inefficient at collecting from overdue accounts. The result may be retraining of some collectors to enhance their collection skills, or perhaps shifting the more difficult accounts to those collectors who are more adept at collecting funds.

A caution when using average days to pay at the collector level is that some customers are more difficult to collect from than others, irrespective of who is handling the account. Thus, an excellent collections person may have been assigned several customers who simply are not going to pay anywhere near the date mandated by their collection terms. Also, if collectors are being evaluated based on this measurement, there may be infighting over who is assigned certain accounts, or perhaps a rush to write off the more difficult receivables. Because of these issues, it may not be wise to rely on measurements at the collector level, at least when making determinations about changes in compensation or promotions.

Collection Dispute Cycle Time

While the days sales outstanding measurement provides a good overview of how long receivables are outstanding, it does little to provide additional detail about why the receivables are outstanding for so long. The next level of detail below DSO is to track the time required to resolve collection disputes. This measurement is called the *collection dispute cycle time*; when applied just to the resolution of payment deductions, it is called *days deduction outstanding*, or DDO. The simplest approach is to use the same case tracking system used by the customer support function, and record within it the beginning and ending dates for each dispute, as well as the amount in dispute, the cause of the problem, and who is handling its disposition. When summarized over a large number of disputes, this information gives management a good idea of the average time required to settle a dispute, as well as which customers are repeatedly involved with the longest-running disputes, what root problems caused them, and which collections staff have the best (and worst) ability to resolve disputes within a short period of time.

When used properly, an ongoing examination of the collection dispute cycle time can result in decisions to eliminate more difficult customers, provide training to those employees who have problems resolving disputes in a timely manner, and correct the underlying causes of disputed payments.

The measurement can be deliberately skewed by altering the recorded beginning and ending dates of dispute cases. To keep this from happening, do not tie any reduction in the dispute duration period to a bonus plan; this ensures more honest record keeping.

Deduction Turnover

If the company deals with a large number of deductions on an ongoing basis, consider calculating the rate of turnover in deductions. This approach is useful for tracking the ability of the collections staff to rapidly settle deductions. The formula is:

$$\frac{\text{(Number of deductions outstanding at beginning of the period} + \text{Number of new deductions created in the period)}}{\text{Number of deductions at end of the period}}$$

EXAMPLE

Milford Sound routinely deals with a large number of customer payment deductions related to its ongoing marketing cost reimbursement programs. The controller wants to know if the collections staff is keeping up with the volume of these deductions, and so compiles the following information for each of the past three months:

	January	February	March
Beginning deductions outstanding	300	325	340
New deductions in period	1,200	1,250	1,280
Ending deductions outstanding	325	340	350
Deduction turnover	4.6x	4.6x	4.6x

The table reveals that the number of new deductions is rising through the period, as is the number of unresolved deductions at the end of each period. However, in comparison to the total volume of deductions under review, turnover has remained the same throughout the period. Thus, if the controller uses a turnover rate of 4.6x as an acceptable standard, then no operational changes are required.

Average Time to First Contact

If a company uses a computerized collection tracking system, the computer should be able to track all collection actions taken through the system, such as issuing dunning letters or autodialing a customer. If so, have the system compare the date when an invoice came due and when the first collection contact related to that invoice was first made. When aggregated, this should result in a fairly consistent average time to first contact.

It is not always a good use of staff time to accelerate the average time to first contact, since many payments really *are* in the mail, and will be received shortly. Thus, a close examination of cash receipts will probably suggest a certain number of days past the due date when it is most cost-effective to contact a customer.

Bad Debt Percentage

The end result of the credit and collection process is the proportion of accounts receivable that cannot be collected – the bad debt percentage. Ultimately, the bad debt percentage, combined with days sales outstanding, are the core measurements of the credit and collection function.

The bad debt percentage is a simple calculation, just the bad debt expense for the year, divided by credit sales. However, be aware that the reported amount can be "adjusted," sometimes by a considerable amount. Under the accrual basis of accounting, bad debts are estimated and charged to the allowance for doubtful accounts, which is a reserve against which actual bad debts are later charged. If the collections manager wants to present a somewhat lower bad debt percentage at the end of the year, he or she can simply underestimate the amount of bad debts expected to be incurred, and reduce the size of the allowance for doubtful accounts. This issue can be mitigated by adopting a standard procedure for calculating the amount of the allowance, and rigidly adhering to that procedure.

EXAMPLE

Quest Adventure Gear, maker of rugged travel clothing, has been experiencing increasing difficulty in collecting from its retailer base of customers over the past few years despite growing sales, which has triggered a discussion to only sell through a website where customers must pay in advance. The controller of Quest accumulates the following information about the company's bad debts to prove the case that collecting from retailer customers is not going well:

	20X1	20X2	20X3	20X5	20X6
Bad debt expense	$35,000	$47,000	$68,000	$130,000	$176,000
Credit sales	2,900,000	3,100,000	3,250,000	3,500,000	3,900,000
Bad debt percentage	1.2%	1.5%	2.1%	3.7%	4.5%

Collection Performance Report

If a manager wants to monitor the daily performance of the collection staff, the following report format can be used, subdivided by individual collector:

+	Funds collected for the period to date
+	Cash expected from post-dated checks in the period
+	Promised funds expected by the end of the period
=	Total expected collections
	Total projected collections ((collections to date per day × days remaining in period) + funds already collected)
	Total period collection goal (for comparison purposes)
	Proportion of goal achieved to date

The total projected collections number in the preceding list is particularly important, since it is used to estimate, based on the historical collection rate, how much cash a collector is likely to take in by the end of the period. This number is usually less than the amount indicated by the promised funds line item, which tends to be overly optimistic.

An example of the collection performance report is shown next, and is stated for a single collector. There are 20 business days in the reporting period shown, of which 15 days have been completed.

Sample Collection Performance Report

Collector: Edith Wharton	
$140,000	Funds collected for the period to date
20,000	Cash expected from post-dated checks in the period
82,000	Promised funds expected by the end of the period
$242,000	Total expected collections
$220,665	Total projected collections (($16,133 collections/day × 5 days remaining in period) + $140,000 funds already collected)
$240,000	Total period collection goal
58%	Proportion of goal achieved to date

In the example, note that both the total projected collections figure and the proportion of goal achieved to date indicate that the collector may have difficulty in achieving her collection targets for the period.

Average Time to Establish Credit

If a company wants to complete a sale to a new customer, it has to complete the credit analysis process quickly and assign credit to the customer. Consequently, the speed with which the credit department can process requests for credit is of some importance. The calculation is based on an internal database of when requests are logged in, and when the corresponding credit decisions are also logged in. The aggregation of these processing time periods results in an average time to establish credit. The same database could then be used to investigate those outlier credit decisions that took much longer than the median time requirement.

Unfortunately, this measurement can be easily manipulated by adjusting the dates and times when credit requests and credit decisions are logged in. Some of the problem can be eliminated by having the sales department log in credit requests, rather than the credit department.

General Management Measurements

There are a variety of additional measurements that can be used to monitor the costs incurred within the department, the performance of employees, and the proportion of costs incurred as a percentage of total credit sales. Consider the following possibilities:

- Employee turnover
- The number of accounts assigned to each credit employee
- The number of accounts assigned to each collection employee
- The average rate of pay as compared to the median pay rate in the area for similar jobs
- The total cost of the credit and collection functions as a percentage of sales
- The amount of credit sales divided by the full-time equivalent number of credit and collection employees

Most general measurement systems in the credit and collection area should focus on the employees, since they comprise nearly all of the expenses incurred in these functional areas, and their effectiveness is central to the success of the company.

Summary

It is by no means necessary to use all of the measurements described in this chapter. Only calculate and report a measurement if it will be used. Thus, if there is no interest in reducing the amount of time taken to resolve payment disputes, do not measure the collection dispute cycle time. It may be that management attention will shift in the future, at which point the mix of measurements will change, and a measurement that was previously ignored is now in vogue. Conversely, if no action is now being taken in regard to a measurement that was actively followed in the past, it may be time to discontinue that measurement, and let managers focus on a different aspect of the credit and collection functions.

Chapter 23
Credit and Collection Laws

Introduction

A number of laws have been passed that apply, either directly or indirectly, to the credit and collection functions. A much larger proportion of these laws apply to the protection of individuals than to any other topics. In this chapter, we provide an overview of the laws and their essential provisions.

CAN-SPAM Act

The CAN-SPAM Act is a contraction of the full name of the act, which is the Controlling the Assault of Non-Solicited Pornography and Marketing Act. This law is intended to control the issuance of unwanted e-mail advertisements. If a business is sending e-mails to its customers regarding existing transactions, or to customers with whom there is an existing relationship, the provisions of the law do not apply.

In essence, CAN-SPAM does not allow an e-mail marketer to issue unsolicited commercial e-mails unless the marketer adheres to the following three rules:

- *Content*. The subject line of an e-mail is not misleading, the "from" address is accurate, and a legitimate physical address for the sender is included.
- *Sending behavior*. E-mails cannot be sent through third-party e-mail servers to disguise the issuing address. Also, e-mails cannot be issued to addresses that were acquired through a variety of e-mail harvesting techniques.
- *Unsubscribe*. The e-mails contain an option for recipients to unsubscribe, with all unsubscribes being honored within ten days. Once a recipient has opted out, the related e-mail address cannot be sold or transferred.

This act does not have a direct impact on collections, since e-mailed collection messages are allowed under the concept that there is an existing relationship with customers.

Equal Credit Opportunity Act

The credit department should be aware of the provisions of the ECOA. This Act prohibits credit discrimination on the basis of race, color, religion, national origin, sex, marital status, age, or because an individual receives public assistance. This discrimination can take the form of discouraging a person from applying for credit, or rejecting an application, or imposing different terms or conditions on credit (such as a higher interest rate or other fees). The Act also prohibits credit discrimination by discounting certain types of income, such as income from pensions, annuities, Social Security payments, child support, or reliable alimony.

However, it *is* acceptable for the credit department to consider a person's immigration status, in terms of whether the individual has the right to stay in the country for a sufficient amount of time to repay the debt. It is also acceptable to ask questions about expenses related to a person's dependents, though not whether the person has plans to have or raise children. Further, it is acceptable to consider a person's age when the individual is too young to sign contracts (usually under age 18). It is also acceptable to consider a person's age when the outcome will tend to be more favorable if the person is at least 62 years old.

The Act also gives a person the right to know why a credit application was rejected. The creditor is obliged to inform the individual the specific reason for the rejection. The person also has the right to learn the specific reason he or she was offered less favorable terms than had been applied for, but only if the person rejects these terms.

Fair and Accurate Credit Transactions Act (FACT)

A number of provisions of this act relate to identity theft, which are unrelated to credit and collections. The provisions of FACT that relate to credit and collection activities are:

- *Fraud alerts.* If an individual notifies a consumer reporting agency that he or she is the victim of fraud, the agency must flag that file with a fraud alert, as well as notify other reporting agencies. This requirement can be used by a member of the military on active duty to request an active duty alert, which requires a consumer reporting agency to exclude that person from any list that is intended for the extension of credit for a period of two years.
- *Credit disclosures.* Mortgage lenders are required to send credit disclosure notices to borrowers that state their credit scores, factors affecting their scores, and related information.

Fair Credit Reporting Act

The FCRA is primarily targeted at credit reporting agencies, so it does not have a direct impact on businesses. Key provisions of the act include:

- *Elimination of negative information.* Credit reporting agencies must delete certain types of negative information from their credit reports after certain intervals have passed, usually seven years from the date of occurrence. This negative information includes late payments, tax liens, bankruptcies, and judgments of various kinds. Information about bankruptcies and tax liens are retained for longer periods.

- *Free reports.* Individuals can obtain one free credit report about themselves per year, which is presumably used by them to see if any reported information is incorrect or disputable.
- *Negative information removal.* When negative information has been removed from a credit report as a result of a dispute, the information cannot be reinserted without prior written notification of the individual to which it relates.

From a credit analysis perspective, the main issue is that information must be dropped from credit reports after a certain period of time, which somewhat limits the basis upon which credit decisions can be made.

Fair Debt Collection Practices Act

The FDCPA is the law with the most immediate impact on the collections function. Its provisions are intended to protect individuals, not businesses. Also, the act is intended to apply to third party collection agencies and attorneys, but has been applied at the state level to the activities of original creditors. Key provisions of the act are:

- *Calling behavior.* A collector is not allowed to call repeatedly with the intent of annoying an individual, or to contact them at their place of employment (if prohibited by the employer), or to contact them when an attorney is representing them. Threats or abusive language are also not allowed.
- *Calling hours.* A collector is limited to calling within the hours of 8 a.m. to 9 p.m. local time.
- *Credit report.* The filing of false information with a credit agency about an individual is not allowed.
- *Deception.* Misrepresenting oneself in order to collect a debt (such as claiming to be a police officer or government official) is not allowed.
- *Halt communications.* A collector is required to cease communications with an individual if the person requests it in writing, which essentially leaves litigation as the only remaining collection option.
- *Justification.* A collector is not allowed to demand amounts that have not been justified.
- *Third party contacts.* A collector is not allowed to discuss the nature of a debt with other parties (other than to obtain contact information), or to publish a person's name and location, or to use any form of communication that would make the debt information available to the public (such as sending an overdue notice on a post card).

In addition, the act requires that collectors identify themselves to individuals and state whom they are representing, make proper notification of an individual's right to dispute the debt in question, and send verification of a debt if requested.

Though the act is intended to only limit the actions of collection agencies, the collections manager could incorporate its provisions into the in-house collections procedure, on the grounds that the provisions of the act are fair and reasonable.

Service Members Civil Relief Act (SMCRA)

The SMCRA applies to all members of the military services, and affords the following protections to them:

- *Evictions.* Service members cannot be evicted from housing while they are on active duty, up to a maximum rent payment cap that is adjusted for inflation.
- *Interest rate.* If a service member has a credit obligation, including credit card debt, the interest rate on it is limited to six percent while the person is on active duty. Also, any excess interest above six percent is permanently forgiven.
- *Lawsuits.* Service members cannot be sued while on active military service, as well as for one year following the conclusion of that service.

If you intend to litigate against a former service member, you bear the burden of proving that the individual is no longer on active service.

The net effect of the SMCRA is that collection activities against members of the military are more difficult to pursue than is the case for other individuals.

Telephone Consumer Protection Act (TCPA)

The following actions are expressly prohibited under the TCPA unless the targeted individual has already given consent:

- *Automated calls.* Solicitors cannot send messages to residences that employ a recorded message. These calls also cannot be sent to cell phones, 911 emergency numbers, hospital emergency numbers, a physician's office, or similar recipients.
- *Call times.* A solicitor is not allowed to call a private residence prior to 8 a.m. or after 9 p.m., local time.
- *Do-not-call list.* A solicitor must maintain a list of consumers that have requested that they not be called. In addition, solicitors must observe the list of consumers noted on the national do-not-call registry.
- *Faxes.* Advertising faxes cannot be sent unless the recipient has expressly allowed them.
- *Identification.* The solicitor must identify himself, the name of the entity on whose behalf the call is being made, and provide contact information.

Note that a "solicitor" as stated in the preceding list also means a collector. Someone receiving a telephone call in violation of this act can sue for up to $1,500 per violation, and can seek an injunction to prevent further calls.

Truth in Lending Act (TLA)

The TLA is intended to force lenders to provide specific types of information to borrowers, so that borrowers can make informed decisions regarding entering into borrowing arrangements. The key information that must be disclosed prior to a lending arrangement being finalized is:

- The annual percentage interest rate
- The term of the loan
- Total costs to the borrower

Additional informative disclosures are required when a loan contains a variable interest rate, so that the borrower understands how the rate change is calculated and when any changes will occur.

The act applies to nearly all lenders, including banks, credit unions, mortgage lenders, finance companies, and credit card lenders. The act provides for specific damages to be paid if the rights of a consumer are violated. The amounts are not large on an individual basis, but can be quite large if a violation of the act can be applied to a large number of customers.

Summary

Because of the various laws noted in this chapter, managers should be vigilant in the following areas:

- *Behavior boundaries.* Establish clear boundaries of acceptable behavior for the collection staff that keep the company from being liable under any laws, and monitor the collectors to ensure that they comply with these restrictions. Since the actions of collection agencies could be construed as the actions of the company, enforce these same boundaries with any agencies that work for the company.
- *Monitoring.* There are ongoing updates to several of the laws, so have someone with legal experience monitor the updates and determine how they may impact the company's credit and collection operations. Also monitor any variations on these laws at the state level.
- *Procedures.* Periodically review and adjust the company's procedures that are impacted by these laws, and train the staff regarding the updates. Also have an attorney review the procedures to ensure that they comply with the law.

Glossary

A

A-B testing. A method for altering messages to customers to see which version maximizes customer response.

Accounts receivable aging report. A report that lists unpaid customer invoices and unused credit memos by date ranges. This report is used by collections personnel to determine which invoices are overdue for payment.

Accrual basis of accounting. The concept of recording revenues only when earned and expenses when incurred, irrespective of the underlying inflow or outflow of cash.

ACH debit. The debiting of a payer's bank account by a payee, with the funds shifting into the payee's bank account.

Allowance for doubtful accounts. A reserve account that offsets the total amount of accounts receivable outstanding in the general ledger. The allowance represents management's best estimate of the amount of accounts receivable that will not be paid by customers.

B

Bad debt. An account receivable that cannot be collected.

Bar date. The date by which creditor claims related to a bankruptcy must be received by the bankruptcy court.

C

C.O.D. An acronym for cash on delivery, where the customer is required to pay in cash at the point of delivery.

Collateral. An asset that a borrower or guarantor has pledged as security for a loan or receivable. The creditor can legally seize and sell the asset if the borrower or guarantor is unable to pay back the loan or receivable.

Collection agency. A third party hired by a seller or lender to recover funds that are past due.

Collections management system. An integrated system that monitors collection activity, and which is used to manage ongoing collection operations.

Contribution margin. Revenues minus all variable expenses related to the revenue.

Credit application. A standard form sent to customers, on which they enter information needed by a company's credit department to determine the amount of credit to grant customers.

Glossary

Credit insurance. A guarantee by a third party against non-payment of an invoice by a customer.

Credit limit. The maximum amount of credit extended to a customer.

Credit memo. A contraction of the term "credit memorandum," which is a document issued by the seller of goods or services to the buyer, reducing the amount that the buyer owes to the seller under the terms of an earlier invoice.

Credit rating. A standard score assigned to an entity, based on its financial and operational condition, and which is used to evaluate the credit terms granted to the entity.

Current ratio. The current assets of a business, divided by its current liabilities.

Customer purchase order. A document that a customer may submit to the receiving company, in which it authorizes the purchase of specific items or services.

Cycle counting. The practice of counting a small proportion of inventory on a daily basis, and correcting any errors found.

D

Debtor. A business or individual that owes money to a creditor or lender.

Dunning letter. A letter sent to a debtor, requesting payment of a receivable.

DUNS number. A unique nine-digit identification number, developed by Dun & Bradstreet and used to access credit and background information about a company.

E

Enterprise resource planning (ERP). An integrated software package that supports all of a company's functional areas.

Escheatment. The concept of remitting unclaimed property to the government.

F

Factoring. An arrangement where a financing company takes over a company's accounts receivable in exchange for an immediate cash payment.

FICO score. A credit quality score calculated for individuals, as developed by the Fair Isaac Corporation.

Five Cs of credit. The examination of a customer's character, capacity, capital, conditions, and collateral when determining the appropriate amount of credit to grant.

Full-time equivalent. The number of working hours that equates to one full-time employee.

Glossary

G

Gross margin. Revenues minus the cost of goods sold. The gross margin reveals the amount that an entity earns from the sale of its products and services, before the deduction of any selling and administrative expenses.

I

Invoice. A document submitted to a customer, identifying a transaction for which the customer owes payment to the issuer.

L

Leading indicator. An economic factor that changes in advance of a general economic trend, and which is used to predict such changes.

Lien. A legal claim against an asset, which can include physical possession of the asset.

Lockbox. A mail box operated by a bank, to which the customers of a company send their payments. The bank deposits all checks received into the company's bank account.

Loss leader. The practice of selling a few products at cost, on the assumption that buyers will purchase other products at the same time that are more profitable.

M

Mail float. The time required for a check payment to travel from the payer to the payee through the postal system.

N

Nexus. When an organization is considered to be doing business within a region, due to its presence in that region.

Not sufficient funds check. A check issued for which there are not sufficient funds in the issuer's bank account.

P

Pick list. A document listing the items to pick from stock in order to fulfill a customer order.

Postdated check. A check that is dated as of a future date, and which is intended to be cashed no earlier than the stated date.

Pretexting. Gathering information under false pretenses.

Q

Quick ratio. The ratio of cash, marketable securities, and accounts receivable to current liabilities. The ratio does not include inventory or prepaid expenses.

Glossary

R

Real property. Land and any property attached to the land, such as buildings.

Remote deposit capture. The use of a scanning device to create a legal, scanned image of both sides of a check, which is then uploaded to a bank as a valid deposit.

Return merchandise authorization. A pre-assigned number given to a customer by a seller, to be marked on a returned product package, signifying that the product has been approved for return.

S

Sales order. An internal document used to specify the details of a customer order. It may be derived from a customer purchase order or some less-formal type of communication.

Shell company. A business entity for which there are minimal assets, liabilities, or business activities.

Shipping log. A document created by a business when it ships goods to customers, noting the date and time of each shipment, as well as the method of transport and the customer name.

Skip tracing. The art of finding a debtor who does not wish to be located.

Sole proprietorship. A business that is not incorporated, so that a single individual is entitled to the entire net worth of the business, and is personally liable for its debts.

U

UCC filing. A lien placed on an asset in order to establish a security interest by a creditor.

W

Workflow management system. Software that monitors the progress of activities related to a process.

Index

Made in the USA
San Bernardino,
CA